DATE DUE			

Valiant Heart

Valiant Heart

A Biography of HEINRICH HEINE

Philip Kossoff

New York • Cornwall Books • London

Cornwall Books
440 Forsgate Drive
Cranbury, NJ 08512

Cornwall Books
25 Sicilian Avenue
London WC1A, 2QH, England

Cornwall Books
2133 Royal Windsor Drive
Unit 1
Mississauga, Ontario L5J 1K5, Canada

Library of Congress Cataloging in Publication Data

Kossoff, Philip, 1907–
  Valiant heart.

  Bibliography: p.
  Includes index.
  1. Heine, Heinrich, 1797–1856—Biography.
  2. Authors, German—19th century—Biography. I. Title.
  PT2328.K58 1983   831'.7 [B]   82-46085
  ISBN 0-8453-4762-4

Printed in the United States of America

Contents

Preface

In the beginning, as the news of his grave illness spread, a constant succession of visitors from all walks of life called on him. In front of his dwelling the carriages of the elite lined up daily, and in his mail came letters from prisoners, telling him that the magic of his mocking verses, stronger than the locks of prison doors, had transformed them into men freer than their jailers. Dumas, Balzac, Victor Hugo, Gautier; de Nerval, Berlioz, George Sand; Meyerbeer, de Musset, Béranger; the great and the near great; children of the neighborhood; statesmen and poets; princesses and shopgirls; all knocked on his door. They came to commiserate; he surprised and delighted them with his wonted sardonic wit, his inimitable bons mots; the fallen Heine remained a sovereign emperor still.

They had left him on this pile of mattresses eight years ago. It had happened on a lovely spring day in the year 1848, that year of revolution. Long a sick man, nearly blind, half-paralyzed, he had ventured out of the house, seeking to bathe in the balmy air, and to hear a woman's voice or a child's shout. Stumbling along, he was suddenly engulfed by a band of running street fighters and was knocked down. Regaining his feet, he saw that he was in front of the Louvre. He staggered into the museum and collapsed at the feet of the Venus de Milo. Compassionately the goddess looked down upon him; she seemed to be saying, "Can you not see that I am without arms and powerless to help you?"

They brought him to a dark, cramped, airless apartment that faced over a treeless, noisy courtyard. Later, Mathilde found more pleasant rooms at 3 avenue Matignon, off the Champs-Elysées. It had a balcony protected by a screen and awning, and he would be carried there on a warm day, to feel the sun and breeze, and to catch glimpses of the trees and grass of the boulevard through a spyglass and of the carriages and pedestrians converging on the Arc de Triomphe.

A caller, if he were asked about his visit, would certainly mention the mattresses in the middle of the room, piled one on top of the other. He might describe the little table to one side, crammed with pain relievers. He would recall the door leading to a second room from which could be heard the clamor of Mathilde singing to the accompaniment of her chattering parrot, Coco. He probably also would talk about the other occupants of the apartment—the two nurses, the secretary, and the maid.

And Heine himself? At the question, the visitor would pause, bemused. How could he convey the pity and the awe inspired by that presence? Perhaps not pity; one did not do that to Heine.

It had seemed to the visitor at first that he had entered a tomb. A dead body was lying before him on the heap of mattresses, barely visible in the greenish light that struggled through the heavily curtained windows. Then he saw the face; it was like a delicately chiseled death mask. The left hand of the corpse moved, and the fingers slowly lifted the eyelid of the right eye. A smile, half-sardonic, half-gentle, lit up the face. A voice called the nurse to prop him up against the pillows. It did not seem possible that those warm, deep tones came from that skeleton. The dead man had come to life. The wit sparkled—the tomb lit up. The visitor laughed. When, eventually, he prepared to leave, Heine urged him to call again soon, for "if you miss this opportunity of seeing me, you will soon have to make the uncomfortable journey to Montmartre Cemetery, where I have already rented an apartment with a view overlooking eternity."

But a man should not take so long to die; eight years can tax the patience of the most faithful. As time went by, the doorbell rang less and less often. And outside, there were those, the minions of hate and envy, who closed in on the warrior-poet with their lies and sneers. Pygmies of the right and left barked and nipped at him. They attacked his integrity, they derided his poetry, they laughed at his *grisette* wife. They threatened and hounded him. They spread rumors that he was a German apostate in the pay of foreign governments, prompting him to write: "They howl, and bark, and grunt—my nose can scarcely bear the reek."

Ah, there had been a time when he had walked the streets of Paris like a German Apollo. In the glory of his youth he had felt so proud and tall that, whenever he passed through the gates of Saint Martin or Saint Denis he would involuntarily stoop, for fear of bumping his head against the arch! Now the warm, amorous odors of May penetrated into the sickroom, and he who so loved life cried, "Heaven is mocking me, with its blue skies of May. Oh lovely world, you are a horror." In despair, he wrote:

> How slowly Time, the frightful snail,
> Crawls to the corner that I lie in;
> While I, who cannot move at all,
> Watch from the place that I must die in.
>
> Here in my darkened cell no hope
> Enters and breaks the gloom asunder;
> I know I shall not leave this room
> Except for one that's six feet under.

(To Lazarus)

Death is calling him. Angrily, and then with resignation, he awaits the coming separation of body and soul. "My body is now a corpse in which my spirit is imprisoned . . . my spirit grows wild, it raves and curses and runs berserk." The curses are futile. He shrugs and advises his soul, "Your most frightful curse would never kill a fly. Endure your lot and try to do your whimpering and praying quietly." Body and soul talk to one another, friendly and comfortingly. The soul says to the body, "Oh, stay, stay with me, you body that I love." The body answers, "Be comforted and do not grieve."

And Heinrich Heine summoned all the strength, all the love, all the wild laughter that was in his lion heart. His spirit crossed the continents and seas and roamed the ages, as he jested at life and death and created immortal, wondrous, touching, life-giving poetry. In the midnight hours, as the pain tore at his body, he proudly hymned:

I am the Sword, I am the Flame.
I've lighted your way in the darkness, and when the fight began, battled ahead in the front lines.
. . . The victory was ours, but here round about lie the bodies of my friends . . . But we have time neither for grief nor for rejoicing. The trumpets sound anew, fresh battles must be fought—
I am the Sword, I am the Flame.

(Hymn)

Acknowledgments

The following publishers have generously granted permission to use excerpts from copyrighted works:

Humanities Press Inc. for stanzas from *The Golden Calf* in *Heine*, by Meno Spann. Reprinted by permission of Humanities Press Inc. Atlantic Highlands, N.J. 07716

New York University Press for stanzas from *Castle of Affront*. Reprinted by permission of New York University Press from *Heine: The Artist in Revolt* by Max Brod. Copyright © 1962 by New York University.

Lyle Stuart Inc. for selections from *The Poetry and Prose of Heinrich Heine* edited by Frederic Ewen. Copyright © 1948. Published by arrangements with Lyle Stuart.

Oak Tree Publications, Inc. for selections in this book reprinted from The Sword and The Flame published by A. S. Barnes.

Most of the poems of Heine published in this work are translations by Aaron Kramer. Versions by Emma Lazarus have been used for selections from *The North Sea, Tannhauser,* and *Donna Clara*, and the poem *My Child, We Two Were Children*. Louis Untermeyer is the translator of excerpts from *To Lazarus, How Slowly Time The Frightful Snail, Jenny, Prologue to the Harz Jouney, Stars With Golden Feet Are Walking,* and *I Love This White and Slender Body.* The lyric *Oh, Let Your Tears with Mine* Bedew is translated by Humbert Wolfe.

I wish to thank Dr. Aaron Kramer of the Department of English at Dowling College for helpful comments on the first draft of *Valiant Heart.*

I also wish to give warm thanks to my agent, Roy Porter, for his patience and his confidence in my work.

And to Esther, critic and indispensable helper.

Introduction

In this biography I have sought to convey to the reader the magic, the wit, and the liberating force of Heine's life and work. I have made liberal use of his poems and prose, his letters and reported conversations. The incidents and events are true in all essential details; in some cases these have been transmuted into dramatic form.

Valiant Heart

1
Düsseldorf: The Early Years (1797–1815)

Düsseldorf, city, Federal Republic of Germany,
capital of North Rhine–Westphalia, at the junction of the Rhine and Düssel rivers. It is a major
industrial and commercial center, a busy inland
port, and an important railway junction. Düsseldorf is also the administrative seat of the Ruhr
iron and steel industry. Chartered in 1288 . . . It
was occupied by the French in 1795 . . . From
1921 to 1925 the French again occupied the city.
In the Second World War the city was bombed
heavily . . . Heinrich Heine was born here.

(Columbia Encyclopedia)

On a pleasant summer day in the year 1796, there arrived in Düsseldorf a
handsome stranger resplendent in a scarlet uniform and surrounded by an
unusual entourage: twelve horses and twelve hunting dogs. It occasioned great
surprise when, after inquiring the way, he headed down the winding dirt lane
that led to the home of the rabbi of the town, Rabbi Abraham Scheuer.

Later, the rabbi let it be known that his visitor's name was Samson Heine,
that he was the son of a merchant in Hanover, and that he had served as
quartermaster to Duke Ernst of Cumberland during the Flanders and Brabant
campaigns. The duke, in appreciation of his quartermaster's services, had given
him the horses and dogs, and—what was of even greater value—had helped
him to obtain a contract to supply cloth to the French military forces in the
Düsseldorf area. Samson Heine wished to settle in the city, and he had come to
the rabbi requesting that he recommend to the town authorities that they grant
him a residence permit.

The rabbi had told Samson that he would have to consult with the responsible
leaders of the Jewish community. He knew that the struggling Jewish merchants of Düsseldorf would not be pleased with the prospect of another business competitor, and especially one from another community. In any event, he
was not favorably impressed with this visitor with the powdered hair, the soft
white hands, and the dogs and horses.

17

But then, one month after Samson's arrival, the Jewish community was shaken and scandalized by the announcement of the engagement of Betty van Geldern to the newcomer. Who could have believed that the proud, self-confident, highly educated, wealthy Betty would permit herself to fall reck-lessly in love with an adventurer who consorted with actresses and played recklessly at the gaming tables!

The van Gelderns had lived in the Rhineland for generations. Some had won high positions in the academic, business, and governmental spheres. As a child, Betty heard stories of ancestors who had been in the service of dukes and emperors. Juspa van Geldern, her great-grandfather, had been the financial agent of the Elector Johann Wilhelm, and he had built a business empire with interests in England, France, Austria, and Holland. He had been granted royal permission to erect Düsseldorf's first synagogue. His own residence was a palace, filled with riches—Oriental rugs and French furniture; silver plate and jewels. Juspa's son, Lazarus, married the daughter of Simon Michael of Vienna, who was a purveyor of gold and silver to the imperial mint and financial adviser to the Emperor Leopold I. Lazarus had emigrated to Düssel-dorf around the year 1700. His son, Gottschalk, practiced medicine and was highly respected in the community. He was the father of Betty and her two brothers, Joseph and Simon.

Betty lost her mother when she was an infant, and she was raised by her father. He taught her to read Tacitus, Caesar, and Cicero in the original Latin. She understood Hebrew, English, and French, and she was familiar with the best literature of the age. Her two favorite authors were Rousseau and Goethe.

She was twenty-five, and considered by the custom of the time already a spinster, when Samson arrived in Düsseldorf in July 1796. Her father and an older brother had died the previous year, and she was lonely and unhappy. Her uncles and aunts and cousins introduced her to eligible suitors; *shadchen* came to her with names of wealthy, well-educated, handsome aspirants to her hand, but she remained aloof. She identified more with the world of Héloise and Werther than with the restricted Jewish community of Düsseldorf. At an early age she had decided that she would marry only when love came, real love that struck like a bolt of lightning, a *coup de foudre*, as the French called it.

Then she met Samson. He was so gentle and kind, and yet he bore himself with such dignity. His voice was deep and resonant; sometimes when he spoke she caught the tones of a cello. The love she had been waiting for had arrived. When she announced her engagement to Samson, family and friends expressed their disapproval and even condemnation. "You would not believe," she wrote to a friend, "that my engagement could make so many enemies. But my Heine makes up for it over and over by his loyalty and devotion!" The general belief was that Samson was an adventurer who had seduced the unworldly Betty for her money. The rabbi refused to petition the municipality for a residence permit for Samson, and he told Betty that he would never sanctify the mar-riage.

He underestimated her strength of mind and character. The year before, she had written to a friend, "Although I combine an ordinary face and figure with an equally ordinary mind, yet I feel that I have the power to rise above the chimeras of prejudice, convention, and etiquette, and to regard decency as the sole restraint." She told the rabbi that if he refused to give his blessing to her marriage, she and Samson would invoke the old Jewish custom whereby a young man took a woman as his wife by placing a wedding ring on her finger and repeating the words, "By the Law of Moses and Israel I take thee for my wife." The rabbi capitulated, the residence permit was granted, and the marriage took place on February 1, 1797.

Betty gave birth to her firstborn on December 13, 1797. In the religious records his name was entered as Chaim, that being his grandfather's name, but at home he was always called Harry, after an English business friend of Samson's. (When he was baptized in 1825, he changed his name to the more German Heinrich, but, he confessed in his *Memoirs*, "I still like to be called Harry," and the family always referred to him by that name. A sister, Charlotte, named Sarah at birth, was born in 1800 and lived to the year 1899; Gottschalk, who changed his name to Gustav, was born in 1803 and died in 1886; and the youngest, Meyer, later called Maximilian, was born in 1805 and died in 1879.

Betty, in preparation for motherhood, reread Rousseau's *Emile,* and thereafter followed the book's precepts on child-rearing. She breast-fed her children and adhered to a strict regimen of fresh air and hygiene. When they grew older, she did her best to shield them from such corrupting influences as the novel, verse, and the dangerous allures of the theater. When she discovered a servant telling fairy tales to Harry, she ordered her never to do it again. (But when his mother was not around, the boy coaxed the maidservant until she gave in to his pleadings and held the young Harry spellbound with ancient folktales that had been handed down from generation to generation.)

Betty loved all her children, but her hopes and dreams were lavished on her firstborn. She was convinced that he was no ordinary child—that he was destined to carry the glory of the van Geldern heritage to new heights.

The boy bubbled with life. He was physically enchanting. He could read and write when he was four. Only one thing worried his mother: his quick and violent temper. Once Samson had to pay a sizable sum for damages because of this trait of Harry's. Betty had engaged a dancing instructor for Harry, but he had difficulty in mastering the steps. When the little dancing teacher with the mincing manner insisted that he do the same step over and over, Harry's temper flared up and he turned on the teacher and pushed him out of the window. It was fortunate that it was a low window and that the fall was cushioned by a trash heap. Even as a mere tot in kindergarten he had displayed this temper. He filled Frau Hindermann's snuff box with sand, and when he was asked why he had done it, he shouted, "Because I hate you." The mother sighed when such stories were brought to her attention. But he will outgrow such tantrums, she assured herself; ordinarily, he was such an affectionate and sunny child. And so devoted to his sister and his brothers.

Betty's ambitions for her son were boundless. The times were such that the lowest became the highest. A Corsican cadet had become emperor of Europe; a friend of hers, the daughter of an ironmaster, had married one of Napoleon's marshals and was now a duchess.

The armies of Napoleon had engulfed the Rhineland and proclaimed the principles of *égalité*. The ghetto walls had crumbled overnight. It seemed as if the Messiah had come. In Cologne the French commissioner proclaimed, "All traces of slavery are now abolished . . . you shall account to God alone for your religious beliefs, and as to your status, all men stand equal before the law." Napoleon himself visited Düsseldorf in 1811. He was greeted by a deputation of the clergymen of all faiths, and their spokesman was Rabbi Abraham Scheuer, who had married Betty and Samson. To the rabbi's welcoming speech Napoleon responded: "Before God all men are brothers. They should love and help one another without regard to differences of religion."

This was the climate in which Betty Heine laid her plans for her oldest son's career. She envisioned him with golden epaulets on his shoulders, a marshal in the service of the emperor; but, knowing that greatness must be achieved and does not come by itself, she carefully planned to train and equip him for his future great role as a strategist or an administrator of a conquered territory, and she arranged private tutoring for him in subjects such as mathematics and engineering, even though he was already taking courses at the lyceum in geometry, logarithms, algebra, and similar subjects. But, alas, the empire fell, and suddenly the bankers and great financial houses were seizing temporal power. She changed her plans for Harry accordingly. Now she envisaged him as a great financier, and she rearranged his studies to include bookkeeping, geography, foreign trade, and English—subjects that would prepare him to become another Rothschild. But he showed no aptitude for business, and this dream, too, had to be given up. Ever dauntless, Betty discovered yet another career for her boy. "She had observed," Heine wrote in his *Memoirs,*

> that for generations . . . the legal profession had been all powerful; that lawyers, in particular, managed through their chattering to play important roles and rise to the highest public offices . . . Since the new University of Bonn had just been established, and its law faculty was composed of the most celebrated professors, she forthwith sent me to Bonn.

The irony is that it was not Harry but the other children who achieved the worldly goals by which she set so much store. Greatness of another kind was reserved for him. Gustav, after failures as a farmer and a merchant, entered the cavalry branch of the Austrian army and rose to the rank of lieutenant. He married, left the service, and established himself as the editor of the Vienna *Fremdenblatt,* which became a widely read, semiofficial publication reflecting the most conservative views. In time he was rewarded for his services to the state with the title of Baron von Geldern, and he died a multimillionaire. Heine's other brother, Max, left for Russia after completing his medical education. He served as a military physician in the war in the Caucasus, was medical officer in a cadet institute, and then physician at the imperial court. There he met and married the widow of the czar's personal physician, Privy Councillor von Arndt, and was given the title of Baron von Heine-Geldern. He wrote a number of medical works and even tried his hand at belles-lettres. They include *Margaret, The Miracle of the Lake of Ladoga; Pictures from Turkey; Letters from Petersburg;* and *Recollections of H. Heine and His Family.* It was one more paradox in a life of paradoxes that, while Harry became the poet and eloquent spokesman for democracy and the cause of freedom, his two brothers were rewarded with wealth and titles for their services to the Hapsburgs and Romanovs, the brutal gendarmes of Europe. Charlotte, too, entered the upper social circles. She married a wealthy Hamburg merchant and bore two children: a daughter, Maria, who acquired the title of the Princess della Rocca, and a son, who became the baron Ludwig von Embden, and whom Heine in his will appointed custodian of his personal papers and letters.

A deep, life-long bond existed between mother and son. Heine's tender love and reverence for his mother glow in his sonnet, *To My Mother.*

> It's been my way to walk with head held high;
> I've got a pretty tough and stubborn mind;
> And if the king himself should pass, he'd find
> That I'm a lad who'll look him in the eye.
>
> And yet, dear mother, this I'll frankly say:
> No matter how puffed up my pride may be,
> When I am near your sweet serenity
> My haughtiness begins to melt away.
>
> Is it your soul that strangely holds my flight?
> Your towering soul, that bravely pierces all
> And soars up flashing toward the heavenly light?
> Or am I tortured now when I recall
> My many wrongs, that filled your heart with woe?
> Your beautiful, big heart that loved me so?

After their marriage, Betty's dowry was used to establish Samson as a dealer in imported English cloth. He gave up the company of actresses and the excitement of gambling, and Betty made him dispose of his horses and hunting dogs, for they consumed too much fodder and meat and brought in no profit. She did allow him to keep one of the dogs; by a quirk, it had nothing of the hunting dog about it, but on the contrary was an ugly, respectable housedog. "Ah, Joli," Samson would sigh, and Joli would wag his tail sadly.

Samson was a man who found contentment in the most ordinary happenings of daily life. He was always cheerful, always serene and "filled with a boundless enjoyment of living." The bolts of silks and satins that he handled in his business were more than merchandise; they were creations pleasing to the touch and eye. When, through an English friend, he discovered the soft English velveteens, he hastened to import great quantities of them, and he proclaimed their beauty to everyone. He was an officer of the municipal militia, and he was never so happy as when he could put on his dark-blue uniform with its sky-blue trimmings and ride past his house, a fine figure at the head of his company, and wave his three-cornered, plumed hat in a sweeping salute to his smiling wife.

Biographers have tended to dismiss Samson as an ineffectual, weak person, lacking in judgment. This is an unjust picture of him. True, he was not shrewd, he was not tough, he was not distrustful of his fellowman. People, wrote his eldest son, sometimes mistook this for a lack of understanding, but this was not true. "He would sense, with his mental feelers, what it took wise men a great deal of time to understand by reflection. He thought not so much with his head as with his heart, and he had the most lovable heart you can imagine." Samson was esteemed by both Jew and gentile. He was not only an officer of the militia, but he also held the post of inspector of the poor in his district, an office that never before had been entrusted to one of his faith; indeed, previously it had always been held by a member of one of the patrician families.

Samson had not moved away from the faith of his forefathers. Each morning he faced east and said his morning prayers as his ancestors had done for centuries past. It never entered his mind to do otherwise. But his moral code embraced more than the ritualistic utterance of the daily prayers. Many a time, when the money in the poor-relief funds ran low, he quietly added from his own pocket. He organized and became the first president of the Society for the Practice of Philanthropy and for Reading the Psalms. So had his father, Heyman Heine, in 1762 been one of the founders of a similar society in Hanover.

All the traditional Jewish holidays were observed at the Heine home: Rosh Hashanah, marking the beginning of the New Year; Yom Kippur, the awe-inspiring Day of Atonement; the festive celebrations, Sukkoth, Purim, and Hanukkah, each with its special games and gifts for the children, special foods and delicacies, special chantings and ceremonies at the synagogue. Passover, particularly, was a joyous occasion. Numerous relatives and friends joined the family around the seder table. Often, Samson would return from the synagogue with a stranger who had been caught far away from home on this precious night. Years later, memories of these wondrous seder nights surfaced to inspire the tender, glowing description of the Passover celebration in *The Rabbi of Bacherach*.

Home was a place of love; the sky was always blue; the breezes were ever pleasant.

Harry's sister Charlotte was his favorite playmate, and the two delighted in crawling into the large hen-coop in back of their house at 10 Bolkerstrasse and playing at being grown-ups. Heine's poem, *My Child, We Two Were Children*, recalls those days:

> My child, we two were children,
> As lively as ever you saw,
> We crept into the hencoop,
> And we hid there beneath the straw.
>
> The chests that lay in the courtyard,
> With paper we overlaid.
> Therein we lived together;
> An excellent house we made.
>
> The old cat of our neighbor
> Would visit us at whiles;
> We gave her bows and curtsies,
> And compliments and smiles.
>
> We talked like grown folks sagely,
> And sat there oft and long,
> Complaining how all had altered,
> Since the days when we were young.
>
> How love and faith and friendship
> Had vanished, the world was bare;
> How dear were tea and coffee,
> And money had grown so rare!
>
> Those childish games are over,
> All things roll on with youth,-
> Money, the world, and the seasons,
> And faith and love and truth.

When Harry was five, Samson told Betty that it was time to send their son to Hebrew school. Betty, the rationalist, argued with him. She saw no necessity to place Harry in a cheder; he could get all the religious instruction he needed at home; she wanted her son to receive a modern, rational education. But on this occasion Samson stood firm. Harry was enrolled in a cheder.

There he was taught in the traditional, orthodox manner. Little Harry learned to read from the Talmud—in the pure Hebrew that is demanded when studying that sacred text, a language distinct from the German-Yiddish dialect spoken by most Jews of Düsseldorf. He was taught the prayers, the commandments, and the taboos. He was a good learner, but his mother's skepticism was reflected in his irreverent attitude toward matters of ritual. Once, on a Saturday, a playmate was horrified to see him bite off grapes one by one from a neighbor's vine. (He was then nine and no longer attending cheder.) "It is true that one is forbidden to pick grapes by hand on the Sabbath," explained Harry, "but the Law does not stop us from biting them off with our teeth."

Harry stayed in the cheder for only two years. Then, at Betty's insistence, he was taken out and placed in the lower school of the Düsseldorf lyceum. It was run by priests and housed in a former monastery.

Napoleon kept changing the colors of the map of Europe. On March 15, 1806 French troops marched into Düsseldorf, capital of the duchy of Julich, and installed Joachim Murat, Napoleon's brother-in-law as the new grand duke. The duchies of Cleves, Berg, and Julich became part of the French empire and henceforth enjoyed the blessings of the Napoleonic Code and *égalité*. Serfdom was abolished, peasants and bourgeois had equal rights with aristocrats, the ghetto was done away with and legal and religious equality proclaimed. "In my childhood I breathed the air of France," wrote Heine.

He was eight years old when the French troops entered Düsseldorf. The streets reverberated to the sounds of trumpets and drums, the clatter of horses' hoofs, and the tramp of soldiers' heavy boots. It was a glorious sight: the horsemen in their bright blue coats, white trousers tucked into riding boots, burnished helmets shining in the sun, sitting up so insolently in their saddles, with polished swords held point upright; and the long, endless lines of foot soldiers—the grenadiers and the guards and the *voltigeurs*. And the drums never ceased beating. The drum major "threw his gold-knobbed baton as high as the second story, and his glances as far as the third where pretty girls sat at the windows." In the marketplace,

> everything was changed, as if the whole world had been freshly painted. There was a new coat of arms on the town-hall; the iron railings of the balcony were hung with embroidered velvet; French grenadiers stood guard; the old councillors had put on fresh faces and wore their Sunday best and looked at one another in the French manner and said "bon jour." Ladies were peering from every window, curious citizens and smart soldiers filled the square, and we boys clambered up the huge horse of the Elector and looked down on the motley crowd in the market place. *(Ideas: Book Le Grand)*

The French soldiers were billeted in Düsseldorf homes for a time, and the Heine family had a French drummer quartered with them. His name was Le Grand, and he was destined to be immortalized by Heine in *Ideas: The Book Le Grand*. Little Harry clung to him like a burr, followed him everywhere, "on guard, to the roll call, on parade." He polished the buttons on the drummer's uniform "till they shone like a mirror," and he whitened his vest with chalk. Above all, he learned the revolutionary language of the drum. Monsieur Le Grand beat out the *Marseillaise*—and the boy understood the meaning of *liberté;* he drummed "Ça ira, ça ira—les aristocrates à la lanterne!" and the boy knew what *égalité* meant. And Monsieur Le Grand told him of the heroic exploits of the great emperor, and each time he spoke of a bold deed he drummed the march to which it was performed; and the boy saw the emperor cross over the Alps, saw the emperor on the bridge at Lodi, in his gray cloak at Marengo, on his charger at the Battle of the pyramids, at the Battle of Austerlitz (my, how the bullets whistled), at the battles of Jena, Eylau, Wagram. Monsieur Le Grand drummed to a wild crescendo so that little Harry's eardrums nearly burst.

Six years later, when Harry was fourteen, he saw Napoleon himself! Down the great avenue of Düsseldorf rode the emperor. He wore a simple green uniform. He rode a white horse, which moved so proudly. One hand held the reins and the other patted the horse's neck, and it seemed to the boy that the trees bent forward, and the sun bathed Napoleon in a golden halo. Down the avenue he rode, and the people shouted, "Long live the Emperor!"

On that day was born the young Heine's hero worship of Napoleon. As he grew older, he saw him as the incarnation of the great ideas of the French Revolution, the genius who swept away the kings and other relics of a dying age. Here he was like hundreds of writers and artists of the period who extolled Napoleon. Goethe told his countrymen, "Just shake your chains, that man is too strong for you." Hegel called him "this world soul." Beethoven named his third symphony the Bonaparte Symphony, then tore up the dedication when he learned that Napoleon had made himself emperor.

In 1828 Heine visited the battlefield of Marengo. He had grown wiser, and he reflected:

> Here it was that General Bonaparte drank so deeply of the cup of glory that, intoxicated by its fumes, he became Consul, Emperor, and conqueror of the world. And he did not become sober until he reached St. Helena. We did not fare differently. We too partook of his intoxication, and dreamed the same dream . . . Do not class me as an unqualified Bonapartist. Unconditionally I worship this man only until the eighteenth Brumaire. On that day he betrayed freedom.

But Heine could not divest himself completely of his past idolization of Napoleon, and he added: "My allegiance is not given to the actions, but to the genius of the man . . . I do not admire the deed—I admire only the human spirit . . . love sometimes clings passionately to old clothes, and thus it is that I am enamored of the cloak of Marengo." (*Journey from Munich to Genoa*)

Yet the importance of Napoleon went far beyond his military conquests. He had revolutionized a decaying society and changed the world in which Harry Heine grew up. When the days of glory had receded into the past, a chastened Napoleon said that he would be remembered more for his civil code than for the forty battles his armies had won; and truly, the Napoleonic Code is his most lasting achievement. For the first time in modern history, a system of uniform law was created, which applied equally to all inhabitants of the state—

rich or poor, plebeian or aristocrat, Jew or gentile. But this was only the beginning of his grandiose plan to reshape France and the empire from top to bottom. Just as he had given personal attention to the deliberations of the commission that drafted the civil code, so he participated in the planning of a centralized educational system throughout the lands of the empire from the North Sea to the Mediterranean. In 1808 an imperial decree ensured that every school in every corner of the Continent would be conducted in accordance with directives drawn up in Paris. All instruction would be in French, and at least one-third of the curriculum had to be devoted to French literature and history.

The Düsseldorf school that Harry attended was now part of this Napoleonic school system. His teachers were priests who were steeped in the writings of Voltaire and Rousseau, priests who in the church celebrated the Catholic services and rites in all their traditional beauty and color, and in the classroom taught according to the principles of the Enlightenment. For the most part, they were a kindly group, so much so, that, as he recounted it in his *Memoirs*, there was a time when he kissed the hand of every Franciscan monk whom he met in the streets of Düsseldorf.

It must have been quite confusing—all these pressures playing on the boy— German, Jewish, French, Catholic.

He was only a fair student. Latin was a torment. Many a time he stood in a cloister of the monastery and prayed to a figure of the crucified Christ, "Oh thou poor, eternally tormented God, if everything is really possible for Thee, help me that I do not forget the irregular verbs." French was painful. L'Abbé d'Aulnoi, who taught French, applied the cane when Harry could not remember the French for *der Glaube*.

> Six times, each time more tearfully, I answered, "It is *le crédit*." And the seventh time the examiner, purple with rage, shouted, "It is *la réligion*." And a rain of blows descended and all my school-mates laughed . . . since that day I never hear the word *réligion* without feeling a cold shiver running down my back, and my cheeks reddening with shame. And to be candid, I have found *le crédit* more useful to me through life than *la réligion*. (Ideas: Book Le-Grand)

But the class in Greek mythology entranced him. Here he first fell in love with the beautiful, serene gods and goddesses.

After school he would seek out Christian Sethe, his closest friend. The pair were a familiar sight: the mercurial, mischievous Jewish boy, and the tall, grave Teuton. They remained friends long after they had both left Düsseldorf. "You were infinitely dear and precious to me," Heine wrote to Christian in 1816, at a time of great suffering for him.

Christian stood loyally by his side through many a boyish scrape. But even Christian was not able to help him on that day when laughter and mockery turned the world into a horrible place. It had begun when he asked his father to tell him about the grandfather whom he had never known. Samson, engrossed in his own thoughts, answered that there wasn't much to tell beyond the fact that grandfather was "a little Jew with a long beard." The next day, when he came to class, Harry could hardly wait to announce this remarkable news.

> Scarcely had I conveyed this piece of information, than it began flying from mouth to mouth, was repeated with all sorts of intonations, and accompanied by all sorts of animal noises. The boys jumped on desks and benches; tore down the multiplication tables from the wall, so that they clattered to the floor along with the inkstands. What a laughing, bleating, grunting, barking and crowing pandemonium broke loose! And the constant refrain was that my grandfather was a little Jew with a long beard . . . Our teacher heard the uproar, came rushing back in a fury . . . it was proved that poor me had caused all the uproar, and I received a good thrashing for my offense . . . the aftereffect of those early impressions has been so strong that whenever I hear of little Jews with long beards, a weird chill . . . creeps up and down my spine. *(Memoirs)*

Harry stood at bay. A wild hatred seethed within him. After school Christian tried to comfort him, but he shook off his hand and ran away. "I hate you, I hate all of you," he shouted. Big, serious Christian gazed sadly after him until Harry was no longer in sight. Harry did not run home. He headed straight for his secret place of refuge, the attic in the home of his uncle Simon.

Simon van Geldern lived in a house that had over its door a carved, brightly colored figure of a Noah's ark, and the house had come to be so named. He was an eccentric old gentleman. He dressed in the old-fashioned style: short breeches, white stockings, buckled shoes—and he wore a long pigtail. He had inherited money after the death of his parents, but his chief occupation was collecting books and manuscripts and writing letters on political topics to the newspapers. He had taken a liking to his bright and eager nephew, and he permitted him to rummage at will through his large library and the contents of the attic.

The loft was filled with marvelous antiques and with old and modern books and manuscripts: travel books, works of philosophy, medical treatises, astrological and alchemistic charts and tables. One other inhabitant shared this hiding place with him, an old Angora cat, which, when the sun shone through the dormer window, was transformed into an enchanted princess.

One afternoon young Harry made a thrilling discovery. He found a journal in one of the trunks, and he began to read it. It had been written by his great-uncle, another Simon van Geldern. It was the story of his life, and no character in fiction ever lived a wilder and more romantic one. He was born in 1720 and died in 1794. He was referred to in the family as "the Oriental," because of his wanderings in the East and his habit of always wearing oriental clothes when he returned home. In his late twenties he had suddenly begun his travels. He turned up in Morocco, where he learned the armorer's craft. He became the sheikh of a warlike Bedouin tribe, which delighted in plundering passing caravans. He made a pilgrimage to Jerusalem. He eventually returned to Europe where he shone at various courts, dazzling everyone with his personal charm, his mastery of horsemanship, his desert dress, and his mysterious necromancy. Unfortunately, he dared to make love to a very exalted lady, and had to flee on his horse, leaving all his other belongings behind him. His flight ended in England, where he pursued a more humdrum existence and wrote stilted French verse.

The story of his great-uncle had an extraordinary effect upon the boy. He began to lead a double life, to a point where he identified himself completely with his great-uncle; indeed, he imagined that he was a reincarnation of the robber chieftain, the desert horseman, the romantic courtier. In his dreams he met strangely attired men with wild, adventurous faces whom he greeted as if they were old friends. Amazingly, he understood their strange language, and to his astonishment he answered them in their own tongue and gesticulated vehemently in a fashion utterly unlike his normal self.

This strange episode of daydreaming lasted for about a year. In his *Memoirs*, Heine observed—perhaps waggishly—"Many idiosyncracies, many extremely annoying sympathies and antipathies not at all in accordance with my nature . . . I explain . . . as after-effects of that time of dreams when I was my own great-uncle."

When he was fourteen Harry passed from the grammar school to the lyceum. The headmaster was Rector Schallmeyer, who was a friend of the Heine family. (Betty's father had saved his life when he had been stricken with a severe illness.) Schallmeyer took a personal interest in Harry, and he invited him to attend his class in philosophy. There he introduced Heine to the pleasures of that subject, ancient and modern; he acquainted him with the world of skepticism and sophistry and with the delights of playing with words. Soon rumors reached Samson that his son had been heard uttering irreverent remarks. Thereupon he lectured his offspring.

My dear son, your mother sends you to study philosophy with Rector Schallmeyer. That is her concern. For my part, I do not like philosophy as it is nothing but superstition, and I need my own wits about me for my business. You can be as much a philosopher as you please, but I must ask you not to say in public what you think. It will hurt my business if my customers learn that I have a son who doesn't believe in God. The Jews in particular will stop buying any more velveteens from me, and they are my best customers; they pay their bills promptly; they are honest, and they love their religion. I am your father and therefore older than you and more experienced; and you must believe me when I tell you that atheism is a great sin. *(Memoirs)*

It was one of the longest speeches Samson had ever made. It was fortunate for his peace of mind that he was kept in ignorance of certain discussions between Schallmeyer and his wife in which the rector urged Betty to send her son to Rome to study theology there. Schallmeyer assured her that he had friends among the top prelates, and that with their help a brilliant boy like Harry was certain to advance to the highest ranks of the Church. Heine learned of these talks in 1843, when, an exile in Paris, he made a secret visit to his aged mother in Hamburg.

It had not been any Judaic convictions that had influenced his mother to reject the churchman's extraordinary advice. Other motives persuaded her to turn down his suggestion:

> At the time she dreamed of lofty, worldly dignities for me. Furthermore, she was a disciple of Rousseau, a strict deist, and it seemed to be quite wrong to put her son in the cassock which displeased her so when worn so clumsily by German priests. She did not know how differently the Roman abbots wore their cassocks, with what grace and what coquetry they shrugged their shoulders clad in the black silk mantles which are the pious uniform of gallantry and preciosity in eternally beautiful Rome . . . In the end I might have risen to the loftiest post of honor, for although I am not by nature ambitious, I would not have turned down a nomination to be Pope. *(Confessions)*

At the age of sixteen Harry met his first love. Her name was Red Sefchen but he called her, affectionately, Josepha, and she was the same age as he. Her grandfather and her father had both been executioners. The father had died when he was quite young, and she had gone to live with her grandfather. He died when she was fourteen, and she was then taken in by her aunt. The two lived on the outskirts of Düsseldorf, ostracized by most of the townspeople because of the stigma of the executioner's calling. But with Josepha, Harry had his first, youthful love affair.

> As she wore no corsets and very few undergarments, her close-fitting gown was like wet cloth on a statue. But no marble statue could vie with her in beauty . . . Her great, deep, dark eyes looked as though they had asked a riddle and were waiting tranquilly for the answer to it; while her mouth with its thin, arching lips and chalk-white teeth, rather long, seemed to say, "You are stupid, and will guess in vain." Her hair was red, red as blood, and hung in long tresses below her shoulders, so that she could bind them together under her chin. When she did that, she looked as if her throat had been cut, and the blood was gushing in red streams. *(Memoirs)*

Red Sefchen knew many old folksongs and ballads, which she sang in a husky, passionate voice. Other times she told him stories of her early life with her grandfather. Shudderingly, she would tell of times when she was left all alone, and the wind howled, and the ghosts of those who had been executed came knocking at the windows and begged to be allowed to come in and warm themselves. Then she would fetch the executioner's sword and whirl it around and point it at them threateningly, and they would vanish like the whirlwind. At this point in her story Josepha stopped and burst into tears, and Harry put his arm around her and kissed her, a trembling, virginal kiss.

> Despite the infamy which fell upon those who came in contact with any of her outcast race, I kissed the lovely daughter of the executioner. I kissed her not only because of my own tender affection for her, but also in scorn of society and all its dark prejudices. *(Memoirs)*

Harry left Düsseldorf within the year, and he did not see Josepha thereafter. But he never forgot this illiterate, superstitious girl whom he saw secretly. She had been the only person to whom he dared show his poems; his mother frowned upon them, and he was reluctant to show them to anyone else. But red-haired, dark-eyed Josepha listened admiringly to them. "She had certainly the greatest influence on the poet waking in me," Heine wrote in his *Memoirs*. "My early poems, the 'Dream Pictures,' written soon after this time, have a grim and gloomy coloring—like the relationship which then cast its bloody shadow over my young life and thoughts."

Impelled by his instinct to side with the victims of prejudice, Heine had sought the company of the executioner's daughter. A similar example of this trait is his relationship with Joseph Levy, a fellow student at the lyceum.

Levy was an object of ridicule as he strolled about the Düsseldorf palace gardens, a work of Spinoza in one hand and a piece of bread and herring in the other, a habit that had earned him the appelation of "the herring philosopher." He was said to be both an atheist and a radical, and he was on bad terms with his father and brother. Heine was the only person who was friendly with him. They went on long walks, discussing Spinoza and Kant while Heine overlooked the smell of herring. Even after Harry had left Düsseldorf, he concerned himself with his friend's welfare. Writing from Hamburg to his friend Christian, he pleaded: "I must beg of you to befriend poor Levy. It is the voice of humanity you hear. I implore you by everything you hold holy to help him. He is in the direst straits. My heart bleeds." It says much about Heine's compassion for a friend that he wrote this letter at a time when he was himself suffering great personal unhappiness. In a separate letter to Christian we find him crying: "I wish to drown my senses. Only in the infinite depths of the mystical can I rid myself of my interminable pain."

2
Frankfurt and Hamburg: Amalie (1815–18)

The French occupation of the Rhineland meant years of prosperity for the merchants of Düsseldorf. Samson did so well that he bought one of the finest houses in the town, and Betty, as befitted a van Geldern, engaged household servants, and also dancing, drawing, and music teachers for the children.

But, seemingly overnight, their comfortable world collapsed. Napoleon lost his *Grande Armée* in Russia, the French withdrew from the Rhineland, and Russian dragoons occupied Düsseldorf in 1813. An economic depression followed; shops and mills closed; and Düsseldorf reverted to being a sleepy river town of fifteen thousand inhabitants. Samson's business was hit hard, and the servants had to be given up. Suddenly the family was thrown into poverty. The blow to Samson's self-esteem was devastating, and he was too dispirited to start over afresh. He fell into a state of lethargy, and Betty more and more took over the handling of the little business that remained.

One day she sat Harry down for a long talk about his future. Writing verses and studying philosophy with Schallmeyer were a sterile existence. They had hoped to send him to university, but that was now impossible. However, the world of business was open to him, and there he could achieve wealth and prestige. Fired with enthusiasm, Betty cited the examples of his own uncles. There were his uncle Solomon in Hamburg, a millionnaire many times over; his uncle Isaac, a banker in Bordeaux; and uncle Henry, a broker in Hamburg. Harry listened dutifully and offered no opposition. He was moved by the revelation of the depth of his mother's fervor.

A short time later his father arranged with a banker friend of his in Frankfurt, a Herr Rindskopf, to accept Harry as a trainee in his bank. Board and lodging would be provided at the banker's home, a fortunate provision as Heine soon found out. The eighteen-year-old boy came to Frankfurt in 1815 in high spirits. After all, he was a bright, imaginative youth, and the unknown future beckoned alluringly, as it always does to the young. Who could blame him if he did dream of emulating Uncle Solomon? But two months later he was back in Düsseldorf.

Nothing in his experience had prepared him for the Frankfurt ghetto. He had not imagined that such vileness was possible. In Düsseldorf Jews and

31

gentiles lived in harmony with one another, and there was no ghetto. His best and most beloved friend was a Christian. He had been taught by Catholic priests and he had learned to love the color, the incense, and the music of the Church. Here in the Frankfurt ghetto the streets were narrow and dark, the moldering houses were crowded warrens, the sanitation facilities were nonexistent. Rooms were workshops during the day and sleeping quarters at night. And the humiliations! Ludwig Börne, a contemporary publicist described them in these words:

> On Sundays, they were not allowed to leave their street, lest they be beaten by drunkards. Before their twenty-fifth year they were not allowed to marry, so that their offspring might be strong and healthy. On holidays they could not take a walk outside of the gate before six o'clock in the afternoon, for fear that the excessive heat of the sun might harm them. They were prevented from using public sidewalks and were forced to betake themselves through the fields, so their agricultural talent might be stimulated. If a Jew crossed a street and a Christian called out: *"Mach Mores, Jud!"* the former had to take off his hat and through his courtesy cement more closely the love between the two religious groups. (Quoted by Frederic Ewen in Introduction to *The Poetry and Prose of Heinrich Heine*)

There had been an alleviation of the harsh treatment of the Jews during the Napoleonic occupation. Indeed, they were granted full civic rights in Frankfurt—although only after the payment of the enormous sum of 450,000 gulden. But after the fall of Napoleon and the return to Prussian sovereignty, the patrician rulers of the city voided the agreement with the Jews and reinstated most of the former restrictions of the ghetto. They refused, however, to return the 450,000 gulden.

Heine walked through the Jews' quarter, sad and trembling with rage. Over the years, under the influences of his rationalist mother and the free-thinking priests, he had given up his belief in the God of the cheder. He had replaced Him with a friendly but irascible God of his own creation, a great jester, at home equally on Mount Sinai, on Mount Olympus, or in Valhalla. He was not sure of his relationship with this deity, but there would be time to figure that out. He had not abjured his Jewish identity; in fact, he thought it gave him a certain distinction. But above all he considered himself to be a German, a German poet. Yet in this strange city he was looked upon as an alien, inferior being. What kind of a world was it? "Ist sie ein Tollhaus oder Krankenhaus?" (Is it a madhouse or a hospital?)

When Heine returned to Düsseldorf two months later he shunned his friends. He spent his time reading in his uncle Simon's library or writing poetry. He never talked about the Judengasse of Frankfurt.

Both her son and her husband were in a state of deep despondency. Something radical had to be done, and the indomitable Betty acted. She wrote to her husband's wealthy brother, Solomon, and begged him to spend a couple of days in Düsseldorf to rescue Samson from impending bankruptcy. She planned, when he came, to wring a promise from him to take Harry into his bank in Hamburg.

Solomon had the aura of success about him. His manner was domineering. When Harry mentioned that he wrote poetry, Solomon jeered, "My boy— poetry—is that a profession?" The remark stung. "A more noble one than banking," the young poet shot back. "Well, well, a firebrand," Solomon snorted. "But I'll make a businessman of you yet." Harry kept silent. He vowed to himself, "The day will come when he will treat me as his equal." It was the opening parry in a lifelong duel between the proud uncle and the equally proud nephew.

Solomon had arrived with his daughter, Amalie. They stayed longer than he had planned. He was shocked at his brother's despairing state of mind, and he tried to infuse new hope into him.

Amalie and Harry were thrown together, and she completely dazzled him. She was an enchantress from a world of splendor. He had never known a girl like this dainty kinswoman of his, this flower of the Heine line. She was sixteen, mature for her years. She was part impish girl, part grown woman; by turn tender and reserved, serious and flirtatious. She enjoyed testing her pow- ers over men. In this forsaken town of Düsseldorf she played a game of love with Harry. She found him really clever, amusing. He was good-looking. Everyone commented that there was a startling similarity between them; he had the same blond coloring as she, the same laughing blue eyes, even the same timbre in the voice.

He took her for a walk in the Düsseldorf gardens. She laughed infectiously at his witticisms. He kissed her, and it seemed to him that she returned his kiss. That evening he composed a poem, struggling over it late into the night. Just before the time of her departure, he handed it to her.

> Tell me who first invented the kiss?
> That was a mouth on fire with bliss.
> He kissed, unthinking, all through the day.
> It was the lovely month of May
> Up from the earth the blossoms sprang,
> The sun laughed, and the birds all sang.

She placed her hand on his arm and looked at him sweetly, then gave him a warm cousinly kiss. He was conscious of her fragrance and the touch of her warm fingers. Then the coach bore her away.

Now he counted the days until his uncle would summon him to Hamburg. Then he would see her. She had trapped him. He could not forget her—her laugh, the way she had looked at him, her kiss, the touch of her hand. Ah, that shimmering world from which she came, he would conquer it.

Sometimes a shred of sanity jolted him. She had never said she loved him. He was a fool. But reason was helpless before the ecstasy and the longing that had seized him. In his dreams she was his.

> . . . And lo, his love enters . . .
> Of shimmering sea-foam her dress is.
> She glows till she grows like the bud of a rose,
> Her veil gleams with gems; and her tresses
> Fall to her feet in a golden array;
> Her eyes are impassioned. The lovers give way
> And yield to each other's caresses.
>
> He holds her so close that his heart almost breaks.
> The wooden one now is afire;
> The pallid one reddens, the dreamer awakes,
> The bashful is bold with desire.
> But she, she coquettes and she teases, and then
> With her magical veil she must blind him again,
> Who blindly does nought but admire.
>
> (Prologue to *Lyrical Intermezzo*)

The rays of the afternoon sun left a golden sheen on the sides of the ships in the harbor of Hamburg. The floes of ice in the water had come rather early this year. Harry Heine, sitting on a bench, listened to the chants of the sailors and watched a ship with raised sails head toward the open sea. His heart was full of yearning. He played with fancies. To what port was the ship sailing? Would its voyage be a calm one, or would it run into storms, as his heart had run into storms in this corrupt town of shopkeepers, profiteers, and whores?

His face darkened as he thought of the humiliating scene he had witnessed yesterday: a rabble of young men and pot-bellied merchants marching down the street, yelling, "Out with the Jews!" and breaking the windows of Jewish shopkeepers as they proceeded.

If only it were tomorrow night and he were already at his uncle's chateau. Amalie would be there, surrounded by her cursed circle of admirers, those sons of millionnaires, high society folk, and assorted lickspittles. Oh Amalie, you with your sweet kisses and words of love, why do you toy with me? Why do you utter words of love and then betray me? Is it all only the game of a vain, spoiled darling?

Harry stood up and strolled away, hands in his pockets. He was hungry. He would stop at the Swiss Café, order a meal, and watch the girls parade along the Jungfernsteg, that beautiful promenade shaded with lime trees and fronting on the Alster Basin.

The café was a tentlike affair, built out into the water, and it was a very nice place indeed. But he had hardly begun to eat when the most horrible, desperate cries put an end to his meal. He walked out to the edge of the pier, and he saw the white swans thrashing around in agony. Their wings had been broken to prevent them from flying away to the warm south when winter arrived. The Alster Basin had frozen over, but the ice had been cut over a small area, and it was there that the swans were screaming. A guard remarked that the cold was good for the swans, but that was not true, thought Heine. It was not good for anyone to have his wings broken so that he could not fly to the beautiful south with its lovely flowers, golden sunlight, and blue mountain lakes.

Solomon Heine, barred from enjoying the honor of citizenship in the free city of Hamburg because of his religion, nevertheless was no meek son of Abraham; he held his head high. He had begun life as a penniless youth, but he was reputed to be worth thirty million marks. The town councillors never failed to tip their hats to him when they passed him in the street. He owned a town house in the city and a country estate on the Elbe. A castle with turrets and battlements, the chateau stood high on a hill. Below, formal gardens, fountains, and statues; parkland and a running brook stretched in all directions; and in the distance one could see the Elbe, its water headed for the North Sea. The chateau itself was furnished with elegance and taste.

On weekends it was quite usual for a circle of Hamburg's social elite to gather at the castle. Harry, who lodged at the widow Robertus's decrepit old house in the Grosse Bleiche area of Hamburg, was often invited there. When he first appeared at these salons, he was a popular figure. The young people, especially, were captivated by his Heinesque humor and irreverent witticisms. He wrote to Christian that the nephew of "the great Heine" was much sought after. "Pretty girls ogle me, their bosom kerchiefs rise and fall, and their mothers calculate." But then his letters to Christian changed. These "diplomatic cocks-of-the walk, millionnaires, sage senators" were not his kind of people, he wrote.

Suddenly Harry became conscious of gossip and ridicule directed against him, the poor nephew who had appeared out of nowhere and won the favor of the wealthy banker, and who assumed such superior airs and smiled so ironically at one. The clique of toadies and relatives treated him as an intruder who did not belong, as someone who was trying to worm his way into the great man's favor and fortune. They loosed upon him their snobbery and refined insults. When he joked, "My mother read fine literature and so I became a poet; my uncle's mother read tales of Cartouche, the bandit chief, and so her son became a banker," they ran to Solomon and gleefully repeated the disrespectful witticism.

Conscious of his worth, and trapped in an alien and hostile surrounding, Heine's defense was an air of superiority and disdain, a mocking smile, and a sharp tongue. In this connection, one may observe that his later unfavorable and satirical utterances against Jewry, particularly against German Jewry, were a reflection of his experiences in this Hamburg period. "When I spoke of Judaism as a disease, I was only thinking of the German Jews," he once stated.

Among his very last verses can be found the bitter stanzas of *Castle of Affront,* in which the pain and humiliation of these days is recalled.

> The years roll on, the castle stands
> With tower and battlements on high.
> The castle and all its stupid folk—
> I can't forget them, though I try.
>
> Still I see the weathervane
> Upon the roof; it used to creak.
> The anxious looks that people cast
> Toward it before they dared to speak.
>
> No one spoke until they knew
> Which way the wind was blowing up,
> For fear the surly Northern bear
> Would snap at them and say, "Shut up!"
>
> . . . .
>
> I do not know a single tree
> Without its tale of jeers and quips
> That fell upon my luckless head
> Alike from coarse and dainty lips.
>
> The toad that listened in the grass
> Told everything to neighbor rat,
> The rat made sure the viper knew
> The viper got the tale off pat.
>
> He told it to his friend the frog,
> And all the filthy clan in town
> At once the gossip heard, and knew
> The insults I had to swallow down.
>
> . . . .
>
> I watched with envy ships that sailed
> To far-off happier, blessed lands
> But alas! The accursed castle stood
> And held me tight in cursed bands.

Yet he stayed and did not try to flee the castle of affront. The truth was that he was trapped in the most hopeless, the most poignant of loves, his love for Amalie.

In order to remain near her, he "swallowed down the insults," stayed, and let himself be held "tight in cursed bands." In the beginning he had convinced himself that she returned his love. "A golden star draws me northwards," he wrote Christian when he left Düsseldorf for Hamburg. Soon enough he realized that he had lived in fantasy, that she had forgotten him. He released his agony in letters to Christian, his faithful confidant:

> She loves me not. You must utter that last word softly, very softly. In the first of these little words there is eternal heaven, but in the last only eternal hell . . . to be near her, and yet to languish for weeks fruitlessly for one of her blessed glances—that, oh that, Christian, can tempt even the purest and most devout heart into wild, insane godlessness . . . I do not know whether the poems I write now are better than those I used to write, only I am sure that they are much gentler and sweeter, like sorrow dipped in honey

He continued to pursue Amalie. His passion was too strong for him to do otherwise. She, sure of herself, accepted his homage. He was different from the general run of her admirers. He wrote poetry (not that she cared very much for poetry); he was rather good-looking; he was good at coining clever remarks.

Amalie was playing with fire. In spite of herself, she began to respond to his lovemaking. Her smiles became promises; the kisses became longer and deeper; the embraces more bold and passionate. She uttered words of love, torn from her in moments when she was carried away, but which Heine took far more seriously than she wanted them to be taken.

Moments of love! He never forgot them. The secluded spot under the giant, shady tree, with the wind off the North Sea. They lie on the thick fragrant grass. She responds to his embrace, and she murmurs words of love, of passion. She is so young and fresh and sweet, and she vows that he is her world.

And he believed her.

Solomon did not understand his nephew. Harry did not show any gratitude for what he was doing for him; he acted as if the fact that he was a poet entitled him to special consideration. What nonsense! Why didn't he apply himself to his business? He had worked hard when he had first come to work for him at the bank, two years ago in 1816. And now when Harry had told him he wanted to go into business for himself as a dealer in textiles, he had put up the capital for his nephew. Sad to say, the lad spent as much time strolling on the Jungfernsteg or sitting in the Swiss Café watching the girls as he devoted to his business. Naturally enough, the firm of Harry Heine, dealer in imported textiles, was on the edge of bankruptcy.

But there was a more urgent reason why his nephew was on his mind these days. He was aware that Harry was pursuing Amalie, and he did not like that at all. None of his possessions brought him the joy and pride that his beautiful, fashionably reared, lovely daughter did. She was the priceless jewel of his house. He would never permit her to throw herself away on a scribbler of verses. Of course, he doubted that Amalie would be so foolish as to let an infatuation run away with her; she was too sensible a girl. Still . . . At the first suitable moment he would have a parental talk with her.

Heine was spending the week at the chateau. His parents, sister, and younger brother were coming for a short visit. He suspected that it was not purely a social call, that his own future would be discussed. He awaited their arrival impatiently.

When they got off the coach, he rushed to hug and kiss them. They passed the evening in an affectionate family reunion. He basked in their love. They were all so sure of his eventual success. Even as a child, he had been the one for whom destiny had surely planned great things—not his sturdy, practical brothers, nor, of course, the girl of the family. Lottie had great news to tell him: she was engaged. He was delighted. His Lottchen was all grace, daintiness, and harmony, and she deserved the good man she had fallen in love with.

But after this happy evening, Heine grew more and more gloomy. Amalie chose to wall herself off from him. She retreated behind an army of cavaliers who invaded the castle that week of festivities. Then came an unpardonable affront.

He was strolling through the castle to get to his quarters, when he heard Amalie's voice reading something aloud and being interrupted by bursts of feminine laughter. Coming closer, he saw her with a group of her friends lounging in a corner of a large room; they didn't notice him. Then he realized that what Amalie was reading and what her friends were giggling and laughing at was a poem he had written to her, and to her alone. He rushed away before he could be seen.

He was blind with humiliation and anger; he must flee the accursed castle. He was stopped by someone's outstretched arm. He turned and saw Karl, Amalie's older brother, looking at him solicitously. "You look angry, Harry. What is it? Is it Amalie again?" Good, kind Karl. He was so different from Amalie, always kind, never snobbish. In fact, Karl had confided to him that he shared his contempt for the aristocracy and admired his poetical talent. They were the same age, and many a time they went exploring in Hamburg. Karl, who affected the airs of a man about town, had taken him to Lorenz's where the best oysters and Rhine wines were served. They frequented the Jungfernsteg and ogled the girls. They had made the acquaintance of Helga and Sybil, the two charmers who entertained the public at the Apollo Music Hall and entertained them privately in their own tawdry rooms. Ah, to flee to Sybil now, and rid himself for a while of his torment.

"Harry, it would be best for you to forget Amalie," he heard Karl say, commiseratingly. Harry opened his mouth to speak, then stopped. His suffering was evident. Suddenly his words came in a rush, yearning and bitter, absurdly theatrical and touching. All the misery of the unhappy poet poured out: "What hellish agony—to be near her, sometimes to have her look at me with affection, and the next moment to see in her eyes haughty disdain. To be near her, to languish for a smile from her, to confide my heart's pain and love in verses that I write for her alone, and then to hear her read those sacred lines to others and laugh at them—that is shameful behavior, and it wounds me. She has pearls and she has diamonds, why does she play with me? But I will not grovel before her, I will not."

Karl waited for Heine to go on. "I'll be leaving soon anyhow." Harry spoke in a more quiet tone. "I'll be off to the university, if your father will listen to my mother and set aside an allowance for me."

Karl changed the subject. "Don't miss tonight's dinner, Harry. Marshal Blücher is the guest of honor." He pulled at Heine's arm. "Come, let's take a walk around the grounds."

The evening was a gala one. The great dining hall was ablaze with light and resounded with laughter and talk. Servants kept coming and going with the endless courses: barley soup, dumplings, meatballs, herring, sauerkraut, stuffed chestnuts, goose, oysters—and brandy, beer, and wines.

Harry hardly touched his food. Not even the playfulness of Lottie, who was sitting next to him, dispelled his gloom. Amalie was torturing him. She sat at the far end of the long table, and she acted as if she was utterly captivated by the blond *Herr* who was making her laugh so delightedly. Why did she place her hand so often on his arm? Harry took another drink. There was a roaring in his ears. Clouds of cigar smoke choked him. Through the fumes, the figures of the diners assumed strange shapes: the men, squat, with red jowls hanging limply, low foreheads, cold eyes, fingers cramming and shoveling food into their immense mouths; the women, bejewelled, big-bosomed, upholders and exemplars of virtue and piety—with each bite of herring biting into someone's good name.

Harry stared at the marshal. He was a man in his seventies, but he ate and drank with gusto. As he did so, he regaled his listeners with tales of his exploits against Napoleon, of how after the great victory at Leipzig he had called for a war to the end. Napoleon could have been finished off then, but the diplomats had overruled him. He had to take to the field again, and five months later he had led the brave Prussian lads across the Rhine and into Paris. Once more the diplomats saved Napoleon, and he came back at Waterloo. What a bloody battle that was! At the end, forty-five thousand dead sprawled over an area of three square miles!

The diners strained to hear the marshal's every word. Harry, too, listened to the story of that legendary day. Wellington, waiting for Blücher and the Prussians to arrive, holding off repeated charges of the French. Blücher, evading Grouchy and his army who are looking for him at Namur, slips away. The Prussians, arriving at Waterloo at 7 P.M., join the British, and Napoleon is crushed.

Blücher finished his thrilling account. The wife of a city councillor turned to Harry and whispered, "Our wonderful Prince Blücher—he is such a grand old man!"; her husband in turn stood up and in a burst of patriotic emotion offered a toast to the marshal and to the greater glory of Prussia. The assemblage rose, clinked glasses; eyes grew misty.

Heine turned to look at Solomon and he was struck by a similarity in the features of his uncle and Marshal Blücher. Both men had proud faces, piercing eyes, eagle noses over thin-lipped mouths and jutting chins. They got on very well with each other, two proud dominating men.

Heine had joined in the toast to the marshal, but his heart was with the emperor, the Little Corporal, who was now in exile on the lonely island of Saint Helena, twelve hundred miles off the west coast of Africa. His armies had toppled kings from their thrones and brought *liberté, égalité, fraternité* wherever they advanced. But now, thought Harry, as he looked around the room, the jackals bark at the lion, and the aristocratic flunkies are in the saddle. He closed his eyes. The buzz and hum of the dinner talk, the deeper voices of the men and the higher voices of the women faded away, and he heard other sounds and saw other sights. He heard the people shouting, "Long live the Emperor!" as Napoleon rode down the great avenue on his white horse. . . .

The dinner came to an end. The waltzing was ahead, but he did not feel like dancing. He wandered out onto the terrace. The music and the laughter penetrated here, but he felt sad and alone. What was she doing? She loves me, she loves me not. Suddenly Amalie had her arms around him, and she was whispering terms of endearment, and she said that she had been looking for him, that she was glad to escape from that boring Johann. "Don't say anything," he whispered, and held her close. He did not ask her why she had flirted so outrageously. The minutes passed.

"Amalie."

"Yes?"

Heine's voice was urgent, pleading. "I will be going off to the university, and it will be ages before I see you again. With all your high society and parties and balls . . ." He stopped.

"Yes, Harry?"

"You will forget me."

"Don't be foolish. How could I ever forget you?"

"Will you remain true to me? I will write such poems about you that all the world will know of our love. But promise me."

"How you talk!"

"This wealth, this luxury, this castle, it's a different world from mine," Heine exclaimed despairingly. "Would you leave it for me?"

"You are my dear, beautiful poet."

She embraced him, but she had not answered his question. In the distance, the plaintive, sweet sounds of the nightingale rose and fell.

The last carriage had rolled away; it was an age when guests did not stay beyond midnight. In one of the large drawing rooms, Solomon, his brother, and the two wives were settled comfortably. Samson waved away a cigar that Solomon offered him, and the latter turned to Betty.

"Well, Betty, I'm sorry I couldn't sit down with you for a long talk before now, but I've been so busy. I know you want to talk to me about Harry. Now, what is your latest plan for that Harry of yours? First he was going to be a diplomat, then a banker, then I set him up as an importer of English goods, but I'm afraid that will not work out either. What do we do with him now?"

"Solomon, it's true that Harry has not yet found himself. But be patient. The three of us have talked it over, and I believe we are on the right track now. We want to send Harry to the law school at the University of Bonn. He will make a good lawyer."

Solomon took a deep puff on his cigar before answering. "Betty, Betty," he teased. Then, suddenly somber, he observed that he was not sure that a Jew would be given a lawyer's license. Betty answered that there were ways to get around that. She went on: "We need your help, dear Solomon. Some day you will be rewarded for all your kindnesses, dear brother-in-law."

"If I help him, he must promise to attend to his studies. I will give him an allowance for three years. At the end of that time, I will expect him to have his doctorate in law, and to begin practicing right here in Hamburg."

"You will not be sorry."

"I trust not."

Aron Hirsch, Solomon's chief accountant, carrying out his employer's instructions, had secured a fine carriage for Harry Heine upon his departure from Hamburg several weeks later. He was rather fond of the harum-scarum young man, and now, as he helped Harry tuck away his few possessions, he chided him gently for having failed to build his career; after all, he was the nephew of the great Solomon Heine.

Harry smiled. Hirsch could not understand how he hated the business world. Hirsch was content to spend each day going through the same motions, like a puppet on a town hall clock; each day calculating: twice two is four. Harry laughed out loud; a sudden fancy had seized him: what if it suddenly occurred to Hirsch that twice two is five—that all his life he had been making a terrible mistake! What a panic would overcome him!

"Never mind, Hirsch, I may surprise all of you yet."

The carriage rolled away. He was headed for home, where he would study and prepare for the entrance examinations to the university. Good, reliable Christian was enrolled at Bonn; he looked forward to his company.

Harry Heine was happy, this summer day in the year 1819. The light breeze from the north felt good. The coach jolted and bumped over the rough road. He was lost in fantasy. He saw Amalie as she lay with him under the trees in the park on the Elbe. Once again he heard her voice on the terrace, murmuring, "You are my dear, beautiful poet." Each passing hour her image became more lovely and desirable. In his fantasies, he returned to Hamburg, a doctor of laws, and he swept her into his arms, his beautiful, his ever beloved bride-to-be.

But Solomon had other ideas for his daughter's future. The day after his nephew's departure he broached the subject. Bluntly, he asked her what were her feelings toward her cousin. She answered that she liked Harry very much.

"He is not for you, daughter. You are too sensible a girl to ruin your life because of an infatuation with a scribbler. A future with him would be an unhappy one. I know, I know."

"I have not said I am going to marry him, Father."

"I am glad to hear that. Remember, you are the daughter of Solomon Heine. There are many men who find you desirable. Why not? Choose a man worthy of you. Johann, for one. Now there is a fine young man. He is a businessman. He has a great future ahead of him. He would take care of you in proper style. He would be a son-in-law I would be proud of. All Hamburg society would come to your wedding; you would visit Italy, France, England for your honeymoon." It was a long speech for Solomon, whose remarks were usually more terse.

"I will think about what you say, father."

Solomon pinched her cheek affectionately. "I know you will do the right thing."

As Amalie sat at her casement window that night, rubbing cream into her face and brushing her hair, she shed a sentimental tear. Maybe it was fortunate that Harry had left Hamburg. Maybe her father was right. Harry was so different from the others . . . His lovemaking had been so intense he had carried her away. Sometimes he had frightened her. He had been bold, very bold. How could she have permitted him to go as far as he sometimes had . . . And he had habits that marked him off from other people. He didn't like to dance, he didn't smoke or drink. He made fun of merchants and bankers, and of people who converted . . . Yes, her father was right. He wasn't of her class . . . All she had promised Harry was that she would never forget him . . . It would be fun to float lazily in a gondola in Venice. . . .

Dreamily she gazed at the reflection of the cold moon in the placid waters of the brook.

3
Bonn and Göttingen: *The Two Grenadiers* (1819–21)

Heine barely passed the entrance tests of the University of Bonn in 1819. The examiners noted that he knew nothing of Greek or mathematics, and little of Latin. They observed that he did display some knowledge of history, and that he did well in his German composition. A hint of the future satirist was already evident in Heine's essay. Ludwig Marcuse, in his biography *Heine, A Life Between Love and Hate* relates the following:

> The subject was "What would you regard as the essential considerations in deciding upon any particular calling" and Heine wrote: "For the instructions given in these lecture rooms the first essential is desks; for they are the supports, the props and the groundwork of the wisdom which comes forth from the mouths of the teachers and which is noted down by careful students. Desks are, moreover, memorial tablets for our names, which we carve with our penknives so as to leave a record for future generations." The chairman of the examining board ascertained two undeniable facts from this essay—first, that Heine had "departed seriously from the subject that had been set"; and second, that he had a "notable tendency to satire."

Although he had promised his uncle that he would apply himself to his legal studies so that he could earn his degree in the shortest possible time, Heine took only one legal subject: a course in Old German political law. All his other studies were in history and literature. What could torts and contracts offer to compare with the excitement of Arndt lecturing on Tacitus's *Germania*, or Schlegel expounding the *Nibelungenlied?*

Equally far removed from the field of law was his involvement with the university chapter of the Burschenschaft, a patriotic, revolutionary fraternity.

During the war of liberation against Napoleon, the German people had been promised a constitution and a parliament. Five times between 1810 and 1820 the king of Prussia had pledged this, and five times he had forgotten his solemn word. Instead, he had joined with the emperor of Austria and the czar of Russia to form the Holy Alliance, whose aim was to stamp out, in the name of religion and the Savior, all movements for freedom and democracy, wherever they arose. The satanic genius of this misnamed alliance was Prince Metternich, who sat in Vienna and thought of himself as "the physician in the great hospital of the world."

The Congress of Vienna, redrawing the map of Europe after the fall of Napoleon, set up a German confederation of thirty-eight states, among which Prussia was predominant. But a movement for a united Germany had been born, and it continued to grow. Metternich and Austria, however, feared the emergence of such a state and used espionage, bribery, censorship, and force to prevent German unity.

It was in this climate that the Allgemeine Deutsche Burschenschaft was founded at Jena in 1815 and quickly spread to other universities. A black, red, and gold flag was adopted as its emblem, the colors symoblizing the bloody struggle against the black night of oppression toward the golden sunrise of liberty. Unfortunately, the university nationalists too often looked back to the Middle Ages and the ancient German society for their inspiration and guidance. The Romantics discovered the *Nibelungenlied;* professors and historians annotated it, and students wrote odes to it. Unfortunately also, the inheritance from the Middle Ages included the hatred of the infidel Jew.

Heine, ardent and eager, joined the Bonn chapter of the Burschenschaft. He took the oath of chastity, bravery, and loyalty to the Fatherland; he was part of the glorious and holy struggle for the triumph of liberty and equality in Germany. Always an enthusiast in whatever he did, he became an active participant in the work of the organization. He wore the red cap of a student corps member; he spoke and wrote. And he was one of the organizers of a torchlight procession to the top of the Kreuzberg on October 18, 1819, the fifth anniversary of the Battle of Leipzig. It was there, too, that his first doubts about the movement surfaced.

One of the speakers was Wolfgang Menzel, president of the student association. His shock of unruly black hair framing a face of ruthless self-assurance, he bellowed to the crowd to show the German world what it could expect from them. Apply the purifying fire to the books that offended their patriotism, he shouted. The students hurled the unpatriotic books and newspapers into a huge bonfire, and since not all the un-German writings were at hand, they copied the titles of books on scraps of paper and threw them into the flames. Heine withdrew into the shadows.

But later he put his uneasiness aside. How pleasant the camaraderie, when of an evening the students gathered around the stove in their special room at the inn, with the wood burning brightly, the candles shedding a soft light, and the voices raised in song. Sometimes they declaimed patriotic poems, such as Grabbe's wild, passionate celebration of the victory of Arminius over the Romans, or Kleist's hypnotic hymn of hate against all foreigners, Germany to Her Children. The barbaric chauvinism of lines like "strike him dead, the law of nature questions not your reason fair" would leave him with a feeling of uneasiness, but then all the more glowingly did he speak of the coming time when Germany would be free, democratic, and united.

But his uneasiness did not leave him; his misgivings grew. At the meetings of the students there were fewer and fewer of those who believed in the principles of the French Revolution; more and more the Burschenschaft was taken over by the Teutons and the followers of Friedrich Ludwig Jahn.

Jahn, one of the founders of the Burschenschaft, had a devoted following among students and peasants alike. His speeches were endless apostrophes to the glorious German past, the German honor, the German soul. He extolled the superiority of the German people and praised brutality as a Teutonic virtue. He called for the moral regeneration of the race, to be achieved by the excision of the alien element—the French, the Slav, and the Jew. Among his dramatic proposals was a fantastic plan for a great, impenetrable forest to be planted along the border with France, with wild beasts set free in it, so that no Frenchman or traitorous German would dare to cross the frontier. Bands of the most fanatical of his followers organized themselves into military orders, wore their hair down to their shoulders, and donned gray cloth uniforms. They lived in camps organized along military lines, and periodically they descended in bands upon a selected city, took over the streets, and terrorized the population. To swell their numbers, they bullied parents into permitting their sons to stay at the camps, where they would be recruited by Jahn's followers.

What Jahn spoke in the streets, the philosophers preached in the universities.

Item: Johann Fichte, author of *Essay toward a Critique of All Revelation*(1792, a work highly praised by the great Kant) and rector of the University of Berlin from 1810 to 1812. Hailed for his *Address to the German Nation* (1808), which was said by many to be a majestic and biblical work, and which contained the following oft quoted peroration: "The state has a higher aim than guaranteeing peace, personal freedom, property, and the well-being of all. Its object is to spread the devouring flame of a greater patriotism." Fichte's concept of "a greater patriotism" included this advice: "The only way I can see to allow Jews to enjoy civil rights is to behead them all in a single night and furnish them with new heads that do not contain a single Jewish idea."

Item: Jakob Friedrich Fries, honored with the chair of philosophy and physics at Heidelberg and Jena. Author of *New Critique of Reason*, issued in three volumes in 1807. Suspended from lecturing at Jena because of "liberal political teachings." These teachings included the thesis that "the Jewish element has always had a devitalizing and demoralizing effect on all classes of society . . . It is necessary that the Jews be entirely destroyed."

Item: The universities of Jena and Kiel conferred the degree of *doctor honoris causa* on Jahn. A famous scholar dedicated his translation of Pindar to him, and another savant hailed Jahn as the author of "the formula for humanity's evolution to the heights."

Disillusioned with the false patriotism of the Burschenschaft, Heine stopped attending their meetings. He discovered and made friends with a group of students who read and wrote poetry; it included Karl Simrock, Johann Baptist Rousseau, Friedrich Steinmann, and his childhood friend, Christian Sethe.

They looked up to him because he actually had had verses printed in the *Hamburg Wächter.* Never mind that the journal had a small circulation and had paid him nothing for his poems; nevertheless, it was agreeable indeed to be held in high esteem by his friends and fellow students. But then he received recognition from the illustrious August Wilhelm von Schlegel!

Schlegel's lectures on literature and prosody drew not only students but also other teachers and scholars. His translations of Shakespeare were remarkable, and he had translated into flowing Germany many lyrics from Italian, French, Spanish, and Portugese. It was said that he could compose verses in any modern meter and thirty ancient ones. He was an authority on the *Nibelungenlied* and was one of the founders of the Romantic School.

Heine submitted some of his poems for criticism: Schlegel was impressed by them and made certain suggestions. Heine rewrote his verses. Then he was given the signal honor of being invited to Schlegel's home. The great man engaged Heine in serious discussion and taught him a new appreciation of the importance of form. When Heine mentioned his admiration for Byron, Schlegel suggested that he try translating him, asserting at the same time that he wondered whether certain portions of *Manfred* could be adequately translated.

Heine wrote to a Düsseldorf friend, Friedrich von Beughem, that he and Schlegel had "chatted for an hour over a steaming cup of coffee . . . His first question is always about the publication of my poems . . . You, too, dear Fritz, ask me the same thing. Unfortunately, I have to take many changes as a result of Schlegel's advice." One detects in this letter of the young poet a suggestion of Heine's manner of work, which already was marked by merciless self-criticism. "Be strict with yourself. Never spare the critical knife, even if it is your favorite child that has come into the world with a hump or a goitre or some other excrescence" was a favorite motto of his.

Schlegel remained his mentor, and he continued to echo the language and symbols of Romanticism in his poems, yet there already is evident in them something new in German poetry. He wrote and rewrote his verses endlessly, never satisfied until he achieved "the note of genuineness and true simplicity for which I always strive," as he wrote in a letter to the poet Wilhelm Müller.

Many years were to pass before the mature Heine, in 1836, wrote *The Romantic School,* in which he excoriated and held up to ridicule Schlegel, his former idol, and the other leaders of German Romanticism. Yet, he could not entirely negate the past, and, even as he pilloried Schlegel in the book, fond memory drew from him a portrait, half ironic and half tender, of the moment when he first met Schlegel.

He was, with the exception of Napoleon, the first great man I had ever seen, and I shall never forget his impressive appearance. To this very day I feel the thrill of awe that passed through me when I stood before his desk and heard him speak. I was wearing a shaggy white coat, a red cap on my long fair hair, and no gloves. Herr August Wilhelm Schlegel, on the other hand, wore kid gloves, and was clothed in the latest Paris fashion. He diffused an aura of good society and *eau de mille fleurs.* He was daintiness and elegance personified; and when he spoke of the Lord Chancellor of England, he added "my friend." Behind him stood his servant in the decorous livery of the Schlegel family, snuffing the wax candles that burned in silver candelabra upon the desk before the great man; there was in addition a glass of sweetened water. A liveried servant! Wax candles! Silver candelabra! Could this be the lecture of a German professor? All this magnificence impressed us young people not a little, and myself not least.

After a year at Bonn, Heine realized that he was making no progress in the purpose for which he had come to the university. Uncle Solomon was supporting him so that he would become a lawyer, not a poet. He concluded that as long as he was near Schlegel and the literary-minded group of friends, he would find it difficult to forget poetry and study law. He decided to leave Bonn and go to Göttingen, where he would be free from such distractions.

He left for his new place of study in September, 1820, traveling on foot, but on the way he made a detour to Düsseldorf. It was a sentimental sidetrip, for his parents did not live there anymore; Solomon had brought them to Bad Oldesloe, a village near Hamburg, after Samson's business failed and left him a broken, melancholy man.

It was on the stopover in Düsseldorf that Heine witnessed a sight that led to his writing his famous poem, *The Two Grenadiers.* The incident is related in his *Book Le Grand.*

But as I was sitting on the old bench in the Palace Gardens, dreaming of days gone by, I heard a confused sound of voices behind me—people pitying the fate of the unfortunate French, who had been dragged as prisoners to Siberia during the Russian War, and had been kept there many years in spite of the peace, and were only now on their way home. Looking up, I actually beheld before me these orphans of *la gloire;* stark misery peeped out through their torn and battered uniforms; hollow sorrowing eyes looked forth from weatherbeaten faces, and although crippled, weary and mostly lame, they still managed to keep a sort of military step, and they were preceded by a drummer who staggered along with his drum.

A strange illusion came over Heine that the drummer was the very same one whom he, as a small boy had followed around in Düsseldorf. He imagined that once again he was listening to Le Grand drumming "the old marches . . . The poplars near us trembled as he again thundered forth the red march of the guillotine. And he drummed as before, the old battles for freedom, the deeds of the Emperor."

The sound of the drum died away. The drummer and the French soldiers were gone. Heine continued to sit on the bench, thinking of the day when, along this very avenue where he was now sitting, the emperor had ridden and the multitude had cried, "Long live the Emperor!"

Only once or twice before, had Heine achieved the power and perfection of

The Two Grenadiers. Gone were the knights and dead lovers and all the stock phrases of his early poems; in their stead arose a miracle of simplicity, realism, and genuine emotion. It was a forerunner of the Heine to come.

Göttingen was a disappointment. A few weeks after his arrival, he wrote to Johann Baptist Rousseau at Bonn, "I am frightfully bored here. The tone is stiff, smug, snobbish. Everyone must live like a recluse. Here one can only be a grind, but after all, that is why I came here." To Friedrich Steinman, he wrote: "If I had not been intimidated by the distance, I would have gone straight back to Bonn. Fops, dilettantes, foolish minds, immobile faces—here you have the students of this place. The professors are even more lifeless."

The social atmosphere of the university was set by a clique of Hanoverian princelings whom Heine detested and despised. They associated in clubs whose membership was based on alleged descent from one or another tribe of the great migrations—Vandals, Frisians, Teutons, Saxons, Thuringians—and they sought to carry on what they believed were the manners and customs of these tribal ancestors. They talked only of dogs and horses and their forebears. They treasured and deemed it a high privilege to have a special table reserved for them at the the Rosy Mill, the Flying Jug, or one of the other inns. He ridiculed them with great glee in *Norderney:*

> The young noblemen grow up just like their fathers. The same conceit that they are the flowers of creation and we the weeds; the same foolish attempt to screen their own demerits behind the merits of their ancestors; the same blindness to the problematical nature of those merits—scarcely one reflecting that patents of nobility are seldom conferred by princes on their truest and worthiest servants, but most commonly on the pander, the flatterer, and other vile parasites.

Heine's scorn grew when, one Sunday afternoon, he witnessed a hunt organized by a group of these noblemen. Only it was a special kind of hunt, a sport in which the hunted animal was a man.

> The wretched man had already run in the broiling heat till he was pretty well tired out, when some Hanoverian young gentlemen who were studying the humanities offered him a few thalers if he would run the course again. The fellow ran, and he was deathly white and wore a red jacket, and close at his heels, raising a cloud of dust, galloped these well-bred, well-fed aristocratic youths on their fine steeds. Every now and then the horses' hoofs struck the gasping, hunted creature—who after all was a human being.

One night, out of curiosity, Heine went to a meeting of the Göttingen chapter of the Burschenschaft. He discovered a boisterous, beer-drinking crowd listening approvingly to an announcement that Jahn had decreed that lists be drawn up to be used by the new order when it came to power. Anyone who was descended even unto the seventh generation from a Frenchman, a

Slav, or a Jew would be exiled. The death penalty would be invoked against anyone who had ever written a word against Jahn, and the instrument of punishment would be the axe, and not that French instrument, the guillotine.

That night was another lesson that Heine never forgot. Years later, in *Ludwig Börne,* he summed up these so-called patriots as

> False revolutionaries who bawled much about love and faith but whose love was nothing but hate of everything foreign, whose faith consisted only of unreason, and whose ignorance knew nothing better than to invent the burning of books . . . The words "Fatherland," "Germany," "Faith of ancestors," and so forth, will always electrify the vague masses of the people far more certainly than the words "Mankind," "World Citizenship," "Reason of the Sons," and "Truth!" . . . I mean to say by this that the representatives of nationality are far more deeply rooted in the German soil than the representatives of cosmopolitanism, and that the latter will always be beaten by the former unless they swiftly forestall them.

Despite what he had written in his letters to Rousseau and Steinmann, Heine eventually attracted to himself a number of friends and admirers. Ferdinand Osterley, a fellow undergraduate at Göttingen, pictured Heine in his university days in very attractive terms.

> With few exceptions he was very open-hearted with friends, was the soul of amiability, showed the utmost delicacy of feeling and was upright and unsparing of himself. He was very boastful and yet in reality no one thought less of himself than he did; he liked best of all to joke about his ignorance of law. Although he suffered from violent headaches, he had an exceptionally cheerful and lively mind, the quality of which was reflected whenever something struck him as ridiculous.

According to biographer Max Brod, Heine's brother Max described him in his university days as "mild, gentle, and soft-hearted, but becoming extremely violent when made angry; sometimes in such cases even belying his normal nature by giving way to deeds of violence." This temper of Heine's—he had had it since childhood—sometimes led to duels, for he never shrank from a fight.

He wore his bright red cap far back on his head to show the dueling scars that testified to his intrepidity. His walk was nonchalant, with his hands usually thrust deep into his yellow nankeen trousers. His shirts and wristlets were always immaculate and trimmed with ruffles. He never smoked, and he drank little.

A few months after his arrival in Göttingen, he had a violent quarrel with one Herr Wiebel, a Junker student and challenged him to a duel with pistols. The rector, hearing of the dispute, called in the two students and tried to effect a reconciliation. Both were refractory, but they finally agreed to call off the duel. Nevertheless, the university authorities were not satisfied. They decided to apply sanctions, although the university code that forbade dueling had rarely been enforced. It was true that no duel had actually taken place, the authorities conceded, but, they argued, the crime had been *contemplated,* and it had not been consummated only because the authorities had stepped in and stopped the duel. After long and grave deliberation, the officials hearing the case delivered their verdict: Herr Wiebel was suspended from classes for one week; Herr Heine, as the challenger, was held to be more guilty and was suspended for six months.

Then, in the midst of this turmoil, a letter came that threw Heine into a frenzy. He learned that Amalie was betrothed to another; her fiancé was Johann Friedländer, a wealthy property owner in Koenigsberg. His anguish and rage were unbearable. It couldn't be true. Oh the stupid little fool, shallow and calculating. . . . But he had always feared it.

Incapable of thinking clearly, not knowing what he would do when he got there, he packed and rushed off to Hamburg.

Whatever intentions Heine had had when he left, he realized the hopelessness of his journey when he arrived. He did not call on Amalie. What he actually did was to show up at midnight before her window and stand there in a freezing rain, and gaze upward. A shadow moved across the blinds—but let Heine himself tell it:

> All the madhouses had let loose their lunatics and driven them at my throat. The mad company celebrated its Walpurgis night in my brain, my chattering teeth provided the dance music, and warm streams of red, red blood gushed from my heart. The waves of blood washed around me, the fragrance of her misty presence dazed me, and she herself nodded and smiled down at me, in all the dazzling splendor of her beauty, so that I thought I would perish in infinite yearning and woe and ecstasy. (Letter to Heinrich Straube)

The letter closes on an ironic, Heinesque note: the slits of the blind moved, and the "bitter-sweet little head covered with curls which nodded down to me so amiably was only the old governness who was closing her Venetian blinds."

Had Amalie ever returned his love? Or had it all been a fantasy on his part, as a few biographers have claimed? Or theatrical posturing, as others have argued? It has been asserted, for instance, that Amalie never wrote to him in all the time he was at Bonn and Göttingen—at least no letters of hers have been found. But is it not highly possible that Heine might have destroyed such letters? Consider the remarks of the biographer Max Brod.

> I consider reticence to be one of Heine's distinguishing characteristics . . . He never breathed a word about the great love of his life. Amalie's name was hedged round in a profound silence, and the strange aftermath, his love of Amalie's young sister Therese—"new folly grafted on to old"—remained undiscovered for many years after Heine's death. Researches carried out

much later . . . show Heine practicing a studied reticence which is deeply moving.

How far this reserve of Heine's went is revealed in a letter to his mother at a later period. Writing to her from Paris in June 1851, he informed her that he had burned all her letters and Lottie's to him, since "I would not do anything in the world to expose you to the rude curiosity of a later generation."

In any event, after the letter to Straube, Heine never again spoke of his heart's pain, and rarely mentioned Amalie's name, except on one occasion many years later in Paris. It was to Gérard de Nerval, poet, and dear and sainted friend—de Nerval, toward the end of his life increasingly lost to bouts of madness, who hanged himself one wintry January night in 1855; de Nerval, who in his lucid moments was the most enchanting of companions, and for whom it was a labor of love to translate Heine's poems into mellifluous French—it was to de Nerval that Heine revealed his heart's buried pain. A dam broke and he repeated to the gentle de Nerval words he had once written to Christian: "I was a mad chess player, and at the very first move I lost my queen, and yet I went on playing—playing for the queen. Rage alone kept back my tears." Heine wept then—uncontrollably, and de Nerval, poor saintly soul, wept with him and confessed that he was suffering from the same malady, trying to sing to death a hopeless passion.

Following the tragicomic episode in Hamburg, Heine left for Bad Oldesloe, where he found an unhappy and gloomy home. His father was deeply melancholic, his mother complained of headaches, and Lottie suffered from catarrh and dreamed of her forthcoming marriage and escape into a happier world. Gustav's ambition was to become a rich landowner, and Max hoped soon to study medicine at the University of Heidelberg, but these plans were dependent upon uncle Solomon's aid.

He had to escape. Where? He could not return to Göttingen, where the suspension still had months to run. Suddenly he thought of Berlin, and the more he thought of it, the more attractive the idea became. He would pursue his law studies at the university there in earnest, he told his mother. He cheered her by suggesting that at the University of Berlin he would meet important people who would be helpful to him in obtaining a professorship or a diplomatic post. He did not mention that in the back of his mind was the thought that he might get a book of his poems published. He spoke in this vein, but still stayed on. Then, with the coming of spring, he acted. He wrote to Schlegel asking him to provide letters of introduction to people in Berlin. Schlegel responded quickly, and with the letters in his pocket Heine left for Berlin.

The date was March 1821. As he rode in the coach, he thought of other times when, with high hopes, he had departed for other places—Frankfurt, Bonn, Göttingen. He was sure that this time it would be different. An exciting world lay ahead. His discouragement and dejection vanished; he became his buoyant self again.

4

Berlin: *Poems by H. Heine, Letters from Berlin, Donna Clara, Essay on Poland,* and *Tragedies with a Lyrical Intermezzo* (1821–23)

It was a zestful, dreamy, scoffing young poet who knocked on the Varnhagens' door and presented a note from the renowned Schlegel, highly laudatory of its bearer. Heine did not know it at the moment, but they—husband and wife—would become the warmest and truest and most understanding of friends. They recognized his unique talent, they realized it might even be genius, but they did not hesitate at the same time to criticize his weaknesses and youthful follies—severely and sharply if they thought it necessary.

August Varnhagen von Ense, of aristocratic lineage and a diplomat, was fourteen years younger than his wife, Rahel, who had been born Rahel Levin and had converted to Protestantism. She was in her fifties, in poor health, small and plain-looking, but Heine was completely captivated by her. He called her "the little woman with the big soul," and "the most intellectual woman in the universe."

Her home was a center, a magnet that drew diplomats and princes, poets and musicians, philosophers and scientists. There they gathered to talk, declaim, argue—about life and death, about music and poetry, about the theater, about eating places, about loves eternal and loves strange.

There were other such salons in Berlin, presided over by women, most of them Jewish. To meet the intellectual and social elite, to make one's literary reputation, to be abreast of the latest ideas, it was necessary to be admitted to these salons. When, after the defeat of Napoleon, the anti-Semitic movement sought to exclude Frenchmen and Jews from German society, it found itself helpless against these salons. Many a prejudiced writer or statesman had to confess defeat and seek entry into one of these centers of culture.

No salon was more famous than Rahel's; even royalty came regularly to the gatherings at her home. She was called the Berlin Madame de Staël, and indeed she rivaled Germaine de Staël in her ability to attract a coterie of the elite, although she was not an author, as was Madame de Staël, who had earned the distinction of having one of her works banned by Napoleon for being "un-

French" and had to flee France to escape his police. Rahel's love life, unlike the Frenchwoman's, was a conventional one.

From her early days Rahel had worshipped Goethe, and she devoted herself to proclaiming his greatness. It was said that it was because of the preaching of the apostle Rahel that Goethe's true stature was universally recognized. Anything that challenged the supremacy of Goethe was met by her instant battle cry.

She had never been a beautiful woman, and now she was ailing. But she was blessed with a gift for inspiring people of the most diverse talents and interests to talk to one another. She had a saying: "Human beings must get together if they want to use their brains, to love, to practice justice."

Heine's friendship with Rahel was one of the most important of his life. They had their misunderstandings and quarrels, but what she meant to him was movingly expressed in the farewell letter he sent her when he left Berlin May 1823.

> I am going away soon and I would like to ask you not to consign me to the lumber room of oblivion . . . If after a few centuries I shall have the pleasure of seeing you again as the loveliest and most beautiful of flowers in the loveliest and most beautiful of all the valleys of Heaven, I hope you will once more have the kindness to greet me as an old friend with your friendly glance and your gracious presence. You did as much in the years 1822 and 1823, when you treated me, a sick, bitter, morose, poetical and insufferable creature, with a tact and kindliness which I certainly never deserved in *this* world, and must owe only to your tender recollections of me in an earlier acquaintanceship.

Varnhagen urged Heine to submit his poems to F. W. Gubitz, the editor of the *Gesellschafter*, and, acting upon the suggestion, he called in person. Thrusting a sheaf of poems upon the editor, he blurted out nervously, "I am completely unknown to you, but through you I hope to get known." Gubitz smiled courteously, took the poems, and perused them with growing interest. He himself wrote poetry and was a discerning critic, and as he read them, he was impressed by the uniqueness of tone and phrase, the commingling of romanticism and realism in the work that had been handed him. He told the author that he would accept some of the poems for publication, but that there were lines that would never pass the censor. Heine murmured, but agreed to revise his verse; the *Gesellschafter* was a widely read publication, and to be published in it would make him known. Five of the poems appeared in the May issue of the periodical, and others were published in later numbers, almost always after first being "gubitzized," Heine's humorous term for the changes he made to meet the restrictions of the censor.

As he came to know the editor better, Heine discovered that Gubitz was a warm-hearted and unusually considerate person. When he became aware of the poverty in which the poet was living, he did what he could to help him. On one occasion, he heard that Solomon was in Berlin visiting the banker Lipke, who, it so happened, was also a friend of the editor. Gubitz thereupon asked Lipke to arrange a small social where he could meet Solomon. When the two met, the editor told Solomon that his nephew possibly was a genius, that he had heard how the uncle was helping him, and that he hoped he would never abandon such a nephew. Solomon responded that he did not intend to do so, but that Heine had to learn how to use money, even if he was a poet; then he turned to Lipke, and after first joking that he hoped Gubitz was right about the genius of his nephew, instructed Lipke to remit two hundred thalers to Heine at once, and an equal sum in each of the next two years.

The generous-hearted Gubitz also took time from a busy schedule to find a publisheer for Heine's first book, *Poems by H. Heine.* It appeared in December 1821. The use of the initial "H" is interesting. Heine must have decided that Harry was too foreign a name for a German poet, yet he could not bring himself to use the German Heinrich. In fact, even after he was baptized a few years later as Christian Johann Heinrich Heine, he rarely signed a letter with the name Heinrich. According to Emma Lazarus, he always insisted that his works appear under the name H. Heine, and when a publisher on one occasion printed the full name he was furious.

He received forty free copies as payment for his first printed book. He must have smiled, a little ironically, but still, there it was, he had been published! He considered how to dispose of the books. The very first copy to Rahel and Varnhagen. One to his old mentor, Schlegel, to friends at Bonn and Göttingen, to his parents and Lottie . . . Then he set about composing a letter to the revered Goethe. He rewrote it several times before he was satisfied with it.

> I could give a hundred reasons for sending your Excellency my poems. I give only one: "I love you." That is reason enough. My versifying I know as yet has little merit; yet I hope that here and there passages show that I may be able to do something in the future. I was long perplexed about the nature of poetry. People told me: "Ask Schlegel." He said, "Read Goethe." That I have done in all reverence, and if I shall ever do something worthwile, I will know whom to thank. I kiss the noble hand which has shown me and the whole German people the way to heaven.

Goethe never replied.

Poems by H. Heine included some sixty poems, a few of which had previously appeared in magazines. Many of them echoed the traditional Romanticism, but there were some that stirred the discerning reader to a realization that here was a poet of more than ordinary talent.

The Two Grenadiers was in it:

> So, like a sentry, I'll lie in my tomb
> And silently take heed

Till at last I hear a cannon-boom
And the trot of a neighing steed.
Then will the Emperor ride over my grave,
While sabres flash and rattle:
Then will I rise uparmed from the grave—
For the Emperor, the Emperor to Battle!

and *Belshazzar,* written when Heine was only sixteen. It was inspired by a few words in the Hebrew hymn sung at the Passover seder service: *Va-yehi ba-chatsi ha-layela* (And it came to pass at midnight).

And with sinful hand the King takes up
A holy goblet, filled to the top.
And hastily he drains it dry,
And with foaming mouth he utters a cry:
"Hear how I mock you, Almighty One!
It is I that am King in Babylon!"
And see! and see! on the walls of white
A hand like a man's began to write;
And wrote, and with letters of fire seared
The wall, and wrote, and disappeared.
The monarch sat and stared ahead,
With shaking knees, and pale as the dead.
Cold sat the courtiers, chilled to the bone,
And made no sound, were still as stone.
The Magi came, yet of them all
Not one could interpret the words on the wall.
But ere the sun rose up again,
Belshazzar was murdered by his men.

For the sentimental reader there was a group of lyrics, like the poignant and nostalgic *Lovely Cradle of My Sorrow,* that captivated with their simplicity and seeming artlessness.

Lovely cradle of my sorrow,
Lovely tomb where peace might dwell,
Smiling town, we part tomorrow.
I must leave; and so, farewell.

The reviews of Heine's first book were on the whole laudatory. He was particularly pleased with the comments by Karl Immermann, the eminent Prussian poet, dramatist, and novelist.

Throughout most of Heine's poems there runs a rich vein of life. He has the first and last prerequisite for the poet; heart and soul and that to which these give rise; an inner story. You can tell that at one time or another he must have intensely felt and lived the content of his poems. He possesses the true spirit of youth, which is a lot in an era when people are born old.

The theologian Schleiermacher wrote that never before in German literature had a poet "bared his inward life with such boldness and such astonishing ruthlessness"; that they bore the stamp of truth, "and since truth possesses a wonderful and irresistible power," that here was another reason for the over-whelming fascination exerted by Heine's poems.

Suddenly Heine became a literary celebrity. Elise von Hohenhausen, Rahel's rival as a literary priestess, introduced him at her Thursday night salons as "the German Byron," a comparison that pleased him greatly; he had long called that poet "my English cousin."

Two months after his book was published, Heine entered a new field, that of social and political commentary. In February 1822, the *Rheinisch-Westfälischer Anzeiger* printed the first of his series of *Letters from Berlin,* which continued to appear until June. He had to skirt thin ice in what he wrote, for the royal power did not permit anything to be published that was even mildly liberal or disrespectful of authority. Ernst Hoffmann's novel *Master Flea,* was banned for satirizing the commission in charge of investigating conspiratorial groups. Plays like *William Tell* and *Egmont* were prohibited. In his first letter, Heine reported that Heinrich von Kleist's *Prince of Homburg* would not be per-formed; it seemed that the censor disapproved its satire of a member of a high aristocratic family. Most of what Heine wrote was mere gossip and light froth: news about the royal family, the opera, the circus, and the fancy dress balls. But now and then the irrepressible satirist in him reappeared and he enjoyed himself jousting with the censor. Thus he wrote that in Berlin, unlike Paris or London, political and social conflicts could not break out because "the royal power, mediating powerfully and impartially, stands at the center." Slyly, he then went on to write that partisanship in Berlin was expressed in taking sides in cultural matters, as in the field of music. Here the censor stepped in, for Heine was referring to the fact that the Berlin public was divided into the Spontini camp, which admired the Italian composer favored by the king, and the von Weber partisans who hailed the German composer. It was forbidden, of course, to question the talent of a musician admired by the royal house. Such writings met with the disfavor of the authorities, and there was a move to banish Heine from the capital. However, friends intervened and he toned down his writings.

But in his final letter, he dropped his caution and spoke up sharply against a move to replace the Napoleonic Code, which was still in force in the Rhine-land, with the reactionary Prussian system. The attempt was defeated, and in fact the Napoleonic Code remained in effect until 1900. Heine's letter was quite bold and ensured that from then on he would remain a political suspect in the eyes of the Prussian authorities:

> The Rhinelanders are begrudged their Rhenish judicial procedures; there is a move to redeem them from those "fetters of French tyranny" . . . May our

beloved Rhineland long bear these fetters, and be loaded with yet others like them! May that genuine love of freedom long flourish on the Rhine, freedom not based on national egotism and hatred of France; a genuine vigor and youthfulness not swilled out of a brandy-flask; a genuine love of Christ which has naught in common with heresy-hunting bigotry and hypocritical proselytization!

A letter that makes pleasant reading is one in which he describes his feelings at a masked ball which he attended:

> Masquerades always delight me hugely. When the drums thunder and the trumpets blare and the charming tones of flute and fiddle intrude their alluring notes, I hurl myself like a mad swimmer into the tossing and gaily lighted flood of humanity and dance and skip and jest and chaff everyone and laugh and chatter . . . anything that pops into my head. And I pressed everyone's hand, and courteously doffed my hat to everyone; and everyone was as courteous to me. Only one German youth played the boor, and growled at me in his Teutonic, beer-drinking voice, "At a German masquerade, a German should speak German." Oh German youth! how your words strike me as not only silly, but almost blasphemous at such moments, when my soul lovingly embraces the entire universe, when I would joyfully embrace Russians and Turks, and throw myself in tears on the breast of my brother the enslaved African!

The masked ball was drawing to a close. He had danced, he had laughed, and he had flirted, and now he was strolling in the gardens with his conquest of the evening. The air was redolent with the incense of flowers and myrtle. He was enchanted by her bold glances, by the pliant body sheathed in a low-cut white gown of the latest French style. Who was behind the mask? Was she the daughter of a countess out for a lark, or was she the countess's nursemaid? Whoever she was, he looked forward to spending the rest of the evening with her.

They stopped under an awning in the shadows. Heine reached out to take off her mask, but at that moment she cried out. He stopped, startled. "What is it, Hilde?"

"Something stung me. It must have been a mosquito. I hate these mosquitoes! Oh, why do we have to have mosquitoes and school lessons and nasty Jews! Why can't we have dances and parties and lovers like you?"

Heine stood stock-still. Even here! "Darling Hilde, what do you know about Jews? Have they hurt you?"

She shook her head. "No, but my tutor says that all Jews should be forced to wear a yellow badge, as in the Middle Ages. He says they are a plague on the Fatherland. And he has a solution." She paused and giggled. "He says that the Jews should be sold to planters in the West Indies to be used on plantations instead of Negroes, and that the men who can't be sold should be castrated, and their wives and daughters put in brothels." Again she giggled.

"Your virgin soul approves of this?"

"We must maintain our German purity, our German morality."

"Yes, Hilde, we must be pure, we must be moral."

As Heine gazed at her, she put her arms around him and pressed her lips against his. But at that moment a warning signal sounded.

"Oh, it's late," she cried. "They let the ball go until past eleven, and I have to go. Tell me, what is your name that you have kept from me? What family do you come from?" She started to remove her mask.

But he restrained her. He pressed a kiss on her forehead. In a manner courtly but mocking, and with a touch of sadness in his voice, he said: "Our pleasure is over. If only your soul were as lovely as your body! That one so young and fair should talk so evilly! You see, your handsome knight, your adored, is the son of the beloved Jewish merchant and well-known officer of the guard, Samson Heine. Shall I escort you back?"

Heine's *Donna Clara* was an outgrowth of this incident. When the poem was published, it was enjoyed by the reading public as a humorous satire. That had not been his intention. When a friend wrote him that he had found the poem very amusing, he answered that he had not intended it to be a work of humor, and in still another letter he reiterated that he had not meant to raise a laugh; that he had wanted to portray in the poem a specific incident that had a general, a universal application; that he had conceived the poem as a serious and melancholy one, in fact, as the first part of a tragic trilogy.

Reading *Donna Clara* in this light, one catches the sadness in the poem. The young poet's heart is full of love, and the world is full of folly, and so he seeks to ease his heart's pain with an anodyne of Heinesque magic. Hilde becomes a senora, he himself is a cavalier, whose zither

> Nightly draws me to my casement.
> As he stands, so slim and daring,
> With his flaming eyes that sparkle
> From his nobly-pallid features,
> Truly he St. George resembles.

As the poem opens, they meet in a garden of the Alcalde's:

> And with love's slight, subtle meshes,
> He has trapped her and entangled;
> Brief their words, but long their kisses,
> For their hearts are overflowing.
> What a melting bridal carol,
> Sings the nightingale, the pure one!
> How the fire-flies in the grasses
> Trip their sparkling, torch-light dances!
> In the grove the silence deepens;

Naught is heard save the furtive rustling
Of the swaying branches,
And the breathing of the flowers.

And against the backdrop of this magic knight we hear the refrain of the Christian woman:

Yes, I love thee, oh my darling,
And I swear it by our Savior,
Whom the accursed Jews did murder
Long ago with wicked malice.
Naught is false in me, my darling,
E'en as in my bosom floweth
Not a drop of blood that's Moorish,
Neither of foul Jewish current.

At the end of the poem the stranger reveals his identity:

I, Senora, your beloved,
Am the son of the respected
Worthy, erudite Grand Rabbi,
Israel of Saragossa.

Despite Heine's intention to write a tragedy, the poem emerged as satire because of its sustained and striking contrast between beauty and vulgarity, young love and age-old prejudice. *Donna Clara* marked a development in his humor. Heretofore his wit characteristically was a reflex action to insult and injury. *Donna Clara*, however, deals with prejudice as prejudice; it heralds the polished satire of later years, which he wielded with such mastery against life's follies and injustices and which entitled him to claim the august company of Aristophanes, Cervantes, Rabelais, Voltaire, Swift, and all the great satirists who have held up to life "the laughing mirror of wit."

Heine's book of poems had been favorably, even enthusiastically, received by Karl Immermann and a few other critics of equal stature, and for a while he knew the pleasure of fame. But suddenly he was aware of a concerted campaign of slander and malicious attacks against his works and himself personally. His poems were called "uninspired aberrations"; his brother Max wrote him that people in Hamburg were saying that Heine didn't understand German!

When his second book was accepted for publication, he was resigned to its getting unfavorable reviews, but the reality was worse than anything he had anticipated. He wrote Karl Immermann that "a clique of toads and vermin . . . have got hold of my book before it is actually published and from what I hear they are going to . . . bring it into contempt in a way which rouses my whole being and fills me with supreme disgust."

Yet he had expected it all. Even when the critics had lauded him, he had been certain that when the Jew-haters became aware of his antecedents they would unleash their hatred against him. Rahel chose not to see what was going on in the country; in her salon she was a queen who reigned over the great and the near great. She uttered hosannas to Goethe and was blind to the rising waters that threatened sooner or later to engulf the land. But he could not forget the pinpricks and insults he had suffered from childhood on, the duels he had fought at college. "Unto the seventh generation," Jahn had sworn. "Make them wear the yellow badge," Friedrich Rühs advocated. "Castrate the men, and place the wives and daughters in brothels," Hartwig Hundt wrote.

Driven by rage and pride, exploding with the accumulated anger of years, he wrote to his old friend, Christian Sethe.

I can no longer be your friend. I have always acted honestly toward you, and do not wish to deceive you now. Everything German is odious to me, and unfortunately you are a German. Everything German affects me like an emetic. German speech shatters my eardrums. My own poems nauseate me when I see that they are written in German. Even the writing of this letter makes me retch because the German script irritates my nerves. I would never have believed that those beasts commonly known as German could be at the same time so tedious and malicious a race. Farewell, dear Christian, and think of me as well as you can under the circumstances.

Later letters show that their friendship was renewed. But Heine's inner conflict was not resolved. He could not brook the fact that the stupid rabble dared to deny him the right to call himself a German poet, he who had always loved everything German, whose heart was an archive of German feeling, just as his two books were archives of German songs. But what was he?

He was a German and he was a Jew. His friend Christian was a German and a Christian. But Sethe was accepted and he was not. He recalled the ghetto in Frankfurt, the pogrom against the Jews in Hamburg. Now, in 1823, the Prussian government had revoked the civil rights granted the Jews in 1812 during the war against Napoleon. The professions were again closed to them, unless they chose the path of baptism. The thought that some day he might have to choose between conversion and leaving Germany flitted across his mind.

But hatred alone was no answer. He wanted a faith to give him inner peace and strength, and he needed to anchor it in a group identification. He was in this frame of mind when he discovered the Society for Jewish Culture and Science.

In the first two decades of the century, thousands of Jews from the educated strata in Germany had converted to Christianity. For many, it was a formal act to enable them to pursue a professional or artistic career. A growing proportion, however, were permanently lost to Judaism.

The Society for Jewish Culture and Science had been founded in 1819 by a group of brilliant intellectuals who wished to halt the tide of conversion and bring about a renaissance of Judaism. They dreamed of bringing about a synthesis of modern science and philosophy with Jewish history and religion, thereby destroying the ghetto mentality and reviving the proud and noble heritage of the Jewish people. They believed that in Germany a new era of enlightenment was dawning, that liberal and democratic ideas would triumph, and that this would lead to the separation of Church and state. In this new age, the Jews would shed their outworn manners and customs and their inner emancipation would be paralleled by the civil emancipation that would come with the triumph of reason.

Prominent among the leaders of the society were several devout admirers of the philosopher whose name was on everyone's lips and who held forth at Berlin University—Georg Wilhelm Hegel. They included Eduard Gans, a legal scholar whom Hegel considered to be his foremost disciple, and Moses Moser, a scholar in many fields who was also a businessman on close friendly terms with Heine's uncle Solomon. Gans and Moser were regularly present at Hegel's lectures, and it was there that they became friendly with Heine, for he too had fallen under the spell of the master. In later life he renounced Hegel, but the student Heine was enraptured by the iconoclast who delighted in shattering old beliefs. In *Confessions*, he etched a picture of the relationship that vibrates with life.

> One starlit night we were standing together at a window. I, a young man of twenty-two, had just finished a good meal and drunk my coffee, and was waxing lyrical about the stars. I called them the abode of the blessed. "Hm, the stars," growled the master. "Hm, a bright eruption on the face of the sky." "Good heavens," I exclaimed, "is there no place where virtue is rewarded after death?" "So," Hegel shot back, looking at me with his keen, pale eyes, "so, you want a tip for taking care of your sick mother and not poisoning your brother?"

His new friends assured Heine that the teachings of Hegel held the answers to the questions that were baffling him. The same dialectic that cut away at his faith in a higher being was used by these young Hegelians to prove that the emancipation of the Jews was inevitable. He listened to their explanations of how the inexorable dialectical process of history and the unfolding of the world idea must lead to the desired outcome. They painted a glowing picture of the Society for Jewish Culture and Science, which, basing itself on an understanding of these laws, would hasten and ease the historic development of the Jewish future.

They persuaded Heine to come to meetings of the society; he became more and more interested in the organization, and on August 4, 1822 Gans proposed him for membership. He was accepted, and, true to his nature, prepared to become active in the work of the society, but postponed this when a student friend, the Polish Count Eugene von Breza, invited him to come to Poland for a few weeks of summer holiday.

Count Eugene von Breza, member of one of Poland's proudest aristocratic families, was one of those beings who, without trying, captivate everyone with whom they come in contact, men and women alike. In one of his *Letters from Berlin*, Heine declared, "He was the only man whose company was always a delight, whose jokes always made me laugh, and whose clean features reflected what my own spirit was like before my life was sullied with lies and hatred."

Among the many women who succumbed to the aristocrat's charm was the duchess of Cumberland. A royal scandal threatened, and the king of Prussia demanded that Breza leave Berlin. The count returned to Poland and promptly wrote to Heine inviting him to spend a few weeks on one of the vast Breza family estates.

While in Poland, Heine moved in the highest circles of the nobility, enjoyed himself hugely, and was a favorite of the ladies. To them he penned a rhapsodic paean in the *Essay on Poland*, which he wrote upon his return to Germany.

> And now kneel down, or at least doff your hats—for I propose to speak of Polish women . . . what are the smudges of Raphael compared to the altar-pieces of beauty, which the living God so happily drew in his most joyous hours! What are Mozartean jangles when set beside the words, the stuffed bonbons of the soul, which gush from the rose-lips of these sweet creatures . . . these lovely ones, whom I . . . will call angels of the earth, just as I will call real angels the Polish beauties of heaven! Yes, my dear friend, whoever gazes into their gazelle eyes believes in heaven!

This tribute to lovely ladies made pleasant reading, and no doubt Heine engaged in a flirtation or two, but the *Essay on Poland* is testimony to the fact that he spent much time closely observing the daily life and customs of the nobility, the peasantry, and the Jews, who constituted the middle class. His comments on the three classes were astute and penetrating. He was filled with sympathy for the Polish struggle for freedom: "If the word 'Fatherland' occupies first place on the lips of the Poles, 'Freedom' has the second." But, he pointed out,

> the freedom of the Poles is not the god-like freedom of Washington. Only a very few, like Kosciuszko, have grasped it and sought to disseminate it. True, many individuals speak enthusiastically of freedom, but they make no attempt to emancipate their own peasants.

He was appalled by the treatment of the peasants. Once, witnessing an act of brutality to a servant, he was moved to anger and violent response. He was enjoying breakfast with his friend von Breza on the terrace of his country manor. While one servant handled the dishes, another one stood at the head of a curving flight of stairs that led down to a grassy courtyard, awaiting orders. The meal began pleasantly enough, but soon the conversation became animated. Waving his arms disdainfully, the count challenged Heine, "What is this Age of Freedom you are prattling about?"

"I am telling you," Heine answered, "That this is the age of emancipation, that the whole world is freeing itself from the rule of the aristocracy."

"Bosh! Some are born to reign, others to serve. That is how it has always been and that is how it will remain."

Heine rose and paced angrily. "Men are not born to be beasts of burden for a privileged few. Or perhaps you can meet Voltaire's challenge and demonstrate that the former were born with saddles on their backs and the latter with spurs on their heels?"

The count too, rose and shook his finger. "My friend, listen. The natural order of society has been ordained by God. Just as in Heaven he has set the angels close to his throne between Himself and men, so on earth the aristocracy is the mediator between king and people. We serve the king and take care of the people. Beware of upsetting the divine order of things."

"And I say, beware of the day that will come when your peasants will follow the example of the French, who, when all other paths were closed to them, enforced equality by tenderly cutting off the heads of their divinely ordained aristocrats."

Von Breza snorted. "We know how to handle our serfs."

The word "serfs" seemed to remind him that a servant was still awaiting his orders. He summoned the servant who was waiting at the head of the stairs. Words went back and forth, and the count began to speak in a sharp, angry voice. The servant's tone was cringing and apologetic. He retreated toward the stairs as his master grew more furious. Suddenly the latter delivered two brutal slaps across the menial's face, then threw him down the stairs. Turning around, the count was met by an infuriated Heine. The two exchanged heated words; they shouted at each other; they shoved. In the course of the fracas the count slipped and fell, and sprained his ankle.

"Glorious angel," Heine murmured, as he helped him up, "do you see how your simile limps?"

Gubitz published the *Essay on Poland* in the *Gesellschafter* in January 1823, but Heine wrote to Christian that Gubitz and the censor had "shamefully disfigured it." The article caused a literary and political uproar. The nationalists were outraged by Heine's condemnation of the treatment of Poles in Prussian-occupied Poland, and his charge that the reports of journalists about Poland were distorted by their prejudices and their habit of looking at the Poles through German spectacles. The wealthy Berlin and Hamburg Jews read the essay and were angered by the way he compared the German and Polish Jews and contemned the former.

I am still horrified when I recall my first sight of a Polish village almost entirely populated by Jews. What abysmal wretchedness . . . They had fled Germany to Poland long ago to escape religious persecution, for in this respect Poland has always distinguished herself for her tolerance. The Jews first brought trade and handicrafts to Poland, and in the reign of Casimir the Great they were granted extensive privileges . . . In those early times, the Jews far surpassed the nobles in intellect and culture, for the latter engaged only in military pursuits . . . The Jews, on the other hand, were at least busy with Hebrew scholarly and religious books . . . But they did not keep step with European culture, and their spiritual world has sunk into . . . hair-splitting scholasticism which has taken a thousand perverted forms. Yet, despite the barbarous fur cap which covers his head, and the still more barbarous notions which fill it, I esteem the Polish Jew more highly than his German counterpart . . . as a result of rigorous isolation, the character of the Polish Jew acquired a wholeness . . . The Polish Jew, with his dirty fur coat, his beard, his smell of garlic, and his queer speech is certainly preferable to many a German Jew who shines in all the glory of gilt-edged government bonds.

Upon his return to Berlin, Heine immediately plunged into the work of the Society for Jewish Culture and Science with all the ardor of a convert; he even became its secretary. He recruited members, laid plans for a women's auxiliary, and taught classes three evenings a week in French, Jewish history, and German history. He took no pay for any of this, although his financial situation was precarious.

A fascinating description of Heine delivering a lecture to one of his classes is this one by a student, as quoted by the biographer Max Brod:

Arminius was for him the model of a great hero and patriot who risked his life, his all, to win freedom for his people and to cast off the Roman yoke. When Heine, raising his voice, cried out, as once did Augustus: "Varus, Varus, give me back my legions!" his fine eyes sparkled, and his manly fetaures radiated joy and ecstasy. We could have kissed his hand, and our admiration for him increased and remained with us all our lives.

The portrait is striking. Some time before, in a moment of despair, Heine had sent the frantic letter to Christian Sethe in which he had renounced everything German, but the act had been an aberration. Later, to another friend, he wrote emotionally that never would he be able "to divest myself completely of my German character . . . I know that I am one of the most thoroughly German beasts . . . I love Germany more than anything else in the world . . . I delight and rejoice in her."

But at the same time he was too proud to renounce his Jewish lineage. Out of pride, out of solidarity with his embattled people, he had joined the society. He was not moved by any religious urge. When, a little later, Charlotte married, he wrote to her husband: "My attachment to Judaim stems solely from my deep antipathy to Christianity. Yes, I am a contemner of all positive religions, and yet I will at some future time probably accept the crassest Rabbinical doctrines merely because I consider them a time-tested antidote."

Disillusioned in German nationalism and unable to believe in any religious dogma, Heine searched for a faith, a cause that would heal the inner dichotomy. He thought he had found it in the Society for Jewish Culture and Science and, as we have seen, became an ardent proselyte.

But the inspiration did not last; his enthusiasm gradually waned. His experiences in Poland had sharpened his perceptions of the actualities and the dimensions of Jewish existence. Soon he came to the conclusion that the Hegelian scholars who guided the society were alien to the spirit and way of life of the masses of Jews: of the millions who led a wretched existence in Poland, and of the poverty-stricken shopkeepers, peddlers and artisans in Berlin itself. Gans and Moser and Zunz did not speak or write in the language of the common man. Their articles and speeches were scholarly, abstract, involved. Heine, the master of simplicity, rebuked them: "I do not demand the language of Goethe, but at least let it be intelligible. I am quite convinced that if I cannot follow an argument, neither will David Levy, Israel Moses, or Nathan Itzig."

The society remained a movement of the intellectuals; the masses spurned what to them was unintelligible jargon about science and history and dialectics. They refused to abandon their ancestral rites and traditions for a program that they suspected would end in self-extinction. In 1824, five years after it was born, the society went out of existence. Looking back in later years to that time of idealism and great hope, Heine concluded that the goals of the society had been illusory from the beginning and never could have been realized. "They tried to revive a long-lost cause, but they succeeded only in digging up the bones of dead martyrs."

His own affiliation with the society lasted only about ten months, nevertheless, it was of lasting value. It stimulated in him an interest in Jewish history and literature, a preoccupation that later was reflected in such works as *The Rabbi of Bacherach,* and still later, the magnificent and exquisite *Hebrew Melodies.* He made friendships that he cherished dearly, particularly the one with Moses Moser, whom he eulogized after the latter's death as "a man fired with a compassion for humanity and the desire to put his learning to practical use in healing its wounds. He never tired of helping others; he was unostentatious in his labors of love." Time and again Heine turned to Moser for help— sometimes for money, other times for suggestions and source material for *The Rabbi of Bacherach* or some other work he was engaged in. Moser was a confidant to whom Heine poured out his troubles in long conversations and in countless letters.

Heine had given up his work with the society and had left Berlin even before the official demise of the organization. But when he departed, he wrote to Moser: "I shall never cease to bestir myself in behalf of the rights of Jews to equal citizenship, and when troublous times come, as I feel sure they will come, from their drinking halls to their palaces, the German mob will hear my voice resound."

Heine's second book of poems, *Tragedies with a Lyrical Intermezzo,* which had aroused so much controversy even before its publication, finally came out in April 1823. It included two plays in blank verse, *Almansor* and *William Ratcliff,* and the wonderful *Lyrical Intermezzo.* The dramas have not stood the test of time, but the poems, a cycle of exquisite lyrics in which the poet tells the

story of his unhappy love, remain as the most widely read and beloved book of
love lyrics in all literature. Great composers such as Schubert, Schumann,
Mendelssohn, Liszt, Wagner, and Brahms have set them to music. It is said
that there are five thousand such songs in existence, and that *Du bist wie eine
Blume* alone has been set to over two hundred tunes.

Heine had written to be understood by the ordinary man and woman, and he
succeeded. The words were so simple, so artless, and the result was pure magic.
Lovers in all times and places have wept over them, the verses that grip and pull
at the heart-strings as they tell the story, by turn rapturous and poignant.

> I've loved you, and love you this very hour!
> And though the whole world crashes,
> Still the flames of my love will tower
> Over the cities' ashes.

> Whenever I hear the song
> My love sang long ago,
> I feel that my heart is wrung
> By a wild, a savage woe.

> Oh, let your tears with mine bedew
> The cheek you lay your cheek on,
> And let the flames of heart on heart
> Blaze in a single beacon.

> My songs, you say, are poisoned—
> How could they wholesome be
> When you with deadly magic
> Have poured poison into me.
> My songs, you say, are poisoned—
> How should they wholesome be
> When I bear a thousand serpents
> And, dear, among them—thee!

> A pine tree towers lonely
> In the north, on a barren height.
> He's drowsy; ice and snowdrift
> Quilt him in covers of white.

> He dreams about a palm tree
> That, far in the East alone,
> Looks down in silent sorrow
> From her cliff of blazing stone.

Karl Immermann praised the *Lyrical Intermezzo,* as did Wilhelm Müller, the
celebrated author of songs and ballads, but most of the Berlin critics were cool,
if not hostile. They could not deny Heine's poetical talent, but they were
disturbed by the new, alien themes they discovered in the poems. They were
accustomed to nightingales and roses, lotus blossoms and moonlight, as proper

subjects for love poems, but their aesthetic tastes were jarred by the mockery and what they called bad taste in so many of these poems. No, the critics agreed, one must condemn this kind of writing; once you begin to weaken your standards, who knows where it will end?

They were right in one respect: this was not the traditional Romanticism. Heine used the forms of the traditional German folksongs, but in tone and spirit his lyrics were the harbingers of a new age. Using the ordinary speech of ordinary people, Heine wrought a new lyrical realism reflective of the times. That this was his conscious aim is indicated in a letter he wrote Wilhelm Müller in June 1826.

My *Intermezzo* . . . owes its intimate style to your songs. I came to know the beloved songs of Müller just as I was writing my *Intermezzo* . . . it was not until I came to your songs that I found the genuine simplicity for which I was looking. How clear and pure are your songs! They are truly folksongs, but my poems, on the other hand, are folksongs only in form; in content they reflect our conventional society . . . reading your seventy-seven poems, I realized for the first time how new forms could be created from the old folksongs, retaining their popular character but without their crudity and awkwardness.

Heine always thought highly of his two tragedies. After the publication of *Tragedies with a Lyrical Intermezzo*, he said that he would be remembered for the plays even if the poems were forgotten. History has judged otherwise; the plays are generally regarded as unconvincing melodrama and poor theater, while the poems are considered a masterpiece of lyrical creation. Nevertheless, there are occasional scenes in the plays, particularly in *William Ratcliff*, when Heine's passionate voice breaks through and he grips the attention of the reader. The plays also have interest because of their evident autobiographical content. Almansor, the Moor, and Ratcliff, the highwayman, are both disguises for Heine; and Zuleima and Maria are transfigurations of Amalie.

He had begun writing *Almansor* as far back as the fall of 1819, when he entered the University of Bonn. Anti-Jewish outbreaks had occurred in a number of German cities that summer, and his anger and scorn were transferred to the play. He set it in sixteenth-century Spain in the period of the conquest and conversion of the Moors by the Christians, whose preaching of love was accompanied by the horror of the autos-da-fé, just as in the nineteenth-century Germany the preaching of the Gospel was accompanied by anti-Semitic violence. When, in the play, Almansor and his beloved leap to their death rather than surrender to the Christians, Heine was expressing his contempt for those Jews in contemporary Germany who chose baptism to escape persecution. He derided those who chose the "new faith with its honeyed accents," and he warned, "Like a plague spot, flee the house where a new faith rears its head." He was afire with inspiration. "I have poured all my wisdom," he said, "all my paradoxes, all my love, hatred, and folly into this drama." Later, however, he judged it more objectively, and he commented that it was "not only not a good tragedy, but doesn't deserve even the name of a tragedy," a statement that was unnecessarily harsh.

But he never had doubts about the merits of *William Ratcliff*. He wrote to Immermann, "I am convinced of the power of this piece, for it is true, or I myself am a lie." As late as 1851 he spoke favorably of it. In a preface to a new edition of the tragedy, he declared that in *Ratcliff* he had been one of the first to raise "the great soup question . . . which now daily boils over . . . furiously"; he was proud of the scene in the thieves' kitchen when Tom, the highwayman, says, "Long ago I divided all mankind into two nations engaged in savage war; the well-fed and the hungry. Because I belonged to the hungry party, I often had to brawl with the well-fed, but I soon saw that the fight was unequal."

This concept of the two parties appears and reappears in Heine's writings, in innumerable variations of language and form. It is basic in his social thinking. In 1828, when he became editor of *New Political Annals*, he wrote: "There are no nations left in Europe, only parties." The thought is there in many of the political articles he wrote as Paris correspondent for the *Augsburg Allgemeine Zeitung* from 1840 to 1844, reaching apocalyptic heights in a vision of a great war between Germany and France and its aftermath

that would only be the first act of the great melodrama. The second act is the European and the World Revolution, the great duel between the haves and the have-nots. There will be no mention then of either nationality or religion; there will be only one fatherland, the globe, and only one faith, happiness on earth . . . Wild, gloomy times are roaring toward us . . . The gods are veiling their faces in pity on the children of men, and perhaps in worry over their own fate. The future smells of Russian leather, blood, godlessness, and many whippings. I advise our granchildren to be born with thick skins on their backs.

But in the spring of 1823, the question of the general social condition was not uppermost in Heine's mind. He was despondent, in poor health, uncertain of his future. In part this was due to his feeling that he was the victim of a conspiracy by anti-Semitic elements to slander and defile his poetry, and to impugn his patriotism because of his article on Poland. At the same time, his financial situation was desperate: the income from his writing was meager; he owed money everywhere, and his uncle would not raise his allowance. Sooner or later he would have to tell him where he stood in his law studies, and the truth was that he had made very little progress there. He had spent far more time in the brilliant company found at the Varnhagens or at the salon of Elise von Hohenhausen than in the study of the Roman Code. To top it all off, the headaches that never left him were getting worse and worse. "Pains like hot lead run through my head and agonize me." He realized he would never be able to finish his law studies amid the distractions of Berlin. He was twenty-five—how much longer could he remain a student?

Once again the wanderer moved on. After two years and two months in Berlin, he left that city on May 3, 1823. His destination was the little town of Lüneburg, not far from Hamburg, where his parents now lived. His two uncles, Solomon and Henry, had found a comfortable home for them there. Solomon, in addition, undertook to take care of the forthcoming wedding of his niece Charlotte, and to provide for the education of his nephews Max and Gustav.

5

Doctor of Laws: *The Rabbi of Bacherach, Harz Journey,* and *The North Sea I* (1823–25)

Heine was indescribably lonely in Lüneburg. He wrote to Moser that he lived "in complete solitude," that the Jews were "insufferable," the Christian middle classes were "fools and animated by a singular hatred," and the upper classes were even worse. "Our little dog is sniffed at and abused in a special way by the other dogs in the street. Christian dogs harbor open animosity against Jewish dogs." He felt suffocated in the dull provincial town. He wrote long letters to his friends in Berlin, asking for news, views, and gossip, and begging them to send him books and journals. Moser particularly was helpful, and sent him the works of Goethe, Gibbon's *Decline and Fall of the Roman Empire,* Jacques Basnage's *History of the Jews,* as well as an Italian reader and grammar. Heine's one faithful companion was the household's little dog, which he named Amichen. We sense his loneliness in a letter he sent to his sister after she moved to Hamburg following her marriage: "When I read, every evening, the nice little animal sits on my shoulders and begins to bark whenever I come to a fine passage in the book. Amichen has more intelligence and feeling than all the German philosophers and poets."

Charlotte's marriage to Moritz Embden took place on June 22. Uncle Solomon, who provided Charlotte's dowry, was the guest of honor, and was quite genial with Harry, perhaps because his nephew had dedicated his second book to him, and the critics in Hamburg, unlike those in Berlin, praised the volume.

Harry took advantage of Solomon's good humor to ask him for a loan to pay for a six-week rest cure at Cuxhaven, a seaside resort on the North Sea. Solomon remained in high humor and, after listening to his nephew's description of his horrible headaches, agreed to give him the money, but laid down the condition that Heine return to Göttingen and complete his studies.

Meanwhile, Heine fell victim to "a new folly grafted on the old," as he described it in a letter to Moser. Solomon's wife and daughter Therese had come with him to the wedding. Therese was sixteen, the same age as Amalie had been when Heine had fallen in love with her. She was the image of Amalie, petite, with the same tinkling laugh. He tells the story in *The Homecoming.*

> The little one's like my sweetheart;
> I hear that laughter again;
> Her eyes are like those others
> That filled my heart with pain.

Years ago—it seemed ages now—Solomon had brought Amalie with him to Samson's home in Düsseldorf, whereupon Heine had promptly fallen in love with her. Now Therese came, and her laugh, if he closed his eyes, was that of Amalie. The visit turned into a play repeated. Therese went back to Hamburg, and he dreamed of her as once he had dreamed of Amalie. His heart throbbed with the old madness. He tried to be sensible. He mocked himself:

> He who for the first time loves,
> Even in vain, is a god.
> He who loves a second time
> And still in vain, is a fool.

He left for Cuxhaven. There he tried to forget her, indulging in flirtations, losing money at the gaming tables. But when the vacation was over, he rushed back to Hamburg. With his usual effrontery he hinted to his uncle that he would like to go to Paris to pursue a diplomatic career there. The suggestion infuriated Solomon, who gave him an ultimatum: to resume his studies at Göttingen or look elsewhere for support. Heine withdrew his request.

He stretched out his stay for three weeks. Therese was there and he could not break away.

> But now your lovely eyes, my dear,
> Have brought me to a firm resolve.

> . . . .

> I could not have believed it true
> That I should ever love again.

It was a strange double love. Now it was Therese whom he loved, now it was Amalie whom he loved and hated. He wandered in the selfsame garden where once Amalie had lain in his arms.

> Here to her vows I listened.
> I stand as in a spell,
> And where her tears once fell
> Serpents are hissing and crawling.

He told Therese that he loved her—"body and soul." She laughed, "long and drolly, and made a twinkling bow." (Letter to Moser). But he did not give up all hope. When he came back with his law degree she would look at him differently then.

He returned to Lüneburg in September and, mindful of his promise to Solomon, buried himself in his law books, planning to enter Göttingen in January. His parents looked at him questioningly, but his dog Amichen "was out of his wits for joy," he wrote Lottie. He dreamed of freeing himself of his dependence on his uncle. "I shall get my lunch from the scale of Themis, goddess of law, and not from my uncle's alms-bowl," he wrote Moser.

But hardly had he settled down to his books than news reached him that a performance of his play *Almansor* had ended in disaster. The poet Ernst Friedrich Klingemann had been persuaded to present the play in the town of Brunswick. It opened on August 20, but before the conclusion of the last act a disturbance broke and prevented it from continuing. The incident was precipitated by a drunken latecomer who shouted that the play was written by "the Jew Heine," and the audience, believing that the author was a local moneylender by that name, had rioted. The night marked the first and last performance of *Almansor;* nor was Heine's other play, *William Ratcliff,* ever produced.

Heine was certain that he was again the victim of a plot by his enemies. He wrote Moser that he recognized the hand of a certain Kochy, an old enemy who lived in Brunswick. "I know how things like that are arranged, and I know, alas, the malice of men . . . It is all very annoying, and it has had such a serious effect on my condition that I don't know what to do. I am not impervious to the attacks of the world and its idiots."

Providentially, out of nowhere a new friend appeared and put an end to his solitude. One day he answered a knock on the door, to be greeted by a smiling young man who said that he wanted to meet the author of the lovely verses that had given him such pleasure. Dr. Rudolf Christiani was a jurist and a member of the town council. He was a charming person, and it did not take him long to break down Heine's reserve. He introduced him to a circle of cultured, friendly people, and soon the formerly lonely Heine wrote to Lottie: "I am greatly honored here . . . Dr. Christiani has made me famous in all Lüneburg, and my verses circulate . . . the people are not bad." To his new friend, Heine wrote an affectionate and playful poem:

> This most amiable of fellows
> Never too much can honored be
> For with wines, liqueurs, and oysters
> Many times he has treated me.
>
> Natty are his coat and trousers,
> And his ties are most appealing,
> And he calls here every morning
> Asks me how I have been feeling.
>
> Of my wide renown he gushes
> Of my charm, my wit and humor;

Zealous, eager to serve and help me
Sorry that he cannot do more.

How delightfully refreshing
In these times to find still here
Such a youth, when daily good ones
More and more do disappear.

(The Homecoming)

Through one of those remarkable coincidences that fate delights in, Christiani later in life met and married a daughter of Isaac Heine of Bordeaux, a younger brother of Samson. In his will, drawn up in Paris in 1851, Heine appointed Christiani to supervise the collected edition of his works.

Heine drove himself to study his law books, but it was torture; from time to time he threw them down and worked at revising and polishing *Donna Clara*, or making notes for the *Rabbi of Bacherach*. And he wrote the letters—those fascinating letters of his in which storm and sunshine alternate so rapidly. He wrote to Moser, to Christiani, to the Varnhagens, to Immermann, and to Lottie, his beloved sister. Depths of love and tenderness are revealed in the letters to her. "The thought of you, dear sister, keeps me upright, when the great multitude bears down on me with its stupid hatred and disgusting love." And in another letter: "I love you inexpressibly, and long intensely to see you again, for there is no one on earth in whose company I am so happy as in that of my sister." And he advises her:

Spare your health; too much housekeeping is not good for you . . . Oh, how beautiful it is when you mutually learn how to tolerate your mutual weak sides! Mutual forbearance, justice, and intelligence are the basis of a good married state. Moritz will soon know how to treat such a dear, pretty, marvellous glass toy as you are.

Within the year Lottie was pregnant and Heine wrote her that the feelings of an uncle already were stirring within him, and he was anxious to know whether he would have a nephew or a niece. How it would delight him to see her in "your present rounded form," and he painted a picture of the delight in the household when the baby arrived: Moritz's delight when he heard the baby's cry; the smell of baking cakes at mama's, and the general rejoicing and excitement. But, he concluded, for all this to come to pass, she must be sure to take care of herself.

Shortly after the new year of 1824 arrived, the money promised by uncle Solomon arrived and Heine prepared to leave for Göttingen. Before he left he wrote to Lottie.

It is now seed-time with me, but I hope for a good harvest. I seek to acquire the most varied kinds of knowledge, and will in consequence be more versatile and completely cultured as an author. The poet is but a small portion of me. I took note of your advice to have as many die as possible in my tragedy. Ah, Lord! I wish I could kill off all my enemies in that way in it.

Heine arrived in Göttingen on January 19, 1824, to try for the fourth time to achieve a law degree. He had just turned twenty-six. No fanfare greeted him. It was as if he had never left. He arrived at night, and in the morning, as he was standing at the window of his room, he saw his old boot-black outside and called him in. He wrote in a letter to Charlotte,

> The droll fellow, without speaking a word, entered and brushed my coat and shoes, still without saying anything, and departed without manifesting the least amazement that I had been absent for three years from Göttingen, because he bore in mind my old injunction never to talk in my presence and ask questions.

The professors and even the students treated him with the respect due one who had had two volumes of poetry published. But in his letters he complained of his headaches and his difficulties with his studies. "Curses! I don't get very far," he wrote to Christiani,

> I still know the titles of Scott's novels and the stories of Boccaccio or Tieck much better than the titles and novels in the Corpus Juris. Oh Saint Justinian, have pity on me! So many a poor drudge has grasped you, and I must despair! Oh, all you Roman Emperors take pity! Oh Gaius, Paulus, Papinianus—you damned heathens—you surely must burn in hell for having made the law so vast.

He wrote to Moser:

> I live here in the same rut; that is, I have headaches seven days in the week. I get up at half past four in the morning, and consider what to begin with. Meanwhile, nine o'clock comes gliding along, and I hasten with my portfolio to my divine Meister . . . Yes, the chap is really godly. He is ideal in his stodginess. He is the perfect antithesis of all that is poetic, and for that very reason a poetic figure. If the material on which he discourses is particularly dry and wooden, he really becomes inspired . . . I let myself become interested in student affairs; I attend duels as a second, or as a referee, or, at least, as a spectator . . . it certainly is better than listening to the superficial chit-chat of the lecturers . . . I am also being ruined by love, but not the one-sided love for a particular individual, such as devastated me in the past. I am in love—desperately—with the Venus of Medici at the library and Councillor Bauer's pretty maid.

He decided to spend the Easter holiday in Berlin. It was a happy decision. Gubitz had printed a cycle of thirty-three of his poems in the *Gesellschafter*, and their publication had revived his fame. Heine wrote to Christiani:

In Berlin I paid court, was the recipient of very gracious and radiant downward glances, reinforced old friendships, ate well, drank even better—à la Hafiz— inhaled a sufficient quantity of incense, accepted a few kisses, spent thirty louis-d'or, listened to interminable and stupid gossip, and enjoyed a few delicious hours . . . While I am writing this, I hear that my cousin, Lord Byron, is dead at Missolough. So that great heart has stopped beating. It was great—and it was a heart, and no hatchery of puny feelings. Yes, this man was great. He defied wretched humans and their still more wretched gods . . . He was a man. Take him all in all, I shall not look upon his like again. I have proclaimed universal mourning.

But not all his time was spent in a round of pleasures. One of the motives for his visit to Berlin was a rather fantastic idea that with the aid of the Varnhagens and other influential people he could obtain a professorship at the University of Berlin. He should have known better. Even if he had not been Jewish, his reception when he went to register his presence in the city should have warned him that he was persona non grata to the authorities. They made it quite clear that the political views in his article on Poland branded him as a subversive, and that if he wished to stay in Berlin he should be careful what he wrote. He listened courteously and indicated he understood. Afterwards, he spent hours seeking the help of every influential person he knew who, he thought, might help him in his dream of becoming a university professor. It all came to naught, and he returned to Göttingen resigned to the prospect of following a law career.

All through the summer of that year of 1824 Heine applied himself to his law studies, determined to complete them by spring. But in his spare time he worked on the project that had engrossed him since the time of his zealous involvement with the Society for Jewish Culture and Science. He had conceived the idea of writing a historical romance that would immortalize the martyrdom of the Jews in medieval times. "It is an offspring of love and not of ambition, it will be an immortal book, an eternal lamp in God's cathedral," he wrote Moser early in 1824. And again, "I am assiduously studying . . . Jewish history . . . because of its connection with my *Rabbi,* and perhaps because of my personal needs . . . The soul of Jewish history becomes clearer and clearer to me, and this spiritual armor will some day stand me in good stead."

Day after day he delved into the chronicles of the martyrdom and the glory of the Jews, and as he did so a forgotten period of his life surfaced from his subconscious. He saw himself, a youth, walking the narrow, sunless streets of the Frankfurt ghetto. He remembered how he had fled from Frankfurt and never spoke of those days to anyone. And now, as he composed the pages of *The Rabbi of Bacherach,* it was as if he were assuaging a hidden hurt. He embraced the people of the ghetto; sat with them in love and tenderness as they worshipped in the synagogue.

Three old men reverently approached the Holy Ark, drew aside its glittering curtain, opened the chest and carefully brought forth that Book which God once wrote with his own hand, and to maintain which the Jews have suffered so much—so much misery and hatred, disgrace and death—a thousand years of martyrdom. This Book—a huge roll of parchment—was wrapped like a princely child in a richly embroidered jacket of scarlet velvet . . . The cantor took the book as if it were really a child, a child for whose sake much has been suffered, and which is, for that reason, all the more precious. He rocked it in his arms, dandled it, pressed it to his heart, and as if awed by such contact, he raised his voice in so jubilant a song of praise, that it seemed . . . as if the pillars of the Holy Ark had actually begun to blossom, and the strange and wonderful flowers and leaves of the capitals were shooting up ever higher; as if the notes of the soprano had become nightingale chants, and the dome of the synagogue would be shattered by the overpowering tones of the bass, and the joy of God flowed down from the blue heavens.

But the book that he had begun with such ardor bogged down; "every line was a struggle." He complained to Moser:

I have completed one-third of the Rabbi. I have been interrupted by racking headaches, and God only knows if I shall finish soon. In this connection, I have come to the conclusion that I am utterly devoid of narrative talent. Perhaps I am unfair to myself. Perhaps it is the material that's really recalcitrant.

He despaired of ever completing the novel, but at the same time it lay on his mind as a duty that had to be completed because it would be "useful and pleasing in God's sight." As late as the spring of 1826 his letters indicated that he was still struggling with the book. After that, silence for years. But he had not forgotten it. In 1840 he wrote a third chapter and published the still incomplete work with a final note, "The conclusion and the subsequent chapters are lost, not from any fault of the author's."

Had Heine written other chapters? Some commentators have concluded that the missing chapters were lost in a fire in his mother's home in Hamburg in 1833. He had been living with her before his departure for Paris in 1831, at which time he had left a number of manuscripts for safekeeping, being uncertain whether he would remain permanently in France. If indeed, drafts or notes for *The Rabbi of Bacherach* were destroyed in the fire, the loss was irreparable, to judge from the fragment that we do have. "What subtle eloquence lurks in that restrained cry of horror and indignation which never breaks forth, and yet which we feel through every line, gathering itself up like thunder on the horizon." (Emma Lazarus, Introduction to *Heinrich Heine, Poems and Ballads.*) It is doubtful, however, that he ever completed more chapters than those we have now. His letters indicate clearly that from the very beginning he had difficulty in shaping the material. His way of writing did not lend itself to the demands in structure and plot of a historical novel. His genius was of a different kind: as a writer of lyrics, ballads, travel reports, essays, journalistic reportage, satire, biography, political and historical commentary. In these fields he was unsurpassed.

Emma Lazarus, in the essay quoted above, and other commentators have expressed the belief that his inability to complete the work was due to an emotional conflict resulting from his baptism. However, he actually completed the greater part of the chapters that have come down to us in the months that followed his baptism on June 28, 1825.

His act was a purely formal one. He was skeptical about all religious dogmas at this time and took the step because he desperately wanted to be free of dependency on his rich uncle, and he saw no way of achieving that unless he entered a profession. But a major obstacle was that, in the Germany of his day, a Jew who wished to practice a profession was required to undergo baptism. Each year hundreds of Jews converted. Even Eduard Gans, who had brought him into the Society for Jewish Culture and Science, had made that choice and had been rewarded with the chair of philosophy at the University of Berlin.

These converts no doubt experienced some soul-searching, but in the end they overcame their inner conflict. Heine was constituted differently. It galled him to be forced to go through the gesture of a baptism, for a formality he considered it to be. Writing to Moser in September 1823, in anticipation of the step, he declared:

> "Baptism is a matter of indifference to me. I do not regard it as symbolically very important, and under the circumstnaces and in the way it is being carried out, it will likewise have little significance for others . . . it may mean that I shall be able to devote myself more fervently to the defense of the rights of my unfortunate co-religionists . . . and yet I think it beneath my dignity and honor to be baptized merely to obtain a post in dear old Prussia!"

Whatever one may think of the merits of Heine's argument that as a lawyer he would be better able to fight for the rights of his fellow Jews, it does underscore his fervent feeling for his people, an attachment that never wavered, no matter how often and how sharply he scolded them. If he found religious dogma repugnant, he at the same time never abjured his tie to the people from whom he sprang. It is in this light that his statement to Ludwig Kalisch in 1850 should be considered: "I make no secret of my Judaism, to which I have not returned, since I never left it."

Summer was over; he had labored diligently, and with the arrival of fall he seized the opportunity between terms to escape into the country. It was an inspired decision, for never did a poet have a happier time than Heine did that fall, as, knapsack on his back, he tramped through the hills and valleys and picturesque towns of the scenic Harz Mountains. The joy of these weeks was recaptured later in the *Harz Journey*, his first major prose work, which, when published in May 1826, became a popular success.

The *Harz Journey* was the story of a tramp through the countryside, but it was different from any travel book that had ever before appeared. It is the diary of a laughing, impudent young poet roaming through the German countryside. He sings of flowers and moonlight and nightingales. He embraces the girls; he makes friends with shepherds and miners and old grandmothers; he mocks the pompous and the pedants. He is tender, ironic, ribald, thoughtful, irreverent, sentimental. He strikes the note at the very beginning in a prologue poem.

> Black dress-coats and silken stockings,
> Cuffs of snowy white—beshrew them!
> Soft embraces, oily speeches.
> Ah, if but a heart beat through them!
>
> If a storm could stir your shirt-fronts,
> Ruffle them in any fashion!
> Oh, you kill me with your maudlin
> Bursts of imitation passion.
>
> I will go and climb the mountains,
> Where the simple huts are standing.
> Where the winds blow fresh and freely,
> And a chest may try expanding.
>
> I will go and climb the mountains,
> Where the mighty pine-trees tower,
> Where the birds and brooks are singing,
> And the heavens grow in power.
>
> Fare you well, you polished salons,
> Polished folk and polished chaffing—
> I will climb the rugged mountains,
> And look down upon you, laughing.

The young poet leaves the town of Göttingen at daybreak on a spring morning. He strides along the highway; early as it is, the road is already alive with travelers. He sees two tender lovers sitting hand in hand under a tree, and he "positively mistakes them for an edition of the Corpus Juris with clasped hands." Milkmaids pass by, and donkey drivers. Occasionally he sees a hack filled with students going away for vacation or even for good. He muses on the endless coming and going of the students, which is like a human tide with only the old professors standing immovable in the midst like the pyramids of Egypt, except that "in these Göttingen pyramids there is no hidden wisdom."

He steals kisses from a fair charmer.

> She retired slowly into the dark corridor; I grasped her hand and said, "I am a lover of flowers and kisses, and what is not freely given to me, I steal," and I kissed her then and there, and when she tried to escape I calmed her fears by whispering, "I'm off tomorrow, and I may never return," and I felt her sweet lips, her little hand coyly returning the pressure of mine . . . I had unconsciously pronounced that charm which serves to win women's hearts—"I'm off tomorrow and may never return."

He muses on immortality:

> Immortality! beautiful thought! Who first imagined you? Was it some Nuremberg shopkeeper, who, with white nightcap on his head and white porcelain pipe in jaw, sat some warm summer's evening before his shop door, and comfortably mused how pleasant it would be if this would only last forever—pipe and breath never going out, to vegetate for all eternity?

The ghost of the late Dr. Saul Ascher, devout follower of Kant, appears to him in a dream to prove that ghosts do not exist.

> Don't be afraid and don't believe I am a ghost. It is a trick of your imagination if you think you are seeing me as a ghost. What is a ghost? Give me a definition. Deduce for me the conditions under which a ghost could be possible. What rational link would such an apparition have with reason? Reason, I say—reason . . . and he demonstrated so eagerly that once, instead of his gold watch, he absently pulled a handful of worms out of his watch pocket . . . the clock struck one and the ghost disappeared.

He stays overnight at the hut of a miner. The miner's little daughter questions whether he has faith in God the Father, the Son, and the Holy Ghost, and he answers that he believes in God the Father, who made the world so lovely, and in the Son who opened the gates of love and for his reward, as usual was crucified, and in the Holy Ghost, who

> . . . has worked amazing wonders
> And the best are yet to be—
> He has smashed the forts of tyrants;
> He has set the bondsman free.
>
> He shall heal the ancient death-wounds,
> Let the old law be renewed:
> All men, equal-born, shall prosper
> In a noble brotherhood.
>
> He has named a thousand champions,

Armoured well, and armed with steel;
Chosen to fulfill his wishes—
And he's flamed their hearts with zeal.

Their beloved swords are flashing;
Their crusading banners fly!
Ah, you'd like to see, my darling,
Such proud knights go riding by?

Well, then look at me, my darling;
Kiss me—do not be afraid!
I myself am such a champion
In the Holy Ghost's crusade.

He apostrophizes the River Ilse, and she turns into his lost love, Amalie.

She comes tripping towards me, dainty and bewitching in mien, form and motion, the very image of the bright being who blesses my dreams; . . . I think of you, and wish I were again there to see you flash down the mountain-side. Best of all would it be to stand in the valley below and receive you in my arms . . . Everywhere miracles are taking place, flowers are bursting into bloom, and my heart, too, will blossom again. It, too, is a flower, a rare, strange flower—no modest violet, no smiling rose, no pure lily, or simple flower that takes a maiden's favor with its gentle loveliness . . . No, this heart is rather like one of those monstrous flowers in the forests of Brazil, which bloom only once in a century . . . Yes, Agnes, not often and not easily does this heart bloom; it has blossomed but once, and that ages ago, at least a century ago . . . now it stirs again, and swells, and bursts in my bosom—do you hear the explosion? Fear not, silly girl, I have not shot myself—but my love is bursting its bud, and is shooting up in lyric flashes, in immortal dithyrambs, in ebullience of song.

On the return part of his journey Heine changed his route in order to get to Weimar, the home of the revered Goethe. The older poet had never acknowledged the books and letters Heine had sent him, but he was determined to talk to the deity face to face. He arrived at his destination on October 1, 1824, and immediately penned a letter to Goethe.

I beg your Excellency to grant me the happiness of appearing before you for a few minutes. I shall not trouble you. I shall merely kiss your hand, and leave immediately. My name is H. Heine. I am a Rhinelander, and now reside in Göttingen. Previously, I lived for some years in Berlin, where I became acquainted with several of your acquaintances and admirers (the late Wolf, the Varnhagens, etc.), and learned to love you more and more. I am also a poet. Three years ago I took the liberty of sending you my *Poems,* and eighteen months ago my *Tragedies with a Lyrical Intermezzo.* I have not been well, and three weeks ago I undertook a journey through the Harz for my health. On the Brocken I was seized by a longing to make a pilgrimage to Weimar and pay homage to Goethe. I have come here truly as a pilgrim, that is, on foot and in weather-stained garments; and now, I await your answer to my prayers. With enthusiasm and devotion, H. Heine.

The worshipful note accomplished its purpose, and the young poet was admitted to the great man's presence. But the visit was a bitter disappointment. Years later in *The Romantic School*, Heine, in an account laced with humor, described the meeting.

> When I visited him at Weimar and stood face to face with him, I involuntarily took a side glance to see whether the eagle was not there with the thunderbolt in his beak. I was on the point of addressing him in Greek, but remembering that he understood German, I remarked to him in German that the plums on the road between Jena and Weimar were excellent. How many long winter evenings had I spent in dreaming of all the profound things I would say to Goethe if I ever saw him! And when at last I did see him, I told him that Saxon plums were delicious.

According to Heine's brother Max, Goethe ended the meeting abruptly when Heine committed the impropriety of boasting that he was planning a Faust, but there are reasons to doubt the account of the not always reliable Max. Goethe noted the fact of the visit in his diary, with no other comment. It is most unlikely that Heine would have confided to his brother about such a humiliating moment had it actually occurred, especially since his relations with his brother were never very close; nor is there any mention of an abrupt dismissal in the letters to Moser and Christiani in which he writes about the visit, although the letters are very interesting.

"Goethe and I are fundamentally opposite, mutually repellent," he confided to Moser.

> He is essentially a man who takes life calmly . . . I, on the contrary, am essentially an enthusiast—one so moved by an ideal as to sacrifice himself for it . . . It is a real question whether the enthusiast, who gives up his life for an idea, does not live more intensely . . . in a single moment than Herr von Goethe in all his seventy-six years of calm and comfortable condescension.

To Christiani, Heine wrote that "I was appalled by Goethe's appearance. His face is yellow and mummylike. His toothless mouth is always moving nervously. His whole body is a picture of human frailty." But then, because he was honest and just, Heine went on:

> Perhaps this is the result of his last sickness . . . his eyes are clear and brilliant . . . I was deeply touched by Goethe's very human concern for my health . . .

In many of his features I recognized the Goethe for whom Life—its adornment and preservation—as well as its practical aspects—represented the highest good.

It is a testimony to Heine's greatness of heart that, no matter how strongly he criticized Goethe the man—the Goethe who was a comfortable state councillor, the Goethe who kept himself aloof from the burning questions of the day—he always acknowledged the supremacy of Goethe the poet.

We who are, most of us, sick men, are far too deeply rooted in our sickly, discordant, romantic feelings to see instantly how sane, harmonious and plastic Goethe shows himself in his works . . . I write against Goethe! If the stars in heaven were to grow hostile to me, would I, in return, say they are only will-of-the-wisps? (Letter to Varnhagen)

Heine placed Goethe in the pantheon of the great poets as equal to Homer and Shakespeare; he called *Faust* "the secular bible of the Germans . . . no less vast than the Bible; it embraces Heaven and earth, humanity and human exegesis included" (*The Romantic School*). But while fully recognizing Goethe's genius, he was aware of his own. In a letter to Varnhagen von Ense, October 30, 1827, he wrote, "No matter how Wolfgang Goethe may infringe the intellectual rights . . . one thing he cannot prevent; that some day his great name will often be mentioned with mine."

After the joyous Harz interlude, Heine spent the ensuing months in heroic concentration on his law studies. Then, in April 1825, he submitted the formal Latin petition that was required of all candidates for the degree of doctor of laws; with disarming candor he stated that, while he had applied himself diligently to his legal studies, "obstinate headaches as well as a chronic tendency to poetry were the reasons why my knowledge is not as great as my application to the task."

When he learned that his examiner would be Professor Hugo, he was in despair. A few months earlier he had written to Moser that Hugo was the friend of his bitterest enemies, and should he become dean, as seemed likely, he was "a lost man." But he had judged wrongly, for not only did the professor pass him, but he added a graceful tribute to his poetical gifts.

But now the moment Heine had so long dreaded was at hand: he could not deliver his dissertation and obtain his degree unless he went through the baptismal rite, that act against which his pride revolted. All his inveighing in *Almansor* against the apostate! All his talk of "spiritual armor"! All his wailing to Moser! It all ended with his doing what he had criticized others for doing.

He waited two more months, but the Rubicon had to be crossed, and finally, on June 28, 1825, at about ten in the morning, he entered the house of Pastor Grimm in the village of Heiligenstadt near Göttingen. Harry Heine, law student, had come to present himself for baptism into the Lutheran church. A second clergyman, Pastor Bonitz, joined in the catechism, which lasted about an hour. The clergymen found Heine's knowledge of Christian doctrine satisfactory. Pastor Bonitz stood as godfather to the convert. Harry was baptized with the holy water and given the names Christian Johann Heinrich. Lunch followed. There was little conversation, and Heine left shortly after the meal was over. His leave-taking was pleasant, even cordial, but when he left the house, his eyes were wet.

He passed his doctoral examination quite creditably. On July 20 he rose in the university auditorium and read his dissertation. He delivered it in Latin and defended it against the objections of opponents. He did this very well, too, although his Latin sometimes was not a particularly classical Latin and provoked some scholarly merriment. Nevertheless, Professor Hugo, in a long Latin oration, expressed his amazement that a great poet should also be such a great jurist, and, no doubt carried away by his own eloquence, mentioned that Goethe too had studied law and even practiced it for a number of years. Later, Hugo invited Heine to dinner. And so it was that after five long, suffering years, Heinrich Heine was formally declared a doctor of laws.

Two days later he presented himself to his uncle Solomon, who was so pleased with his nephew that he did not grumble when the young man asked one last favor of him. Heine explained that his headaches were bothering him again, and he would like to take a rest cure at a seaside retreat before he opened a law office; he was sure the ocean would cure him: it always had a magical effect. Solomon gave Heine fifty louis d'or, and he left for the island of Norderney, one of the East Frisian islands off the North Sea coast, inhabited by fishermen and vacationers.

He took a sail boat from Hamburg. It started out in fine weather, but suddenly the wind sprang up, then turned into a gale. The passengers huddled below, but Heine held on to the rail of the ship, held on for dear life and was wildly exhilarated.

Heine's stay at Norderney gave birth to the first of the two cycles that comprise the *North Sea* poems. He had always loved the ocean, but now on the island he fell under its spell as never before, an enchantment that remained forever. "I love the sea as my own soul," he wrote in *Norderney*.

Often do I fancy that the sea is in truth my soul. And as in the sea there are hidden water-plants, which come to the surface only at the moment they blossom, and sink again the moment they fade, so at times there float up from the depths of my soul wondrous flowers of fancy which shine and bloom and die.

The sea sang to him, mighty symphonies, but when he tried to capture them in verse, he found that the music of the ocean moved to different rythms from that of the land, and that the accustomed verse forms would not do. He created an unrhymed free verse in which the thunder of the ocean alternated with the lilt of a song. Once again, and not for the first or the last time, he experimented with new forms and new language and opened horizons for future poets. Anticipating the reaction of the reading public, he wrote to Karl Simrock, whom he had first met in Bonn and who was now a fellow poet, "The unusual, irregular meter [of the *North Sea* poems] may make the average reader, accustomed to sugar-and-water, seasick." And in fact, it took many years before the general poetry public appreciated the turbulence and restlessness of the *North Sea* cycles. Even a critic like Max Brod, who highly esteemed Heine's works, called the poems "insincere." But George Brandes, the eminent Danish critic, wrote: "In Heine's *North Sea* poems we hear, for the first time in German poetry, the roar of the ocean, with all its freshness and in all its might. Here for the first time we have shells in the sand beneath our feet, and seagulls in the air above us" (*Main Currents in Nineteenth Century Literature*). Louis Untermeyer, too, used the image of the seagull: "Heine sees himself riding desperate waves with his favorite bird, the homeless, restless, wind-driven wandering seagull."

His songs mirror the shifting moods of the sea. He bares his heart:

> The ocean has its pearls,
> The heaven has its stars,
> But oh, my heart, my heart,
> My heart has its love.
>
> Oh little, youthful maiden,
> come unto my mighty heart.
> My heart, and the sea, and the heavens
> Are melting away with love.

(Night in the Cabin)

and asks the age-old questions:

> "Oh solve me the riddle of life!
> The cruel, world-old riddle,
> Concerning which, already many a head has been racked.
> Heads in hieroglyphic-hats,
> Heads in turbans and in black caps,
> Periwigged heads, and a thousand other
> Poor, sweating human heads.
> Tell me, what signifies man?
> Whence does he come? whither does he go?
> Who dwells yonder above the golden stars?
> The waves murmur their eternal murmur,
> The winds blow, the clouds flow past.
> Cold and indifferent twinkle the stars,
> And a fool awaits an answer.

(Questions)

In *A Sea Ghost* the poet peers into the ocean on a calm day and sees in the depths a sunken city, and at the window of one of the gabled houses is his long lost love. He calls to her and is about to plunge into the water to join her.

> But just at the right moment
> The captain seized me by the foot.
> He dragged me to safety
> And cried, angrily laughing,
> "Doctor, have you lost your mind?"

In this poem Heine made use of his famous *Stimmungsprechung*—a sudden and unexpected shift of mood from soft sentimentality to bitterness or mockery. Heine's use of the device has been misunderstood by some critics, who charge him with playing with his reader. Actually, the mockery is self-directed often to mask his own pain. *Stimmungsprechung* is not found in the great poetry of his later years.

In *Poseidon* he talks familiarly with the Greek gods and sees himself in proper perspective. Sitting on a sand dune, he puts down the book of Odysseus the wanderer and calls out to Poseidon that he is afraid of his own homecoming. And Poseidon rises from the sea and, guffawing, answers him:

> "Have no fear, little poet!
> I have no intention of harming
> Your poor little ship.
> For you, poetling, have never offended me.
> And never have you been sagely counselled and protected
> By the goddess of wisdom, Pallas Athene."
> Thus exclaimed Poseidon,
> And plunged again into the sea.
> And, at his coarse sailor-wit,
> Laughed under the water
> Amphitrite, the fat fishwoman,
> and the stupid daughters of Nereus.

He lazed away the summer. His headaches left him, and he was content. No medicine could rival Mother Sea.

When his money ran out at the end of summer, Heine did not go to Hamburg but returned to Lüneburg. He still could not bring himself to take the first steps to build a law practice. Something in him kept clamoring "No" to a life that would be bounded by torts and contracts and warned him that such an existence would be death to his free spirit. Instead, he wrote letters to friends in Berlin, still pursuing the will-of-the-wisp of a professorship, and still hoping to escape the life of a lawyer. But such hopes quickly evaporated, and in November, he left for Hamburg. Just before his departure, he wrote to Sethe that he hoped soon to be able in inform him that he was a practicing lawyer in Hamburg and was married. It was a surprising statement, for Therese certainly had not encouraged him.

It did not take long for him to discover that he had deluded himself. His cousin was flattered by poems he wrote for her, but she did not carry their relationship beyond the flirtatious stage. Uncle Solomon was curt, and the band of in-laws around Solomon carried on a vendetta against the sharp-tongued nephew who, they said, sponged on his uncle's bounty and now lived a dissolute life, gambling and writing impudent and sacrilegious verses. Harry had nothing but scorn for them.

He was angry at himself for his apostasy; when the temple Jews taunted him for his conversion he could not answer them. Writhing, he turned against Gans, who had converted in August and had then been appointed to the chair of philosophy at the Berlin University. He could have forgiven that. He would allow only one excuse for converting: as an act of expediency to earn a living. Any other motivation met with his anger and scorn. What aroused his contempt was that Gans began to preach Christianity. When he heard the news, he wrote to Moser, "If he's doing this from conviction, he's a fool; if from hypocrisy, he's a scoundrel." Heine never changed his beliefs on this point. Twenty years later he expressed the same convictions in a letter to Ferdinand Lassalle (February 11, 1846), in which he commented on the action of the composer Felix Mendelssohn: "I am angry with him for turning Christian. I cannot forgive this man of *independent means* (emphasis added) for putting his great, his prodigious talents at the service of zealots. The more I am impressed by his talents, the more I am outraged by their vile misuse."

Heine concluded this letter with a bit of typical Heinesque humor.

Last Saturday I went to the Temple and had the pleasure of hearing, with my own ears, Dr. Solomon blasting all baptized Jews, and particularly taunting those who allowed themselves to be seduced from the faith of their fathers in order to obtain a position. I assure you the sermon was good, and I am planning to pay the man a visit one of these days. Cohn is very generous toward me. I eat at his table on the Sabbath. He heaps the most glowing kugel on my head, and contritely I munch that sacred national dish, which has done more to preserve Judaism than all the three issues of the Journal. Of course, it's also had a greater circulation . . . I get to be a real Christian now; I sponge on the rich Jews.

There was often a large dose of hyperbole and deliberate play-acting in Heine's letters. If, at Christmastime, he began a letter to Moser, "I'll give you something very special for Christmas; namely, my promise not to shoot myself; at least not yet," that was not meant to be taken too seriously. And when he wrote to another friend, "I suppose you can say that I exist; but you cannot call it living," that was nonsense. For, as the commentator Hermann Kesten said, "Heine enjoyed life and the world, women and poetry, happiness and smaller troubles in a magnificent, poetically wasteful mood." Few men have lived life more fully than Heine. This paean to life is from his *Book Le Grand:*

Life is all too wondrously sweet, and the world is so beautifully bewitched; it is the dream of an intoxicated god who left the carousing multitude of immortals, and lay down to sleep in a solitary star, and knows not that he himself created all that which he dreams . . . The Iliad, Plato, the battle of Marathon, Moses, the Medician Venus, the Cathedral of Strassburg, the French Revolution, Hegel, steamboats, etc., etc. are other good thoughts in this divine dream . . . I live! If I am but the shadowy image in a dream, still this is better than the cold black void annihilation of death . . . God be praised, I live! Red life boils in my veins, earth yields beneath my feet, in the glow of love I embrace trees and statues, and they live in my embrace. Every woman is to me the gift of a world. I revel in the melody of her countenance, and with a single glance of my eye I can enjoy more than others with their every limb through all their lives . . . I need no priest to promise me a second life, for I can live enough in this life . . . the evening breezes lie like flattering maidens on my wild heart, and the stars wink to me, and I rise and sweep over the little earth and the little thoughts of mankind.

6

Hamburg and London:
Travel Pictures and *English Fragments* (1826–27)

Julius Campe, head of the firm of Hoffman and Campe, had the reputation of being a daring and successful publisher who specialized in handling books that other publishers turned down because they were too controversial and might be confiscated by the authorities. No work was too bold for Campe to publish and promote. He was under constant surveillance by the police, but the game of matching wits with them added a fillip to his daily routine. He printed his books outside Germany and Austria, and then smuggled them in, operating with a network of agents, couriers, and booksellers; he even had people in government on his payroll.

One day in January 1826, a young man appeared in the Hamburg bookshop where Campe was usually found, and asked to look at a book of H. Heine's poems. When the clerk showed him a copy, the stranger began to speak in a derogatory fashion about them. Thereupon Campe, who was standing nearby, chided the young man and warmly praised the art of the poems. The argument went on for a while; then suddenly the caller revealed that he was really Heine himself, and that if Campe thought so highly of his abilities, he had a manuscript for him to handle. He was looking for a new publisher, particularly one who knew how to circumvent the censor, and he had been advised that Campe was the one for him.

It was in this somewhat dramatic fashion that author and publisher met and began a permanent but stormy relationship. Heine soon enough discovered how grasping a businessman Campe was, but he also realized that no other publisher would do for him and his works what Campe did, and therefore, despite quarrels and recriminations, despite offers from other publishers, Heine stayed with him to the end.

There is much that is unpleasant in the story of Campe's treatment of the author who made him famous. One example out of many: in October 1827, he paid Heine fifty louis d'or (about $200) for the rights in perpetuity to the *Book of Songs*. It was a sharp action. He told Heine that he did not expect the book to achieve a great success, and the poet signed the contract. While sales at first were slow—it took several years for the first edition of five thousand copies to be sold—later, the demand was so great that new editions were printed every other year to keep up with the demand. The fame of the *Book of Songs* spread far beyond the borders of Germany and it was translated into many languages. Campe made a fortune out of the book, but he kept to the letter of the contract even while the author of the songs was in dire financial need in Paris. Witty but sad is the remark that Heine made to his brother Max who, visiting him in 1852, thought to cheer his sick brother by prophesying that the city of Düsseldorf would some day erect a monument to him. "I already have a monument," said Heine. "It is Campe's grand mansion in Hamburg. If you turn to the left beyond the Boersenplatz, you will find this gorgeous monument of stone built in grateful memory to the many editions of my *Book of Songs*." In fact, by the time of Heine's death in 1856, no less than thirteen large editions had been sold.

The manuscript that Heine had offered to Campe included the scintillating *Harz Journey,* the *Homecoming* (the Amalie-Therese sequel to the *Lyrical Intermezzo*) and the first cycle of the *North Sea* poems. Campe published the three titles in one book, *Travel Pictures I.* This was in May 1826.

The response exceeded all expectations: five hundred copies were sold in the first weeks in Hamburg alone. A literary career now seemed within the realm of practicality, and Heine completely abandoned the thought of practicing law. He at once began work on a second volume of *Travel Pictures.* But he envisaged it as a work of far greater scope than the preceding book. Indeed, it would shake the heavens. In January 1827 he wrote Friedrich Merckel: "The book will cause a sensation. I have blazed a new trail at the risk of my life. Napoleon and the French Revolution are in it—as large as life. I scarcely dare tell Campe what the book is really about." He was writing with a new confidence and a concept of himself as an implacable foe of injustice and privilege. "In the succeeding volume of *Travel Pictures* you will find much that is mad, harsh, offensive and angry," he wrote to Wilhelm Müller. "The times are evil indeed, and he who possesses strength and a free spirit is in duty bound to engage seriously in the battle against evil that struts about so blatantly, and against the commonplace that swaggers insufferably!" A reckless spirit seized him, fanned perhaps by the fact that he now seriously thought of leaving Germany for a place where a thinking person, a liberal, a Jew, could breathe fresh air: London, or Paris, or Amsterdam, or even America. In October 1826 he confided to Karl Immermann: "What nobody knows, what I tell only to you—and what you must not repeat to anyone—is my resumed plan to leave Germany forever, after staying in Hamburg for some time this winter, where I'll have the second volume of the *Travel Pictures* printed. From there I shall go by sea to Amsterdam and on to Paris."

All that summer and autumn and early winter he worked on the book. As the pages took shape, he grew ever more audacious. He wrote Varnhagen: "If there is any special person you wish exposed, or any idea you wish expressed, do not hesitate to let me know. Better still, copy my style, and I will sew the patches into the book, and you can be sure I will keep it confidential. It doesn't matter whether I have another dozen enemies; I dare write anything now." He wrote to Christiani that they "had forced him to take the sword, he who was meant to be a singer of soft ballads," and he would become a worthy swordsman, even though he knew well enough that "he who took up the sword would perish by the sword."

Travel Pictures II was published by Campe in the spring of 1827. Like the preceding volume, it was a miscellany of prose and poetry, but the heart of the book was the section called *Ideas: The Book Le Grand*, Le Grand being the name of the French drummer who had been billeted in the Heine home in the days of the French occupation of Düsseldorf.

From beginning to end the book laughed at the aristocrats, feudal Junkers, censors, Jew-baiters, intellectual swindlers—and Heine enjoyed himself hugely. He thumbed his nose at the censors: for instance, chapter 12 of *The Book Le Grand* consisted of one page, as follows:

Chapter 12
The German censors of the press _ _ _ _ _ _ _ _ _ _ _ _ _ _ _
_ _
_ _
_ _
_ _ _ _ _ _ _ _ _ _ _ BLOCKHEADS _ _ _ _ _ _ _ _
_ _
_ _

But there was more in the book than just ridicule of the censors. This was not what caused the book to be banned immediately in every German state; it was the incendiary political message of *Le Grand*. Not all Germans were blind; many yearned for liberty, equality, and fraternity, and Heine was inciting them, extolling the ideas of the French Revolution, through the person of the little French drummer.

In Vienna, Prince Metternich communicated with his chief assistant, Friedrich von Gentz: the secret intelligence must watch this audacious poet who wrote such lovely verses but whose revolutionary incitements could not be tolerated. Heine was ridiculing the most sacred institutions, even royalty itself! And Metternich underlined for Gentz's benefit, a passage in *The Book Le Grand*.

Monsieur Le Grand . . . could make himself perfectly understood on the drum . . . The taking of the Bastille, of the Tuileries, etc. are never fully realized till one knows to what beat of the drum they were taken. In our history primers we read merely: "Their excellencies the barons and counts and their noble consorts were beheaded; their highnesses the dukes and princesses and their very noble consorts were beheaded; his Majesty the King and his most noble consort were beheaded," but when one heard the drums beating the bloody guillotine march . . . one perceives the why and the wherefore. A truly marvellous march, Madame . . . I was glad when I forgot it. One does forget such things as one grows older . . . But strange to say, Madame, I was dining the other day with a regular menagerie of counts, princes, princesses, chamberlains, ladies in waiting, court butlers, mistresses of the robe, keepers of the plate, mistresses of the chase . . . while I sat idly by unheeded and unserved, with nothing to occupy my jaws, making piles of bread crumbs, and drumming on the table to while away the time—and to my horror I found myself drumming the bloody long-forgotten guillotine march!

"And what happened?" Madame, these people never let themselves be put out when eating, and do not know that other people when they having nothing to eat take suddenly to drumming, and drum very curious marches, supposed to have been long forgotten.

The more the authorities tried to suppress the book, the greater grew the demand for it. Campe's underground apparatus of distribution was kept very busy outwitting the police.

On the day *The Book Le Grand* came out, the author left Germany, heeding the advice of friends who urged him to leave the country and not to return until the furor aroused by the book died down. He felt there was nothing to be gained by doing otherwise. He would have preferred to go to Paris, but he decided that under the circumstances it was more politic to choose London.

He carried with him a draft on the Rothschild bank in London in the amount of four hundred pounds, a very large sum in those days. Somehow he had talked his uncle into entrusting him with an instrument. Perhaps Solomon's vanity had betrayed him, for when he handed the draft to Heine he told him that he had made it out for such a large amount because he wanted his nephew to do credit to the high rank of the Heine family when he presented himself to the London banker; but that he was to draw on it only to the extent necessary to meet his expenses.

But Heine, as soon as he arrived in London, cashed the letter of credit for its entire amount. He wanted, he said later, to live like a true robber banker, and, he acknowledged, he enjoyed the experience. But he did not spend all of his unexpected fortune; he sent a part of it to Varnhagen in Berlin, asking him to put it away for him as a reserve for a future day of need. He also paid off a number of small debts he owed back home. Then for the next four months he lived royally until the money ran out.

He did not like the rush and the noise and the pushing, the "damned pushing!" as when, idly looking into an art dealer's window, he was jostled by a Londoner in a hurry, who said merely, "God damn!"

He had been gazing at a picture of the French army crossing the Berezina River during its retreat from Moscow. He turned around and looked at the roaring London street, and it seemed to him as though all of London was a Berezina Bridge where everyone fought to save his own life; where the arrogant rider trampled down the poor pedestrian; where he who fell was lost forever; where one's best friends stepped indifferently over the bodies of friends; and where multitudes of exhausted, bleeding creatures grasped vainly at the planks of the bridge and plunged into an icy grave.

He wandered about the huge city and witnessed a public double execution: one man hanged for stealing a sheep, and another for forging a check; and he commented, "These people talk always about Christianity, and go to church every Sunday morning, and flood the world with Bibles." The streets grew more dismal and wretched; the faces revealed only misery and despair. What he saw, he set down in vignettes that haunt the reader.

> Here and there, at the entrance of some dark alley, a ragged woman stands mutely with a suckling babe at her exhausted breast, and begs with her eyes. Perhaps if those eyes were still beautiful, one glances into them and shrinks back at the world of wretchedness visible within them. *(English Fragments)*

And from the same book:

> She stares with eloquent, mute, beseeching eyes at the rich merchant who hurries past, busy, jingling his coins, or at the idle lord, who, like a surfeited god, rides by on his high horse, now and then glancing with an aristo-cratically blasé air at the crowds below—as if they were a swarm of ants, or a herd of baser creatures whose joys and sorrows had nothing in common with his feelings . . . Poor poverty! How agonizing must your hunger be, when others wallow in arrogant surfeit! And when a man, with indifferent hand, throws a crust into your lap, how bitter must be the tears with which you wet it.

He could not adjust to the vast mechanical desert that was London. "Send a philosopher to London, but never a poet! This dull earnestness of all things, this colossal uniformity, this machine-like movement, this speeded-up Lon-don, smothers the imagination and tears the heart." A sudden yearning for his homeland swept over him; from a distance it was transformed, and he wrote nostalgically:

> How much more pleasant and home-like it is in our dear Germany! In what comfort, in what Sabbath-like repose all glides along there! Calmly the sentinels are changed, uniforms and houses shine in the quiet sunshine, swallows float over the flag-stones, fat Court-councillors' wives smile from the windows, while along the echoing street there is room enough for the dogs to sniff at each other, and for men to stand at ease and chat about the theater, and bow deeply—oh, how deeply!—when some small aristocratic scamp or vice-scamp, with colored ribbons on his shabby coat, or some Court-marshal low-brow struts along as if in judgment, graciously returning salutations. *(English Fragments)*

Frequently, Heine could be found attending a debate in the House of Commons, particularly when the great Canning himself was to speak.

I shall never forget the occasion when I heard George Canning speak about the rights of the peoples and listened to those liberating words which rolled like divine thunder over the whole earth and left a consoling echo behind them in the huts of Mexicans and Hindus alike . . . In the violence of his speech he once tore his glove from his hand, and I thought for a moment that he was going to fling it down before the feet of the whole of the aristocracy of England, the challenge of insulted humanity. *(English Fragments)*

He spent many evenings at the Drury Lane Theater, where the great Shakespearean actor Edmund Kean was giving his memorable performances. There King Richard "moved my soul so mightily when he rushed desperately across the stage crying: 'A horse, a horse, my kingdom for a horse.'" There Shylock made his great speeches of pride and scorn and hate and of love for his daughter, Jessica. "Behind me in the box stood a pale British beauty who wept bitterly at the end of the fourth act and who frequently cried out, 'The poor man is wronged.' Her face was of the noblest Grecian cut, and her eyes were large and black. Never will I forget them, those great black eyes which wept for Shylock." *(Shakespeare's Girls and Women)*

He attended a trial at the Old Bailey. Heine's report in *English Fragments* is a masterpiece of drama and suspense. He paid an older porter a shilling for a seat in the gallery and learned that the jury was deliberating the fate of Black William. The change was forgery, which was a crime punishable by hanging. Looking around, he noticed the judges.

They sat around a long green table on high chairs at the upper end of the hall just where a Scripture text, warning against unjust judgments, is placed before their eyes . . . On the judges' table I saw . . . a rose. I know not why it was, but the sight of that rose affected me strangely. A red blooming rose, the flower of love and of spring, upon the terrible judges' table of the Old Bailey!

In the gallery, the spectators had formed their own jury and were passing judgment.

A fat woman above whose red, bloated cheeks two little eyes glittered like glowworms, remarked that Black William was a very good-looking fellow. But her neighbor, a delicate, piping soul in a body of bad post-paper thinks that he "wears his black hair too long and matted," and that his eyes gleamed like those of Kean in Othello; "while Thompson is a very different sort of person . . . a very well-educated person, too . . . he plays the flute a little, and paints a little, and speaks French a little."

It appears that Edward Thompson and Black William had been old friends, they had lived and eaten and drunk together, and now upon Thompson's testimony Black William might die.

"Pshaw!" cried the lean woman, and smiled with her thin lips: "If they didn't hang such a forger, no rich man would ever be sure of his money; for instance . . . our friend Mr. Scott has worked so hard to get his money— trouble enough, mem, I assure you—and folks do say that he got rich by taking other people's diseases on himself. Yes, mem, they say the very children run after him in the street and cry "I'll give ye sixpence if you'll take my toothache!" or "We'll give ye a shilling if you'll take Jimmy's hump- back!"

But just at that moment the jury filed in, and there was a hush as everyone strained to hear the verdict. "Guilty!" In words that linger in the reader's memory and do not go away, Heine captures the next moment.

As Black William was led from the hall he cast a long, long glance upon Edward Thompson.

There is an Eastern legend that Satan was once an angel, and lived in heaven with other angels, until he sought to seduce them from their al- legiance, and therefore he was thrust down into the endless night of hell. But as he sank from heaven he looked ever on high, even at the angel who accused him; the deeper he sank, more terrible and yet more terrible became his gaze. And it must have been a fearful glance, for the angel whom it met became pale—red was never again seen in his cheeks, and since that time he has been called the Angel of Death.

Pale as that Angel of Death grew Edward Thompson.

In July Heine spent a fortnight at the seaside resort of Ramsgate, where the ocean had its usual restorative effect. There, too, he enjoyed a passing affair with a pretty Irish girl. Back to London, he lost over three hundred guineas as a result of "adventures, bad luck and stupidities," he wrote Varnhagen. Some of this money was spent on a mysterious Kitty Clairmont, who, several years later, pursued him to Paris, and who inspired a cycle of amorous and sensuous poems. By September he was back in Hamburg. An angry Solomon berated him for his misappropriation of the four hundred pound letter of credit. But Heine, with a teasing smile, further enraged Solomon by saying calmly: "My dear uncle, did you expect to bear my name for nothing?" Solomon was so infuriated that he raised his cane threateningly, and Heine left his presence. Solomon never forgot this remark, although eventually he found it possible to look back at the incident with some amusement. A letter to his nephew written in 1839, and another one in 1843 were both signed, "Uncle, who also bears your name."

7
Travels: *Travel Pictures III* (1827–31)

On October 19, 1827, Campe published Heine's *Book of Songs.* By an ironical coincidence, the day marked the fifth anniversary of Amalie's marriage. He went to the family gathering and saw her for the first time since that day he left for college; and he learned that Therese soon would be announcing her engagement to a young lawyer named Halle. "The world is stupid, and reeks of withered violets," he wrote to Varnhagen.

Once again he was faced with the problem of a livelihood. The *Book of Songs* had brought him all of fifty louis! He had sworn not to ask his uncle for further help, and he was determined not to turn to the practice of law. At this critical time in his career, it was Varnhagen von Ense, true and loyal friend, who suggested to the publisher Cotta that the author of the *Book of Songs* and of *Travel Pictures* would bring distinction and sparkle to Cotta's recently founded journal, *New Political Annals.*

Baron Johann Friedrich von Cotta was a long-time admirer of Heine's writings, and he seized upon Varnhagen's idea. Losing no time, he offered Heine the prestigious position of coeditor of the journal, at a generous salary of two thousand gold marks a year, plus the opportunity to earn additional money by contributing literary articles to other periodicals owned by Cotta. Finally, he added the attractive stipulation that Heine would be free to write on any topic without restriction.

Cotta's newspapers and journals were liberal-orientated and reflected the fact that he was an admirer of two of Heine's own heroes, Napoleon and Channing. His intention in launching the *New Political Annals* was to make it an organ of the German Transpartei, a movement which worked for a union of the small and medium German states as a counterpoise to the two great powers, Prussia and Austria. The movement had great support in western and southern Germany, not only among intellectual figures, but also among a number of the German princes. Although Heine was in sympathy with the movement, he was skeptical of the future of the Transpartei in view of the growing military and economic superiority of Prussia.

Alluring as Cotta's offer was, Heine did not immediately accept it, but in fact hesitated for some time. He was afraid of becoming bound by political fetters, and he did not wish to become a political journalist. Cotta again assured him that he would be able to write as he pleased, that his editorial duties would be kept to a minimum. Dr. L. Lindner, his coeditor, would bear the day-to-day editorial responsibilities. Heine's name alone, Cotta said, was worth what he would be paying him. Finally, with no other prospect in sight, Heine accepted the post but would bind himself for only six months, with an option to renew if at the end of the period he so desired.

Since the *New Political Annals* was published in Munich, it was necessary for him to move there. He secured a generous advance from Cotta, then set out for Munich, traveling leisurely and in comfort, combining family visits with calls on writers and artists who might be persuaded to contribute to the *Annals*.

His first stop was in Lüneburg, to spend a few days with his parents, whom he made happy beyond measure by the news that he was now the editor of an important journal, which paid him a princely salary. When he departed, he left them a generous sum of money.

His next destination was Göttingen, where he sought out Georg Sartorius, the one teacher there who had shown understanding of his prose and poetry and helped him in his troubled hours; their reunion was a pleasant one. He then went on to Kassel, where he spent a week with the Grimm brothers, who showed him the most friendly hospitality. The two older ones, Jacob and Wilhelm, were already famous for their collection and popularization of old German fairy tales such as "Snow White and the Seven Dwarfs," "Hansel and Gretel," "Cinderella," "Rumpelstiltskin," and many others. Heine was himself an enthusiastic collector of old tales, and they had a delightful time discussing the history and varied versions of the popular legends. The third brother, Ludwig Emil Grimm, was an engraver, and he made a profile study of Heine, which portrays a man of keen and forceful, but sensitive mien. Beneath the engraving, Heine wrote: "With moody thoughts in a sad heart I gaze gloomily on a cold world." The words, in the Byronic style, are deliberately exaggerated, but they reflect the Heine who felt the world's follies and cruelties; the man described by Robert Schumann (the composer who set to music many of Heine's poems) in these words: "About his mouth lay a bitter, ironic smile, but it was a smile only for the pettiness of life, and a scorn only for petty people."

Leaving the Grimm brothers, Heine went to Heidelberg to see his brother Max, who was studying medicine at the university there. The visit was marred by an unpleasant incident. Max had arranged an affair in Heine's honor, across the border in Württemberg; but the police appeared and asked if the guest of honor was the author of *Travel Pictures;* when he declared he indeed was, they escorted him back across the border.

On to Frankfurt, where he spent three happy days with Ludwig Börne, whom he had admired from his schooldays, and who was the outstanding spokesman for liberalism in Germany. In later years, when both were exiles in Paris, Börne became his bitter enemy, but now, "he would not let me go. With droll kindness he won from me a promise to give him three days of my life . . .

and I had to go about the town with him and call on all sorts of friends, both men and women . . . The three days passed in almost idyllic peacefulness."

From Frankfurt he moved on to Stuttgart and spent a day with Wolfgang Menzel. Many years had passed since the night of the torchlight procession to the top of the Kreuzberg on the fifth anniversary of the Battle of Leipzig, when Menzel had called for the burning of unpatriotic books. Since then he had had a book of verse published and had acquired a reputation as a literary historian. He was esteemed as a liberal, and Börne had given Heine a warm letter of introduction to Menzel. This was enough to convince Heine that Menzel had changed, and he greeted him as a new friend. A few years later, Menzel went over to the extreme right, and Heine wrote a pamphlet, *The Informer*, in which he castigated and pilloried him.

The weather was cold and blustery when he finally arrived in Munich. It was late November in the year 1827.

In the course of his long journey from Hamburg he had discovered that his writings were talked about everywhere—enthusiastically praised, and as vehemently condemned; he was indeed a famous writer.

He did not want Campe to think that because he had moved to Munich he would forget him, and almost as soon as he arrived, he wrote to him: "I owe this fame to two persons: H. Heine and Julius Campe. These two must stick together. I certainly shall not readily part to better myself or for unseemly greed. I believe that we shall grow old together, and always understand each other."

Heine was content to leave to his associate, Dr. Lindner, all the detail connected with the publication of the *Annals*. He won the esteem of his colleagues by his consideration and concern for their personal welfare. He contributed a few articles, the best of which were later incorporated in *English Fragments*. But it soon became evident that the old dream of an academic post was still an obsession with him; he began to concentrate all his energies on securing an appointment to the chair of German literature at the state university.

It was self-delusion to think that the German establishment would ever allow the author of *Travel Pictures* and similar writings a forum for his ideas at a state university. It was true that he had grounds for believing that the situation in Munich was more favorable for him than in Berlin. Ludwig I, the king of Bavaria, whose royal signature would be needed for an appointment at the university, was a patron of the arts and was receptive to liberal ideas. His minister of the interior, Eduard von Schenk, a poet and dramatist, was an admirer of Heine's poetry and he was introduced to him by Cotta. Heine proceeded shamelessly to laud Schenk's rather mediocre verses in order to curry favor with him. He cultivated the aristocratic favorites of the court and became quite friendly with "the lovely Baronness Bothmer" and her brother-in-law, Baron Tjutschew. The latter was an attaché at the Russian embassy in Munich, and he had translated a number of Heine's poems into Russian.

But, although for ulterior purposes he hobnobbed with the aristocracy, he was quick to take offense if he felt he was being patronized or treated as a menial. When a certain princess sent him an imperious command to come to her mansion immediately and partake of coffee with her guests, he sent her footman back with a message conveying his profound respects to Her Royal Highness and his regrets that he was accustomed to take his coffee where he had lunched.

In July he was assured by Schenk that the papers for his appointment had been drawn up and were awaiting the king's signature, which, he assured Heine, would be forthcoming for a certainty. Thrilled at the news, and relying completely upon Schenk's promise, Heine resigned from his editorship of *New Political Annals.*

He had been plagued by a persistent cough, which he blamed on the Munich climate, and he decided that now was the opportune time to take a long-dreamed of vacation in sunny Italy and to recuperate in "the land of Dante, Machiavelli, Leonardo da Vinci, Michelangelo." He wrote to Varnhagen in Berlin, asking him to send the money he had placed with him for safekeeping when he had cashed Solomon's letter of credit in London. Two weeks later, July 1828, Heine was on his way. Before he left Munich, he arranged with Schenk to send word to him in care of the FLorence post office as soon as his university appointment was signed by the king.

He traveled in style. He visited Milan, Leghorn, Genoa, and Florence. He spent several weeks in Lucca in the Apennines, where he took the famous baths, wrote, dreamed great deeds, and pursued amorous adventures.

Cotta wrote to him, pressing for his return to Munich where he had plans for another journal, but Heine was relying on Schenk's promise; and besides, the women of Italy were too alluring.

> I love these pale, elegiac countenances from which great black eyes shed forth their love-pain. I love the dark tints of those proud necks . . . I love even that overripe bust with its purple points, as if amorous birds had been pecking at it. But, above all, I love that genial gait, that dumb music of the body, those limbs that move in sweetest rhythm, voluptuous, pliant, with divine enticement. (Quoted by Alfred Werner, Introduction to *The Sword and the Flame*)

In Genoa, a jealous swain threatened to stab him, and the police advised him to leave the town, warning that such men made good their threats, but, he wrote Moser, he did not permit himself to be cowed, and nothing happened.

On September 15, in a rush of sentiment, he wrote a long letter to his uncle Solomon.

> I have been thinking so much of you these days, and I have so often longed to kiss your hand . . . I will not think of things I might complain of in you,

which are more considerable than you suspect. So I beg you, cease some of your complaints against me, since they all involve money. If they were reckoned down to the last penny, they would amount to no more than what a millionnaire could quite easily throw away. But my complaints against you are incalculable, infinite, for they are of a spiritual kind rooted in the depths of offended sensibilities. If by a single word or a single look I have ever been wanting in respect for you, or for your house—I have loved you only too well!—then you would have the right to be angry. But not now; for if all your charges against me were added up, they would fit comfortably into a purse of no great dimensions. And even if the money bags were too small to hold all that Solomon Heine complains of in me, and were to burst—do you think, dear Uncle, that it would matter more than a heart that breaks, because it has been filled too full with sorrows? But enough! The sun is shining, and the vine-clad hills are smiling. I will not complain. I will only love you, as I have always done, I will think only of your great soul, which is grander and more beautiful than all the splendor I have seen in Italy . . . Farewell, and give my love to your family, to Hermann, Carl, and little Therese. With certain reservations I was glad to hear of her marriage. After myself, there is no one to whom I would have yielded her so willingly as Dr. Halle . . . Goodby, my dear, good, magnanimous, penny-wise, noble and infinitely beloved uncle."

Heine arrived in Florence on October 1. He hastened to the post office, confidently expecting to find a letter from Schenk, but it had not arrived. He was not too disturbed: the letter might have been misdirected; the king might be away. But days, then weeks passed, and no word came to end the suspense. The tension of waiting for a letter that never came brought back his headaches. He sent increasingly frantic letters to Munich, but after two months had passed, he could no longer evade the truth: Schenk had failed him, and his dream of a professorship had been just that—a dream. Then suddenly a frightening premonition seized him that something had happened to his father, a conviction that he was dying. He packed and fled. In Venice a letter from Max caught up with him, and he learned that his father had had a stroke. He pushed on, but when he arrived in Würzburg another letter awaited him, and he learned that Samson had died in Lüneburg on December 2, and that Solomon had rented a house for Betty in Hamburg. He headed there to be at the side of his bereaved mother.

He had always been unusually close to his parents, and now his grief was overwhelming. He found it difficult to accept the fact of his father's death. Even twenty-five years later, in his *Memoirs*, he still mourned his loss.

In all the world there was no one I loved as much as him. He has been dead for over twenty-five years. I never thought that I would lose him; and even now I can scarcely believe that he is gone. It is so hard to convince oneself that poeple we love very much are really dead. But they are not dead; they live on within us and in our souls. There has scarcely been a night when I did not think of my father. When I wake up in the morning, it often seems to me as if I were hearing the sound of his voice, like the echo of a dream. And then I have the feeling that I must dress quickly, and hurry down to him where he is sitting in his living room—just as I used to do when I was a boy. He was in the habit of rising very early, and applying himself to his affairs . . . I would usually find him sitting at his writing table. Without looking up, he would reach out his hand to me to be kissed. Such a beautiful, sculptured, distinguished hand, which he would always wash in almond powder . . . I seem to breathe the fragrance of the almonds—and my eyes fill with tears . . . One morning he embraced me with unusual tenderness and said: "I dreamed fine things about you last night, and I am very well satisfied with you, my dear Harry." As he spoke these naive words, a smile played about his lips, as if to say: "No matter how naughty Harry may actually be, I shall always dream nice things about him, so that I may love him undisturbed."

Hamburg held too many unhappy memories to allow him to stay there for more than a few weeks, and he left for Berlin in February 1829. Cotta again wrote to him to consider working on his new periodical in Munich, but he spurned the thought of returning to the "beer Athens" where he had been slandered, deceived and betrayed, for he had learned what had gone on in that city during his stay in Italy. He had been the victim of a campaign organized by a reactionary clerical circle, which had spread false and distorted reports of statements attributed to him, and had instigated a slanderous attack against him in an anti-Semitic journal, *Eos.* Schenk had tried to defend Heine before King Ludwig, but he had refused to sign the papers that would have given Heine the appointment he sought.

In April Heine moved to Potsdam, where he lived in solitude for the next few months and worked on the third volume of *Travel Pictures.* He rose at dawn and worked all day at his desk. "For company, I had only the statues in the garden of Sanssouci. I kept from all contact with the ouside world." Sometimes, however, the breath of spring, or a letter from a friend concerned about his welfare, drew him out of his room. Friederike Robert was such a friend. She was the very beautiful wife of Ludwig Robert, the brother of Rahel. Heine's affection for her bordered on love, and for years he had carried on a chivalrous sort of flirtation with her. They were in the habit of writing long letters to each other, and now he wrote her such a letter from Potsdam. Written in May 1829, it revealed his loneliness, the still sharp pain of his father's death, his anger at his enemies, and the sweet memory of his Italian trip.

Lovely, generous Friederike! If a man has crouched at his desk from five o'clock on, he may be tired and stupid by noon; especially if he has a sick heart. Still, I must hesitate no longer to thank you for your last letter, for this wonderful spring letter that drove me into the open with delight—though of course, the old melancholy soon came sneaking after me on its iron crutches . . . Here I am no longer quite a solitary Robinson Crusoe. Several man-eating officers landed near me last night, in the New Garden. I even got into a company of ladies and sat among some female Potsdamers like Apollo among the cows of Admetus . . . Alas! I am sick and wretched, and as if in self-mockery, I am now writing about the most glorious period of my life, when, drunk with pride and happiness in love, I ran about the peaks of the Apennines, rejoicing, and dreamed of great wild deeds which would spread my fame all over the earth, even to the farthest isle, where the seafarer would tell of me nights by the fire. How tame I have grown now, after my father's death! Now, on such a far island, I'd like to be just the kitten that sits on the warm oven, listening to the tales of famous deeds.

Heine had completed *Journey from Munich to Genoa,* the first section of *Travel Pictures III,* in the summer of 1829 and was well into the *Baths of Lucca* when, in July, Campe came to Potsdam and brought with him *The Romantic Oedipus,* a so-called comedy that contained a number of gibes directed at Heine. The author was Count August von Platen, and Heine suspected that he had been directly involved in the machinations that had influenced King Ludwig to withhold the professorship he had sought. The same issue of *Eos* that had viciously attacked Heine had carried glowing praises of Platen.

The count's ire had been aroused by some mild ridicule of his poetical talents that had appeared in the second volume of *Travel Pictures.* Heine had appended a few epigrams by the respected poet Karl Immermann, which lampooned those who, in imitation of Goethe in the *West-Eastern Divan,* were turning out *ghasels* (poems in the Persian style). The criticism was mild, but Platen, who considered himself to be a modern Aristophanes, set out to punish his detractors. In a letter to Count Fugger, the Christian nobleman asked, "How dare the Jew Heine treat so unmercifully someone who is plainly greater than he, who can crush him?" Platen's revenge took the form of *The Romantic Oedipus,* a comedy in which the wit was nonexistent and the satire vulgar. He referred to Heine as the "Pindar of the little tribe of Benjamin"; "baptized Heine, the pride of the synagogue"; "his kisses smell of garlic"; "small Jew canker worm." Heine was infuriated. He had been attacked as a Jew, and that he would not forgive.

He needed time; he needed the medicine of the sea to steady his nerves and inspire his pen. He told Campe to go ahead with the publication of *Journey from Munich to Genoa,* and then left Potsdam for the island of Heligoland, where he stayed until October. His only companions were "two little English women, some sea-gulls, the clouds and Tacitus." The sea worked its magic, and he felt serene and cheerful. Invigorated and refreshed, he worked on *The Baths of Lucca;* he would use it to teach the foolish count a lesson. He finished by November and returned to Hamburg, where he polished the manuscript, read proofs, and made sure that Campe made no changes in his copy. The last copy of *The Baths of Lucca* was off the press on December 29, 1830 and Heine smiled grimly. He knew that he would be denounced for his attack on a count, and he wrote to Immermann, "For three months I pondered over what to do, and then I did only what absolute necessity demanded."

Journey from Munich to Genoa had been published in 1829 and was the subject of conversation not only in Berlin, but also in Paris, Vienna and St. Petersburg. There were readers who found it supremely witty and entertaining; others were enthralled by the descriptions of nature, of art, and of lovely women. But the pillars of society—the nationalists, the clergy, the aristocracy, the wealthy bourgeoisie—read the book with horror. It was immoral, seditious, blasphemous, they raged. And in a way they were right, for *Journey from Munich to Genoa* was nothing less than an assault on the feudal and aristocratic institutions and beliefs of the time. It was replete with passages assailing tyranny, declaring the dignity of all humankind, and passionately calling for the triumph of justice and freedom.

Ostensibly a book of travels, it gives much more information about Heine than about Italy. It is Heine himself—man and poet—who takes over the stage. The *Travel Pictures* celebrate himself in the same way that *Leaves of Grass* was "an attempt from first to last to put a human being (myself, in the latter part of the nineteenth century, in America), freely, fully and truly on record" (Walt Whitman, *A Backward Glance Over A Traveled Road*). It should occasion no surprise that the poet of American democracy hailed Heine as a kindred spirit. Whitman discussed the German poet with his confidant, Horace Traubel, who reports him as exclaiming:

> Heine! Oh, how great! The more you stop to look, to examine, the deeper seem the roots; the broader and higher the umbrage. And Heine was free—was one of the men who win by degrees. He was a master of pregnant sarcasm; he brought down a hundred humbuggeries if he brought down two. At times he plays with you with a deliberate baffling sportiveness. *(With Walt Whitman in Canada)*

Heine must have realized that in writing as he did he was bringing closer the day of his forced departure from German soil. Yet he could not write otherwise. He foresaw the new Europe that was emerging.

> Nations no longer exist in Europe—only parties; and it is an instructive sight to see how quickly these parties recognize one another in spite of their varied colorings and differences of language . . . just as the smallest conflict between two most insignificant powers can turn into a general European war—so the slightest strife cannot occur anywhere in the world today without the most remote and diverse parties being forced to take sides for or against . . . two great hostile camps are lining up and fight with words and looks . . . Time presses for fulfillment of its great task.

And what is this great task of our day, he asked, and answered,

It is emancipation. Not simply that of the Irish, Greeks, Frankfurt Jews, West Indian blacks, and other oppressed people, but the emancipation of the whole world, and especially of Europe, which has come of age.

The *Baths of Lucca*, unlike *Journey from Munich to Genoa*, did not deal with questions of history and the destiny of humanity, but was a witty, farcical, and in spots a hilarious tale. It is a story told in the first person by H. Heine, Doctor of Laws; that is, until the eleventh, final chapter, when Heine breaks off the storytelling and then uses the concluding pages to dispose of Count von Platen.

The two characters who give the book its vitality and exuberance are the Marquis Cristoforo di Gumpelino, a baptized Jewish millionnaire from Hamburg, and his servant, Hirsch-Hyacinth, at one time a lottery ticket seller in that town. Some commentators have maintained that the two figures are spiteful caricatures of people whom Heine had known in Hamburg. That they had their real-life counterparts is undoubtedly true; but there is nothing malicious about the portrayal. Gumpelino, with all his pretensions and absurd hyperboles and redundancies is treated with light-hearted good humor, and Hirsch-Hyacinth, a German Sancho Panza, is an immortal creation. Hirsch boasts to Doctor Heine of his own great honesty: "If you've no objection, I'd like to tell you of a noble trait in my character, and you'll be astonished at it."

He then proceeds with a truly cosmic tale of the time when he had actually collected and then turned over to a client, Herr Christian Hinrich Block, fifty thousand marks won in a lottery, although he could have pocketed the prize money and no one would have been the wiser. One of his most treasured possessions was the receipt for the fifty thousand marks that Herr Block had given him, which he always carried about with him. He shows Doctor Heine the document.

"When I die," said Hyacinth, "this receipt must be buried with me, and on the judgment day, when I must give an account of all my deeds, then I will go with this receipt in my hand before the throne of the Lord, and when my evil angel has read off the list of all the evil deeds I've been guilty of, and my good angel has read off in turn all my good deeds, I'll say, calm and easy, "Be quiet! All I want to know is if this receipt is correct?—is that the handwritting of Herr Christian Hinrich Block?" Then a little angel will come flying up, and he'll say that he knows Block's hand perfectly well, and he'll tell the whole story of the honorable business I carried through. And the Creator of Eternity—the Almighty who knows all things—will remember it all, and he will praise me before the sun, moon, and stars, and reckon up at once in his head that if the value of my evil deeds be subtracted from fifty thousand marks, that there'll remain a balance to my account, and he'll say, "Hirsch, you are appointed an angel of the first class, and may wear wings with white and red feathers."

Hirsch does not hesitate to hold forth on any subject. Launching into a dissertation on religion, he begins by declaring that he can see no pleasure in the Catholic religion: "It's such a religion as if God (God forbid it!) had just died." He finds the Protestant faith no more satisfactory.

> That is . . . too commonsense like, and if the Protestant churches hadn't an organ, it wouldn't be a religion at all . . . I once came to the conclusion that it was a very enlightened religion, without any visionary notions or miracles, though I still think that a Church must have a few visionary notions and trifles in the way of miracles to be one of the proper sort.

As for the Jewish religion: "The mischief take the old Jewish religion! I don't wish it on my worst enemy. It brings nothing but abuse and disgrace. I tell you it isn't a religion, but a misfortune." But then Hirsch goes on to reflect that perhaps for the common man the old Jewish religion is satisfactory, and he is reminded of Moses Lump, a humble peddler, who ran around all week with a pack on his back to earn a few miserable marks. But on Friday evening:

> He goes home and finds the seven-branch candlestick all lighted, a clean white cloth on the table, and he puts off his pack and all his sorrows, and sits down at the table with his sorry-looking wife and his sorrier-looking daughter, and eats with them fish which has been cooked in nice white garlic sauce, and sings the finest songs of King David, and rejoices with all his heart at the Exodus of the children of Israel from Egypt . . . the man is happy; he does not torment himself with worldly concerns; he just sits content in his religion . . . and if the candles should happen to burn a little dim, and the Christian woman who snuffs them on the Sabbath isn't there at the moment, and if Rothschild the Great should happen to come in with all the brokers, discounters, forwarders, and head clerks . . . and say, "Moses Lump, ask whatever you like, I will see that your wish is granted," I believe that Moses would say, quiet and easy, "Trim the candles for me." And the great Rothschild would cry in admiration, "If I weren't Rothschild, I'd like to be just such a Moses Lump!"

When he first read *The Romantic Oedipus* in July, Heine had already completed the greater part of *The Baths of Lucca*. But he was so infuriated by Platen's vile satire that he decided to change the ending he had planned for own book and use the *Baths of Lucca* to annihilate Platen. With this aim in mind, he first devised an incident that could have fitted into Balzac's *Droll Stories*.

The Marquis Gumpelino had been ardently pursuing Lady Julia Maxfield, but was unable to consummate his heart's desire since Lord Maxfield, her brother-in-law, kept close watch. So strong is Gumpelino's passion that he avers he would rather enjoy one divine hour with Julia than win the great one hundred thousand marks prize in the Hamburg lottery. This remark causes Hirsch to cry, "What a crazy notion . . . That any man could prefer love to the great prize!" Hirsch was convinced that his master was suffering from depression and persuaded him to take a powerful dose of salts to rid himself of it. But no sooner had Gumpelino swallowed the laxative than a messenger arrived with a note from Lady Maxfield inviting him to call immediately for their first and last rendezvous before she left the following morning for England. Gumpelino rushed despairingly back and forth, and wailed: "Woe me, fool of fortune! Love holds out to me this nectar cup, and I, alas, have already drained a goblet of Glauber salts! Who can get the accursed stuff out of me? Help! Help!" "No earthly living man can help you now!" sighed Hyacinth.

The marquis was unable to sleep that night. But fortunately he found a book: a collection of poems by Count August von Platen, a book of "gems" he explained the next day to Doctor Heine.

> I swear sir . . . that these poems haven't their equal! You know that I was in a state of desperation yesterday evening . . . because Fate forbade me to possess my Julia. Then I read the poems, one every time when I had to get up, and the result has been, that I feel so indifferent to women that my own passion has become repulsive to me. And that is the beauty of this poet, that he only burns with friendship for men. Yes, he prefers us to women; and for this very preference we ought to be grateful to him. How much greater he is in this than common poets! You do not find him flattering the everyday tastes of the masses; he cures us of that passion for women which causes us so much suffering.

Heine had now made the transition to enable him to launch his attack on Platen. "Who, then, is Count Platen, whom we have in the previous chapter learned to know as a poet and warm friend?" With this question he began the last chapter, amiably and gently, and then proceeded, skillfully and surgically, to cut Platen apart as a poet and a man. He derided Platen's poetical talent.

> This troubador of misery, weakened in body and mind, has striven to imitate the most powerful, the most imaginative and the most witty poet of the youthful Grecian world . . . there is nowhere in this work [*The Romantic Oedipus*] a trace of that profound world-destructive imagination which underlies every Aristophanic comedy . . . the poor Count was capable of imitating only some of the externals of Aristophanes—only the dainty verses and the coarse expressions.

Since Platen had used the most insulting and vile terms to assail him, Heine felt he was justified in using similar tactics against the count. He took note of Platen's predeliction for the company of boys. "I would much prefer having it reported that he hated me to my face, than that he loved me behind my back," he wrote. And, "As for winning the willing love of Genius, it is beyond his power; he must breathlessly run after his youth, as after others, being content with the outward form."

It was to be expected that the upper circles of German society would be appalled and enraged that an "ill-mannered Jew," the son of a merchant, dared to strike so venomously at one of the nobility. Even liberals criticized him, saying that he had gone too far. Contemptuously, Heine wrote to Varnhagen: "The charge against me that I, the commoner should have refrained from attacking the nobly born is ludicrous. That was my very motive: to make an example, no matter what it cost." But friends, too, turned against him, among them Moses Moser. His desertion was a particularly bitter blow to Heine, for he himself was loyal and loving to his friends. Only Varnhagen stood by his side, and to him Heine wrote long letters in January and February 1830, explaining the considerations that had moved him: there had been a plot; others might retreat or cower, but he did what had to be done—fight evil whatever the cost. He would not be cowed, he would not beg forgiveness.

No one knows better than I that I have done myself incalculable harm with the Platen chapter, that I should have handled it differently, and that I have offended the better class of the public; but at the same time I feel that with all my talents I could not have done better, and that—cost what it might—I had to make an example . . . When the clericals in Munich first flung the Jew in my face, I laughed—I thought it was mere stupidity. But when I scented a systematic attack, when I saw that the absurd bogey was turning into a menacing vampire, when I perceived the aim of Platen's satire, when I heard from booksellers that similar productions steeped in the same poison were being secretly passed around in manuscript, then I girded my loins and struck as quickly and as hard as I could. Robert, Gans, Michael Beer, and others have always borne these attacks like good Christians, and maintained a prudent silence when they were attacked. I am a different kind of man, and that is well. It is good when the evil ones find a man who will fight ruthlessly and mercilessly to vindicate himself and others.

Heine sensed that time was running out for him. He was being shadowed by the police. More and more he thought of leaving Germany. He grew accustomed to the realization that sooner or later he would have to join the exodus of the best sons of Germany. Prince Metternich, nicknamed Prince Midnight, had triumphed, and the very word "freedom" had become anathema.

Exile himself from Germany? He loved his homeland, the land of his childhood and youth. To cross the Rhine, never to return, was an agonizing thought. And if he did flee, where would he go? Metternich and his agents were in power everywhere on the Continent, and England was a nation of shopkeepers. He thought of going to America as once he had advised his students to do, but would he be any happier there? The American Declaration of Independence had inspired all humanity with its bold statement that all men were created equal and was one of the sources of the Declaration of the Rights of Man proclaimed by the French revolutionary assembly of 1794; but now in that great land across the Atlantic millions of human beings were treated like animals because of the color of their skin.

His despondency grew. He was tired and longed for a rest, yearned to get away from politics and self-torture for the sake of Hans, who kicked him for all of his pains. Once again he turned to the sea, his "natural element." He left for the island of Heligoland. It was June 1830. He took only a few books with him: the Bible, Homer, and a history of the Lombards.

He fell into a pleasant routine; he flirted with the girls, talked with the fishermen, argued with a Prussian lawyer from Koenigsberg about anything and everything. Walking along the shore at twilight, he surrendered himself to reveries. "What an irony that I who most dearly love to pass my time in watching trailing clouds, in solving metrical word sorcery, in eavesdropping on the secrets of the elemental spirits, felt I had to further the interests of the day, arouse revolutionary action." He stopped short. Yes, he would forget politics and enjoy the world of nature and art. Why continue to torture himself? He was thirty-three. It was time that he saw the world as it really was. He had thought that great causes ultimately triumphed, even if individual soldiers in humanity's war of liberation fell in the battle. But was that true? In 1793 a king was guillotined, but now France was again ruled by a king.

And then, like a thunderclap came the stupendous news. It was in the newspaper that arrived with the mail this day early in August 1830. He reread it. The words were sunbeams splashed on the printed paper. He ran around the inn, kissed the fat landlady, embraced the lawyer, was unable to restrain himself. Then he sat down and wrote to his friends:

Lafayette, the Tricolor, the Marseillaise! My longing for peace is gone! I know now what I must do! I am a son of the Revolution and I take up the charmed weapons upon which my mother has breathed her magic blessing . . . give me my lyre, that I may sing a battle hymn . . . Words like flaming stars have shot from heaven to burn palaces and illumine novels . . . Words like bright javelins, will go whizzing up to the seventh heaven and smite the pious hypocrites who have crept into the Holy of Holies. I am all joy and song, all sword and flame . . .

Perhaps I am quite mad . . . One of those sunbeams wrapped in printed paper has flown into my brain, and all my thougts are in a white glow . . . Even the poor Heligolanders are jubilant, although they understand the events only by instinct. The fisherman who ferried me yesterday to the little island where I bathed, laughed and shouted, "The poor people have won!" Yes, instinctively the people understand these events better perhaps than we with all our learning!

Heine returned to Hamburg, where he stayed with his mother. At his uncle's he found much discussion about the possible effects the revolution in France would have elsewhere. For a short while it seemed that the revolution would spread. There was an uprising in Poland against Czar Nicholas I; Belgium declared herself independent of Holland; in Germany, the regent of Brunswick was driven from the throne and there were scattered uprisings in other parts of the country. But the insurrections were quickly crushed.

If Heine had ever thought that the fires of freedom would spread to Germany, events in the free city of Hamburg quickly put an end to this dream. Two weeks after his return from Heligoland, a violent *Judenkrawall* broke out in Hamburg, possibly instigated by government provocateurs. It began one evening when, at exactly nine o'clock, every Jew found in a restaurant or other public place was thrown out. The next day mobs hunted Jews in the streets and wrecked synagogues and Jewish-owned shops. On the third day of the rioting, the civil guard was called out and order was restored. Thus had the revolution sputtered and been extinguished in Germany.

The rule of the privileged had never really been threatened; nevertheless, the July events in France and the repercussions in Germany prompted the authorities to clamp down on all "troublemakers" at home. There was talk of imminent arrest of all radicals; if that took place, Heine would certainly be on the list of those apprehended.

An old councillor told him that in the fortress prison of Spandau in Berlin the irons were heavy, and he added that they were particularly uncomfortable in the cold winter. Heine remarked that it was very un-Christian not to warm the fetters a little, and since his legs were not trained to wearing chains, prison would not be good for his health. And he would also miss the oysters, which the councillor told him were not served in Spandau. But he would not flee in panic. He would strike a final blow for German freedom before he left.

His action took the form of a book, *Supplement to Travel Pictures*. It was published by Campe in January 1831 and was immediately proscribed as "blasphemous, indecent, subversive, replete with lèse majesté." And indeed, the audacity, the verve, and the poetical fire of the book make it stirring reading even today:

> I am only a Don Quixote. I was a child when I read the great novel by Miguel de Cervantes, and in my childhood innocence took everything at face value, and shed bitter tears over the blows and ingratitude the Knight received for his magnanimity, and thought that to be hurt and despised was a part of heroism. That was long ago . . . Perhaps the reading of all kinds of wonderful books has turned my head, as it did that of the Knight of La Mancha . . . Naturally, the madness and fixed ideas which I drew from those books are altogether different from those of the Knight of La Mancha. He wished to restore decaying knighthood; I, on the other hand, want utterly to destroy what has survived from those day . . . My colleague regarded windmills as giants; I, however, see in the giants of today only noisy windmills . . . He mistook every beggar's inn for a castle—every donkey-driver for a knight, every stable wench for a lady of the court; I, on the other hand, look upon our castles as disreputable inns, on our cavaliers as donkey-drivers, on our court-ladies as stable-wenches. Just as he took a puppet play to be a noble affair of state, I hold our affairs of state to be wretched puppet plays.

Yet just as bravely as the bold Knight of La Mancha do I fall upon the wooden company.

The book was inflammatory, but it was impossible for the reader to lay it down. What a clever rogue the author was! Here was a story that began in a tone so properly patriotic that even the censor would approve of it. It was about the Emperor Charles V, a tale about the time when he was in captivity in the Tyrol.

The poor Emperor . . . was forsaken by all his knights and courtiers . . . who fawned upon and toadied him with such devotion when the sun of good fortune smiled on him, and now left him alone in his dark plight. But suddenly the prison doors opened and . . . the Emperor recognized his faithful Kunz von der Rosen, the court fool.

He has come to console his Emperor. A truly lovely story of devotion to a king, certain to please the heart of any censor. But suddenly the sly Heine exclaimed:

Oh German Fatherland! dear German race! I am your Kunz von der Rosen. The man who in happier days entertained you breaks into your dungeon in time of need . . . If I can't set you free, I will at least console you, and you shall have someone to chat with you about your black misery, to keep up your courage, to love you—someone whose best jests and best blood are at your service. For you, my people, are the true Emperor, the rightful lord of the land. Your will is sovereign, and far more legitimate than any "divine right." . . . the day of freedom draws near, a new age begins. My Emperor, the night is gone, and the red light of morning gleams.

After such words, Heine could hardly hope to remain on German soil much longer. Yet he had one more challenge to fling. He had been asked to write an introduction to a liberal pamphlet, *Kahldorf on the Nobility*, and in a white heat he dashed it off.

He began by discussing the nature of revolution, contrasting the violence that accompanied the great French Revolution of 1789 with the peaceful course of the July 1830 Revolution, and asking which course a German revolution would follow. It would be a mistake, he said, to think that a German revolution would necessarily resemble one or the other. Only similar conditions produced similar results.

The character of the Revolution of 1789 was determined by the fact that the lower classes had been culturally neglected, and kept from every aspiration by a narrowminded despotism . . . political education was lacking not only in the lower, but also in the upper strata of society. The latter understood only the miserable maneuvres of rival corporations, mutual attempts to weaken one another, traditional routines, the art of equivocation, the influence of mistresses . . . The French were forced to learn the great science of freedom—politics—and the study of the first rudiments cost them their best blood.

It was the fault of the stupid obscurantist despotism that the French had to pay so high a tuition fee . . . it had even suppressed, in the most ridiculous fashion, the press, that mightiest instrument for the advancement of popular knowledge . . . censorship, while it may for the time being given an advantage to despotism, in the end destroys despotism along with the despot. Where once the guillotine of thought has done its work, then censorship of human beings is soon introduced. The slave who has been the executioner of thought will soon with the same equanimity erase his own master from the book of life.

These thoughts led Heine to examine the events of the July 1830 Revolution in Paris when on July 5 the Bourbon King Charles X and his minister Polignac had suspended freedom of the press. The next day the people of Paris came out on the barricades; three days later the revolution triumphed.

There were no atrocities committed then, no wanton murders . . . the French press had made the people of Paris more receptive to finer sentiments and less sanguine jests. It had weeded out ignorance from their hearts and planted intelligence. And the fruit of that seed was the legendary moderation and touching humanity of the Paris population during that great week. And indeed, if Polignac did not later lose his head, physically, he owes his good fortune solely to the mild aftereffects of that very freedom of the press, which, in his folly, he had sought to extinguish.

Which course, then, would a possible German revolution follow? It was an important question, for on its answer depended not only the fate of Germany, but also that of Europe. He did not expect a German revolution to come soon, but when it did, its character would be determined by the "cultural and political education of the German people"; and, he maintained, it would depend upon freedom of the press whether the word "revolution" would be "uttered in discussion by quiet assemblies or in rage by an uncontrollable mob."
He was writing his swan song.

Alas! our whole history today is nothing but a chase—a grand hunt against all liberal ideas, and the high nobility are more zealous than ever, and their uniformed huntsmen shoot at every honest heart in which liberal thoughts have found refuge, and there is no lack of learned hounds who with their fangs drag the bleeding word as they would rich booty. Berlin is fattening the best leash of hounds, and I can already hear the pack howling at this book.

He had stayed long enough; any further delay was foolhardy.

Duty and prudence alike counselled departure. I had to choose between laying down my arms completely and life-long combat. I chose the latter, and certainly not lightly. That I did take up arms, however, was forced on me by the way in which I found myself scorned, by the insolence of those who arrogantly claimed a superiority of birth—in my cradle were my marching orders for the rest of my life. (Letter to Varnhagen from Paris, 1833)

Before he left Germany Heine swallowed his pride and once again went to Solomon for help. His uncle gave him money and promised an annual allowance of four thousand francs, but neither one dreamed that Heine would become an exile for life.

He left Hamburg late in April 1831 for Frankfurt where he was feted in liberal circles, but, at the end of a week, word reached him from friends in high quarters that he would be wise to leave at once. Journeying by way of Heidelberg and Karlsruhe, he crossed the Rhine at Strassbourg into France.

8

Paris: *The Romantic School* and *Religion and Philosophy in Germany* (1831–32)

Heine spent his first night on French soil in Saint Denis, rose early, and in twenty minutes was in Paris. He was thirty-four, a poet, and the great city lay before him like a lovely bouquet. The sights and the sounds intoxicated him. Later he was to become more sober, but now he was enchanted. "I heard loud Gallic laughter . . . It is good-tempered and mocking at the same time, like the delightful noble French wines or a chapter of Rabelais. Nothing is more infectious than such gaiety, and I began to laugh with a heartiness that I had never been able to achieve in the home country."

He was impressed by the courtesy of the people.

The men were all polite, and the pretty women smiled so graciously. If someone accidentally jostled me without immediately begging my pardon, I could safely wager that it was a fellow countryman; and if a pretty woman looked somewhat sour, then she had either eaten sauerkraut or could read Klopstock in the original . . . I found the restaurants to which I had been recommended. The proprietors assured me that they would have made me welcome even without letters of introduction, for I had such an honest and distinguished appearance . . . never had a German restaurant-keeper addressed me in this fashion, even if he thought so . . . In the manner and even in the speech of the French there is so much delicious flattery, which costs little and yet is gratifying and refreshing. My poor sensitive soul, which had so often shrunk back with shyness from the rudeness of my German Fatherland, again expanded in the genial warmth of French urbanity. God has given us tongues so that we may say something pleasant to our fellow-men. *(Confessions)*

And what charmers the Parisian women were!

I know nothing more apt than the legend that Parisian women were born with every possible fault, but that a good fairy took pity on them, and lent to each of their faults a charm which turned it into a fresh allurement.

Heine describes one early encounter thus:

> My French was rusty, but after a half-hour's conversation with a pretty flower-girl in the Passage de l'Opéra it soon flowed fluently again. I managed to stammer forth gallant phrases, and explained to my little charmer the Linnaean system, in which flowers are classified according to their stamens. The little one followed a different system, and divided flowers into those which smelled good and those which smelled bad. I believe that she applied a similar classification to men. She was amazed that, despite my youth, I was so learned, and she spread the fame of my erudition through the whole Passage de l'Opéra. I drank in with rapture the delicious aroma of flattery, and had a good time. *(Confessions)*

Often of an evening Heine sauntered along the boulevards of Montmartre or Montparnasse and looked for and met them, the delightful, charming girls of Paris. He tarried with them, had brief love affairs, celebrated them in *New Spring*, a collection of light love poems.

> Over me a melody
> Softly steals; oh, ring!
> Ring out, sing out far and free!
> Little song of Spring.
>
> Ring out till you reach the place
> Where the flowers grow
> Should a rose turn up her face,
> Say I said Hello!
>
> Stars with golden feet are walking
> Through the skies with footsteps light,
> Lest they wake the earth below them,
> Sleeping in the lap of night.
>
> Hush, who called there? My heart trembles
> As the dying echoes fail.
> Was it my beloved, or was it
> Just a lonely nightingale?

Dating from this time too are the amatory poems in the *Miscellany* section of *New Poems*. Cynical is the touch in

> I love this white and slender body
> These limbs that answer love's caresses,
> Passionate eyes, and forehead covered
> With a wave of thick, black tresses.

You are the very one I've searched for
In many lands, in every weather.
You are my sort, you understand me;
As equals we can talk together.

In me you've found the man you care for.
And, for a while, you'll richly pay me
With kindness, kisses, and endearments—
And then, as usual, you'll betray me.

Jenny was published posthumously but may have been written in this period. It is a cry from the depths.

In eighteen-seventeen a maiden
Became my sweetheart, fond and true;
Strangely like yours her form and features,
She even wore her hair like you.

That year before I left for college,
I said, "My own, it will not be
Long till I come back home. Be faithful!"
"You are my world," she answered me.

Three years I toiled, three years I studied,
And then—it was the first of May—
In Göttingen the tidings reached me;
My love had married and gone away.

But still I lived. And now my health is
Strong as an oak that seeks the sky
Yet, Jenny, when I look upon you,
The old dream wakes that will not die.

And the cycle *Abroad* ends with a poignant cry of homesickness.

I dreamed I had a lovely fatherland.
The sturdy oak
Grew tall there, and the violets gently swayed.
Then I awoke.

I dreamed a German kiss was on my brow,
And someone spoke
The German words: "I love you!" (How they rang!)
Then I awoke.

Day after day he explored every nook and corner of the silver-gray city. The streets were lined with chestnut trees and innumerable little shops—a *boulangerie*, a *boucherie*, an *épicerie*, a *poissonnerie*, a *pharmacie*, a *librairie*, a *bureau de tabac*. In the late morning he liked to sit at a small table in a sidewalk café and, while drinking his *café au lait*, listen to the chatter around him and watch the passersby. Sometimes he scribbled a few lines in a notebook that he always carried with him.

Leaving, he picks up a flower at a flower-stand, then saunters on his way. Perhaps he finds himself treading the stones of the spacious place de la Concorde. Voices from the not too distant past murmur and swell. On this spot stood the guillotine that beheaded Louis XVI and Marie Antoinette. He strolls westward down the wide, tree-lined Champs-Elysees, peering about him as he walks, until he comes to the Etoile, a vast square at the intersection of twelve radiating streets. Here, Napoleon had begun the building of his Arc de Triomphe in 1806, but twenty-five years later it is still not completed. He has read that when finished, it will be 164 feet high and 148 feet wide and will stand on an elevation in the center of the Etoile.

Paris! City of light, city of culture and pleasure, city that offered haven to exiles from tyranny, city of the great revolution of 1789, city where every street was alive with history. Here Danton proclaimed to the assembly of nations, "We hurl at your feet the head of a king." Here the drummer boy beat "Ca ira—les aristocrats à la lanterne!" Here Lafayette proposed to the Assembly the adoption of the Declaration of the Rights of Man.

He was astounded when he first stood before the Louvre. It stretched along the Seine for a half mile and was connected with the Tuileries palace and gardens by the Grand Gallery. Kings and emperors had crammed its endless halls with the art treasures of the ages.

Everywhere he turned he saw beauty: the Luxembourg Palace, the Pantheon, where Voltaire and Rousseau were buried, the Cathedral of Notre Dame, the Madeleine, the Sacré Coeur, which stood on the highest of the hills of Montmartre and was topped by a white mosquelike dome glimmering in the Paris sunlight.

A year after his arrival, Heine wrote to the composer Ferdinand Hiller, "If anyone asks you how I am, tell him, 'like a fish in the sea,' or rather tell him that when one fish in the sea asks another how he is, the answer comes back, 'I feel like Heine in Paris.'" He had come with letters of introduction from Varnhagen, Cotta, and Solomon to important people in Paris, but it was the brilliance of his writings that, with astonishing rapidity, won him an enthusiastic audience, and it was his wit and eloquence that completed the conquest.

In December 1831 Baron Cotta engaged him as the Paris correspondent of the *Augsburg Allgemeine Zeitung* and the *Morgenblatt*, journals that were respected in liberal circles throughout Europe. The *Revue des Deux Mondes* published a French version of the *Harz Journey* and of *The Book Le Grand* and *The Baths of Lucca* in June and December 1832, and their appearance created a stir in literary circles. His reputation was further enhanced with the appearance in *L'Europe Littéraire* and the *Revue des Deux Mondes* of essays that later were expanded into *The Romantic School* and *Religion and Philosophy in Germany.* He also turned out in this period the fascinating *French Painters, The French Stage,* and *Letters on Music.*

Paris welcomed him as Berlin never had. Heinrich Laube, the dramatist and novelist and a confidant of Heine's, commented in amazement: "All doors, even those usually most firmly closed, opened to him, and the George Sands, Balzacs, de Vignys, Victor Hugos, Janins and all the rest of them treated him as their equal."

His reputation as a master of the pointed epigram spread and his remarks were picked up and repeated. Said the poet Gautier, "He was like a god, mischievous as the devil, but good-natured with it all, whatever people say to the contrary." De Musset, too, was of the opinion that Heine was "beautiful as a god." Dumas declared, "If the Germans don't want Heine, we will adopt him," then added, "Unfortunately, he loves Germany more than she deserves." And Balzac said: "Ah, the other day, Heine, Heine the famous Heine, Heine the powerful, came to see me. He came unannounced, and although, as you know, I am myself not a nobody, still, when I heard who it was, he took possession of my entire day."

He had entrée to all the literary, artistic, and musical circles in Paris. He knew Lafayette, and was on friendly terms with the celebrated musicians of the period, Chopin, Berlioz, Liszt, Wagner, Meyerbeer, Mendelssohn, Donizetti. Society ladies, too, vied for his presence, but he turned down their invitations, "rather curtly," reported one observer, "The forms of Western European social intercourse seemed to him so much false flummery." However, he was a frequent visitor at the mansion of Baron James Rothschild, with whom he established a relationship that he described as "famillionnair." He found him to be "an old lion who roared now and then but was good and noble at heart," and he maintained an admiring and affectionate friendship with Betty, the baron's gentle and talented wife. The baron admired Heine, and found ways to help him financially in tactful ways. Once he turned over a large sum of money to Heine, explaining that he had played the stock market and had invested a sum for him as Heine had once asked him to do, and if he had lost, Heine would have owed him money. The baron also passed on political and economic information that was of great help to him in his articles on French political affairs.

When he first came to Paris, Heine used to visit, almost daily, the bookshop of Heideloff and Campe in the rue Vivienne, for it was a meeting place for visiting or resident Germans in Paris; there he renewed old friendships and made new ones with such notables as Felix Mendelssohn, Michael Beer, Alexander von Humboldt. He stopped going there when he began to suspect that Austrian and Prussian spies found the bookshop a convenient place to engage him in conversation. Heine's convictions that he was surrounded by Prussian spies were treated later by some biographers as figments of his imagination.

They dismissed as mock heroics a letter to Laube in 1833 in which he wrote that he was afraid of momentary arrest. "I am writing these lines in the bed of my charmingly insistent ladyfriend, who would not let me go last night for fear I should be arrested." But a belated corroboration of Heine's claims came to light in 1912 with the publication of *Secret Reports on the Literary World of the Pre-1848 Revolution*. It revealed that spies for Metternich had indeed frequented the Heideloff and Campe bookshop for the purpose Heine had suspected.

Heine never directed his humor at the weak or the suffering; the objects of his wit were always the pompous, the hypocritical, the arrogant ones. Gautier, his dear friend and admirer, once wrote, "When Heine spoke, the barbed and pointed arrows whistled forth from their red bow; winged darts of sarcasm which never failed to reach their target, for never was anyone so cruel to the stupid; to the divine smile of the leader of the Muses succeeded the mocking laughter of the satyr." But underneath the biting words and the witticisms, Heine was an unusually soft and tender and compassionate person, an impassioned defender of the insulted and injured: the Jews in the Frankfurt ghetto, a despairing mother in a back street of London, the slaughtered Silesian weavers, the kidnapped Negro slaves, a procession of exiled German peasants plodding along the seashore on their way to Algiers.

He would give away his own possessions to help a friend. "He helped me in everything like a brother," said Laube. "He is extremely soft-hearted. He often apologized for it and called himself a silly old woman, but while he apologized he continued to give." Gerard de Nerval reported that helping friends was a fixed principle with Heine, that he would lend money freely, never asking for a note or a receipt, and never pressing for repayment. This habit of Heine's became well known in the circles of German expatriates in Paris, not all of whom were high-principled. They asked for loans as a matter of right from a man whose uncle was a multimillionaire, but they did not hesitate the next day to turn against him and slander their benefactor. Bitter experience finally changed his attitude to these compatriots, but unfortunately not before he incurred a crippling debt of 20,000 francs as the result of lending his signature on a note.

"Heine is capable of any sacrifice for a friend," declared August Lewald. Just how faithful a friend Heine could be, he proved during the cholera epidemic in 1832, when he remained in Paris to save the life of his cousin Karl, at the risk of his own.

It was in the year 1817 that a report reached Europe of a cholera epidemic that had broken out in India. It was shrugged off as of little consequence. In 1823 the plague surfaced in Asia Minor. It was a horror, moving westward relentlessly. It came to European Russia in 1830. London was attacked in January 1832. Then, on March 29, at the height of the carnival season before Lent, the first cases of cholera were announced in Paris.

The Parisians reacted with bravado, perhaps encouraged by news that the plague had caused comparatively few deaths in London. The city officials, unbelievably, took no measures of hygiene and quarantine. The cholera, finding fertile soil in the miserable sanitation conditions, swept through Paris as if with an invisible scythe.

Heine considered leaving the city as most of his friends had done, but then he learned that his cousin Karl, the brother of Amalie and Therese, the one with whom he had roamed about in Hamburg, had contracted the disease. If he died, it would be a terrible blow to Solomon, whose oldest son, Hermann, had died in Italy not too long ago. He told Lewald that he considered it "a sacred duty to preserve this son of Uncle Solomon." He moved into Karl's lodgings and became his nurse. He washed him, cooled him, poured down his parched throat the fluids his dehydrated body begged. Karl's illness ran the usual short course of cholera and he recovered. He expressed his eternal gratitude to Harry and returned to Hamburg.

Heine was now free to report on the events that were unfolding in Paris. He felt as if he were stationed in the midst of a mighty battlefield, and that the outcome of the battle would shake the foundations of society. He roamed the city, observing and reporting.

Enormous crowds surged up and down the boulevards. They wore masks and costumes deriding cholera, seemingly under the delusion that mockery would render it harmless. They crowded the ballrooms, dancing wildly and licentiously.

Suddenly one and then another of the dancers feel a chill. They clutch at their throats and take off their masks and reveal violet-blue faces. At first the other dancers laugh, thinking it is some new bit of deviltry, but then the laughter dies down as they realize they are looking at the faces of cholera victims. Now wagons are summoned and the victims are brought to the Hotel Dieu, the central hospital. There they die quickly, they die in agony, and the deaths occur in such numbers that there is no time before the burials to take the fools' clothing off the corpses. In one day two thousand people die. Coffins give out, and the dead are buried in sacks. "They were piled high, one on top of the other . . . hundreds of white sacks each containing a corpse . . . I remember two little boys who stood by my side with sad faces and how one of them asked me if I could tell him in which sack his father was." *(French Affairs)*

The authorities finally took the indispensable measures of public hygiene. A sanitation committee was set up, first aid stations were established throughout the city, and ordinances were enacted to deal with the problems of sewage and filth in the streets.

One of the main causes of the rapid spread of the cholera was the fact that in the poorest quarters of Paris, waste, rubbish, and even dung piled up daily. The *chiffoniers*, scavengers, of whom there were several thousand, were accustomed to sift through the garbage, then sell the evilsmelling pickings to *revendeuses*, unclean creatures who put the stuff up for sale along the quays. The authorities ordered that the refuse be removed immediately from the streets and that the waste matter be loaded on carts and taken outside the city limits, where the *chiffoniers* and *revendeuses* would be permitted to carry on their business. But, claiming they had been deprived of their property rights, the two groups combined forces and launched a small-scale insurrection against the government. They smashed the new sanitation carts, threw the pieces into the Seine, and put up barricades. The armed forces were called out, the stock market dropped, and the Carlists, followers of the deposed Bourbon king, plotted to benefit from the disturbances.

Ever more gruesome and dreadful sights were described by Heine, in his reports to the *Allgemeine Zeitung* as a kind of madness descended on Paris. The theaters and restaurants were empty, and the few people seen on the boulevards hurried by with hands or handkerchiefs covering their faces. Heine wrote of the growing anger of the people as the wealthier classes fled the city, taking their drugs and doctors with them. "It seemed to the poor," he wrote, "that money had become a prophylactic even against death."

Ugly rumors filled the city, each one wilder than the other. One story that spread like wildfire—the city was ablaze with it—was that it was not cholera but poison put into food by enemies of the people that had caused so many deaths. Heine saw groups gathering and organizing, stopping individuals and searching them.

> Woe to those in whose pockets anything suspect was found. Like beasts, like maniacs the people fell on them . . . There is no more dreadful sight than such popular anger thirsting for blood and throttling its defenseless victims. A dark human flood rolls through the streets, with workers in shirtsleeves foaming up here and there like whitecaps, and howls and roars mercilessly. In the Rue Saint Denis I heard the well-known cry, "*A la lanterne!*" and voices trembling with rage told me that a prisoner was being hanged. In the Rue Vaugirard, where two men were killed who had white powders on them, I saw one of these unfortunates when he was still breathing and the old hags were pulling the wooden shoes from their feet and beating him on the head with them until he was dead. He was quite naked and bloody and mashed; they had torn not only his clothes but his hair, his genitals, his lips, and his nose, and one ruffian tied a rope to the feet of the corpse and dragged it through the streets, shouting constantly, "Voilà le choléra-morbus." A very beautiful female, pale with rage, with bare breasts and bloody hands, stood by and kicked the corpse as it came near her. (*French Affairs*)

The day after these murders, the newspapers announced that the victims had all been innocent, that the powders found on them were cholera preventives, and that there had been no poisoning—all who had died had been victims of the epidemic. Then who had originated the rumors of the poisoning? Heine suggested that the royalist party was responsible; that they had paid a few dupes to incite the people against the government. But the Carlists had fallen into their own trap; the people uniformly ascribed the poisoning to the royalists. "The power of the elder Bourbons will never again thrive in France," wrote Heine. "I heard the strongest words from different groups; I have looked deep into the heart of the people—it knows its men." (*French Affairs*)

The cholera epidemic eventually ended, the theaters reopened, the boulevards again became crowded, and the wealthy returned from their places of refuge. But France was not the same. The fissures in French society had deepened; Franch was a divided nation.

In 1789 and again in 1830, the middle classes had united with the city poor and the peasants to overthrow the power of the Bourbons. But now the rich governed. In a population of thirty million, only two hundred thousand could vote. The bankers, big merchants, and industrialists had chosen Louis Philippe to be the new king. Instead of a crown, he wore a white felt hat, carried an umbrella, and proved his democratic sentiments by parading the streets to shake hands with tradesmen and laborers. He was paid eighteen million francs a year. He was "a pot-bellied bourgeois, with a fat smiling face," wrote Heine.

Louis Philippe was the perfect middle-class king. His backers grew ever richer. Securities on the stock exchange ballooned. Paris was resplendent with balls and entertainments and festivities. From 1830, when one revolution put him in power, until 1848 when another deposed him, he earned his keep.

But listen, Heine warned, and you may hear, from deep underground, ominous sounds.

> Everything is still as on a snowy winter's night. No sound but a soft, monotonous dripping. That is the interest dripping continuously into the capital, which continually increases; one seems actually to hear the riches of wealthy men growing. In the intervals comes the gentle sobbing of poverty. Occasionally, something rattles like a knife being sharpened. (Quoted by Ludwig Marcuse in his *Heine*, A Life Between Love and Hate)

The people of France, he observed, had not yet gained what they had sought when they initiated the French Revolution, and as long as this remained true they would periodically "develop a high fever and tear the strongest bandages and the soothing lint from their wounds . . . and writhe in agony and unrest" until their needs were met. (*French Affairs*)

There was no dearth of prophets, each one proclaiming that he had the answer to the problems of the people, that he would lead humanity into a better world. The movement that at this time had the widest following among the people was Saint-Simonism. It was strongest in France, where it had arisen, but it had won many converts in England and Germany and elsewhere. Among the notables who had been drawn to it were Augustin Thiery, George Sand, and Franz Liszt in France; Thomas Carlyle and John Stuart Mill in England; and the Varnhagens in Germany.

The founder of the movement, Claude Henri de Rouvroy, Compte de Saint-

Simon, was born in 1760 of an old and noble famaily. Before he was twenty he went to America and served with distinction in the campaign against Lord Cornwallis. He returned to France in 1783, supported the revolution, and surrendered his titles. He made and then lost a fortune speculating in the estates of nobles who had fled from France. He became in turn a salesman, merchant, adventurer, engineer, and soldier of fortune. Meditating on the nature of the world and society, he saw that the promises of the French Revolution had not been realized. The middle class had been freed, but the lot of *"la classe la plus nombreuse et la plus pauvre"* had not improved. He began to turn out his blueprints for a better social order, and a group of brilliant young followers gathered around him; but when he died in 1825 his work was still largely unknown.

In his last work, *The New Christianity,* he proclaimed the principles of a "physico-political science" for the reorganization of the social structure. In the new social order all men would work, and the equal claims of each individual for moral, intellectual and physical well-being would be met. Science and industry, under the leadership of scholars, bankers, and industrialists, would find the solutions to the ills of the world. With a naive faith, he called upon the reigning rulers of Europe—the old princes and the new bankers—to renounce their power:

> Princes: Hearken to the voice of God who speaks to you through me. Be good Christians once more. Cease thinking that your hired armies, your nobles, your heretical clergy and your corrupt judges are your mainstays . . . use all your energies to increase as quickly as possible the social well-being of the poor.

The last words of the Count de Saint-Simon were: "My whole life can be summed up in one desire: to ensure to all men the freest possible development of their capabilities."

His disciples continued his work, but they soon quarreled over the mantle of leadership. The most prominent of Saint-Simon's successors were Prosper Enfantin and Amand Bazard. In 1829 they published the *Doctrine of Saint-Simon,* in which they reinterpreted and developed the ideas of the master into a universal system covering every field of human endeavor and aspiration. Reflecting the scientific and rationalist ideas of Bazard, the work presented plans for modernizing the banking and credit system, for promoting advanced technology, for building canals and railroads, and for the eventual public control of all means of production. Key points in their program were the abolition of the right of inheritance and the gradual emancipation of women. During the turbulent days of the July 1830 Revolution, the Saint-Simonists began to hold public meetings; they published a newspaper and established schools. Saint-Simonism seemed well on the way to becoming a power. But animosity between Bazard and Enfantin weakened the movement. Enfantin took over control, but under his leadership the movement degenerated into a cult and engaged in ever more eccentric practices. He combined mysticism and a religious eroticism. He called himself the Supreme Father. He became convinced that the Supreme Being was androgynous, and this led him to the search for a High Priestess to take her place beside himself. He began to talk of a new woman and a new morality. The number of his followers dwindled to a handful, and he returned with them to his estates at Ménilmontant, where they set up a monastic community. They took vows of celibacy, but there were rumors of immoral sexual practices. Finally, in 1833, Enfantin was put on trial and sentenced to a year in prison. After his release he made his peace with established society. He found employment as an engineer engaged in the construction of dams on the Nile and later became a successful industrialist. By then Saint-Simonism was a historical relic.

Heine had become interested in Saint-Simonism while still in Hamburg. How far he had traveled in his embrace of the new gospel was indicated in a letter he wrote to Varnhagen on the eve of his departure for Paris: "Every night I dream that I am . . . going to Paris to breathe the fresh air and give myself up completely to the ecstasies of my new religion, and perhaps to be ordained as its priest."

Within twenty-four hours of his arrival in Paris, Heine called upon Michel Chevalier, the editor of the Saint-Simonist paper, *Le Globe*. He was received enthusiastically; *Le Globe* announced his coming in glowing terms.

> The famous German writer Dr. Heine . . . is one of those courageous men who defend the cause of progress without fear of . . . the enmity of court lackeys and aristocrats. Monsieur Heine is a generous-hearted man of sparkling wit who employs his pen to defend the people's interests in Germany.

The paper went on to prophesy that Heine would play a "magnificent role" in the great cause, which had as its aim the uniting of the people of France and Germany in sacred friendship.

Heine attended meetings of the Saint-Simonists—as he did those of other socialist-oriented societies—and he met many of the leaders of these groups. He was in full sympathy with the idea that the progress of industry and economy had reached a point where the material needs of the people could and should be met. But it seemed naive to him to appeal to industrialists and princes to unite in a crusade to do away with poverty. The aristocracy and the wealthy bourgeoisie would not divest themselves of their riches and power in response to appeals to their Christian virtue.

It was not the political-economic theories of the Saint-Simonists that most appealed to him. As he wrote to Varnhagen in May 1833, "My interest is in the religious concepts, the ideas which, sooner or later, will be incorporated into all existence, into ordinary living." This meant an understanding that bread alone was not enough for the people's happiness. Their spiritual and aesthetic needs had to be fulfilled equally with their physical wants, for to satisfy one at the expense of the other was fatal to human development. The sensual and the spiritual, the physical and the aesthetic were complementary, not opposites.

Saint-Simonism proclaimed the demise of the Judeo-Christian dualism of body and soul and taught that men and women must stride the earth like gods. Inspired by his new faith, Heine added his own vision to the promise of the French Revolution.

> We interpret the words of the Revolution—"bread is the right of the people," as meaning "bread is the divine right of man. In this, and in many other respects, we differ from the men of the Revolution. We do not want to become sans-culottes, or frugal citizens or economical presidents. We prepare to establish a democracy of equally glorious, equally holy and equally happy gods. You ask for simple dress, austere manners, and unseasoned joys. We, on the other hand, demand nectar and ambrosia, purple raiments, costly perfumes, luxury and splendor, dances of laughing nymphs, music, and comedy. Oh, do not be angry, virtuous republicans! To your censorious reproaches, we say with the fool in Shakespeare, "Dost think because thou art virtuous, there shall be no more cakes and ale?" (*Religion and Philosophy in Germany*)

The influence of Saint-Simonism is felt in Heine's two great prose works, *The Romantic School* and *Religion and Philosophy in Germany*. As we have noted, portions of these books appeared originally in French. He wished to correct misconceptions that were prevalent in France about German literature and philosophy, and at the same time he wanted to warn the French against the dangers that could come from a chauvinist and reactionary Germany. He hoped tht his words would help the peoples of the two great nations to understand each other better and to become friends who would no longer "permit themselves to be provoked by the hireling scribblers of the aristocracy into hatred and war."

The Romantic School opened with a review of the political and social conditions that prevailed in Germany at the time of the wars against Napoleon. Poverty was widespread; the national pride was humiliated. To rouse the people against the conqueror, the German poets and romanticists glorified the past—the age of feudalism and the Holy Roman Empire. When victory had been won and German nationalism had triumphed, the leaders of the Romantic school continued to extol the Old German, feudal-Catholic heroes. They spoke the language of medievalism, obscurantism, submissiveness, and death, and thereby became the upholders of reaction and despotism.

Heine paid full tribute to the services Catholicism had rendered Europe in an earlier age when a cruel and colossal materialism prevailed within the Roman Empire and threatened to destroy the spiritual grandeur of humanity. It was Christianity that chastened and spiritualized the barbarians, and for this, Heine wrote, "the Catholic Church has the strongest claims upon our respect and admiration." But that day was past. The Church, "by teaching the rejection of all earthly goods, and by inculcating dog-like humility and angelic patience, became the surest support of despotism." However, Heine asserted, mankind "cannot now be put off with promissory notes on Heaven; they know that matter, too, has its good side, and is not wholly the devil's; they now claim as their inalienable birthright the enjoyment of this earth, God's beautiful garden."

He discussed many other themes, but the central one was always the age-old struggle between sensualism and spiritualism. There was not a dull page in the book—whether he wrote about the *Nibelungenlied,* or Lawrence Sterne, or Aristophanes and Euripides, or Calderón, or Racine. Rarely had deep learning been presented with such grace and sparkle, and the French readers of *The Romantic School* were captivated by its pages.

Goethe had not been kind to Heine, but Heine paid full justice to his genius. Goethe's prose, he said, was as "translucent as the green sea becalmed . . . everything he wrote turned into well-rounded works of art . . . They are the great ornaments of our Fatherland." But, observed Heine, they were ornaments

much as beautiful statues adorn a garden . . . they are only statues—they are sterile. The poems of Goethe do not produce action—as do those of Schiller . . . The deed is the child of the word; and the beautiful words of Goethe are childless. This is the curse that befalls all that is born of art alone. The statue which Pygmalion fashioned was a beautiful girl—even the master himself fell in love with her. She grew alive under his kisses. But so far as we know, she never bore any children.

Art that is aloof from life is sterile, Heine was saying.

German philosophy, too, had forgotten the language of freedom and reason and was now the ally of reaction. Philosophy in Germany had been born with Luther, he averred, and had continued through Spinoza, Mendelssohn, Lessing, and Immanuel Kant. Kant, in *The Critique of Pure Reason,* had destroyed the basis for faith in a personal God, but then, terrified at his own conclusion, had reconsidered, and in *The Critique of Practical Reason* "revived the corpse of deism which theoretical reason had slain." Did he do this out of pity for distressed humanity, or out of true conviction, Heine speculated.

He declared that, after Kant, German philosophers

no longer soar in the realm of ideal abstractions, but seek, instead, for grounds on which to justify that which exists. They have become apologists for that which is [and] wear the resplendent livery of power. They have become state-philosophers, that is, they have concocted philosophical justification for all the interests of the state, in whose employ they are. Thus Hegel, a professor in Protestant Berlin, has taken into his system all of the Evangelical-Protestant dogma. And Herr Schelling, a professor in Catholic

Munich, now justifies in his lectures the most extravagant doctrines of the Roman Catholic Apostolic Church. *(The Romantic School)*

Some of Heine's arguments and conclusions are questionable. To take only two examples: contrary to his expectations, the political and social influence of Catholicism has not diminished; and in the area of Judaism, it must be pointed out that his presentation of Judaism as an ascetic religion is completely untenable. As was pointed out by Dr. Hugo Bieber in his biographical anthology of Heine, "Neither biblical nor post-biblical Judaism preached denial of life. On the contrary, the daily rituals ordained thanksgiving to God for enjoyment of earthly life."

But whatever criticisms one may make of *Religion and Philosophy in Germany* and *The Romantic School,* they nevertheless are brilliant works that make rewarding reading even today. No reader can ever forget Heine's portentious vision of a European Armageddon brewing in the witches' cauldron of German philosophy. The concluding passage of *Religion and Philosophy in Germany* is one of the most remarkable prophecies in all literature; it begins on a joyful and idyllic note. He speaks confiently of the day, not too far distant, when pantheism will triumph over deism and usher in an age of universal joy and harmony. The peoples of Germany and France will lead the way into this beautiful world of the future; he even thinks that Germany offers "the most propitious soil for pantheism," for belief in the "spirits of nature" has never died out among the German people, and pantheism was the religion of Germany's greatest thinkers and artists.

At this point in his argument Heine suddenly stopped short. What would actually happen in Germany on the morrow of a philosophical revolution, he asked—and recoiled in alarm. He recollected that once, in a beer-hall in Göttingen, he heard a Junker declare that Germany must avenge the death of Conradin von Hohenstaufen whom the French had beheaded in Naples. That had happened in 1268 and the French had surely forgotten it long ago, but the Germans forgot nothing.

He had asked what would follow the de-Christianizing of Germany begun by Kant, Fichte, and Hegel. Suddenly the pantheistic vision of a world that gleamed so beautifully in Paris was transformed into its opposite in Berlin.

Christianity—and that is its greatest merit—has somewhat mitigated that brutal German love of war, but it could not destroy it. Should that subduing talisman, the cross, be shattered, the frenzied madness of the ancient warriors, that insane Berserk rage of which Nordic bards have spoken and sung so often, will once more burst into flame . . . The old stone gods will then rise from long ruins and rub the dust of a thousand years from their eyes, and Thor will leap to life with his giant hammer and smash the Gothic cathedrals . . . Do not smile at my advice—the advice of a dreamer who warns you against Kantians, Fichteans and philosophers of nature. Do not smile at the visionary who anticipates the same revolution in the realm of the visible as has taken place in the spiritual. Thought precedes action as lightning precedes thunder. German thunder . . . comes rolling somewhat slowly, but . . . its crash . . . will be unlike anything before in the history of the world . . . At that uproar the eagles of the air will drop dead, and lions in farthest Africa will draw in their tails and slink away . . . A play will be performed in Germany which will make the French Revolution look like an innocent idyll.

Heine wrote much more of his vision and concluded with a warning to the French that whether the crown prince of Prussia or Doctor Wirth, the leader of the German republicans, eventually ruled in Germany, Frenchmen should remain on their guard and be prepared. "On Olympus . . . among the naked gods and goddesses who there rejoice over nectar and ambrosia, you may see one immortal who even among all this festivity and gaiety always wears a coat of mail and bears a helmet on her head and a spear in her hand. It is the Goddess of Wisdom."

Heine's prophecy must be read in its entirety to gain its full import. A hundred years after it was written, the Nazi onslaught against civilization gave terrible witness to the wisdom of his warning.

9
Mathilde (1834)

She stood in the doorway of her Aunt Maurel's glove and shoe shop in the passage Choiseul, a busy shopping street off the rue de Strassbourg. She was at home on the little street. Hardly a moment passed without a clamorous exchange between her and a passer-by; she was enjoying herself hugely.

Now she noticed him. She observed his fashionable attire: a blue jacket, a light-colored cashmere waistcoat, a silk hat. This was a handsome fellow. He strolled by a second and then a third time. He tipped his hat to her. She looked him up and down, her arms akimbo.

"Ah, monsieur," she bubbled, "you'll wear out your shoes walking up and down our passage. And to tell the truth, your shoes do not do credit to the rest of your costume. Perhaps I can help you: our shop carries the finest shoes for gentlemen."

"And boasts the sauciest seller of shoes in all Paris."

"So I've been told." She was in high spirits. "But you do not speak French like a Parisian," she half teased, half inquired.

"I do what is more important. I admire beauty like a Parisian."

"Ah, you are a flatterer."

"Only when the mademoiselle inspires flattery. But you are right, these shoes are a disgrace, and it will be a delight to be sold new ones by someone as charming as you."

"Then come in, come in, Monsieur. Monsieur? . . .

"I am called Henri—Henri Heine. And what should I call you?"

"Crescentia Eugénie Mirat, Monsieur Heine."

He followed her into the little shop and was greeted by the owner, a buxom, friendly woman in her forties, who, he learned was the girl's aunt. The saucy shopgirl danced and chattered as she went about finding a pair of shoes for the hard-to-please customer.

Heine was captivated by the fresh beauty, so obviously and happily aware of her physical charms. She was no more than seventeen or eighteen, a young woman ripe for love. As she moved about with a catlike grace, excitement gripped him. He closed his eyes, opened them; his hand moved and touched her. She smiled and danced away.

He talked disconnectedly. He asked her if by chance she had read any of his poems; she answered simply that she never read anything. A customer came into the shop. Heine told her to wait on the newcomer, that he was in no hurry. As she coquetted and prattled with the customer, her aunt sat down next to him and they exchanged pleasantries. Later, when he left the shop, he said "au revoir," not "adieu," and Crescentia and the aunt joined in assuring him that they would be delighted to wait on him again.

He came back the next day; it seemed that he was in need of a pair of gloves. He presented Crescentia with a posy of violets. She smiled and patted his cheeks. And with that touch she trapped him forever.

He did not yet realize what was happening to him. He had entered the shop, flowers in hand, expecting to embark on one more amatory adventure, one more fleeting affair such as he had experienced so many times with young ladies of this type. For he, a world-famous poet, was fond of dallying with these girls. They were honest; they did not deceive. No lies. They kissed and they tumbled with abandon, and when it was over, no false promises had been made.

But Heine's game of love took a different turn from what he had planned. Crescentia showed that she liked him. She smiled at his honeyed phrases that were strange and exciting, but she made this elegant foreigner pay court to her. He had to take her to fine restaurants, to the theater, to the circus, and—her chief delight—to the dance halls in Montmartre. There she enjoyed the abandon of the masked *contredanses* while he watched dourly. She had him in thrall.

His intimates sought his company in vain. The weeks went by, and he was not seen or heard from. What had happened to him? Was he ill? Had he been kidnapped by agents of the Prussian government? Gradually the story emerged. The great poet, it was reported, had contracted a mésalliance with a common shopgirl. Tongues clucked and heads wagged, reprovingly or knowingly.

Heine's obsession was complete and overwhelming. He importuned Crescentia to live with him, but she refused to take this final step. Her resistance only fed his passion.

Crescentia Mirat had grown up in the fertile countryside northeast of Paris. Her mother, Heine learned from Aunt Maurel, came of peasant stock, but her father was a man from the upper classes, who had seduced the mother, then deserted her before the child was born. Crescentia had been a good daughter, cheerfully tending the cows, keeping the fires going in the kitchen, and sometimes roaming the countryside. By the time she was fifteen the boys were flocking about her. Once, her mother, searching for Crescentia, found her in a meadow with a village boy who was fondling her. The mother boxed their ears; later she gave Crescentia a lecture about the value of what a girl gives a man.

Her daughter must aim higher than some village lout. It was at this time that the mother got in touch with her sister in Paris and asked her to take Crescentia in as her apprentice.

Sensing an ally in the aunt, Heine often spent time with her when Crescentia deserted him. Tonight was such a time. Crescentia had wanted him to take her to a disreputable dance establishment, and, when he refused, she left, dressed provocatively, and shouting, "Jean will take me." He and the aunt were alone. It was late, and the shop had been shuttered for some time.

"Yes, Monsieur Henri, Crescentia is a most invaluable assistant to me. You have seen for yourself how she captivates the men. But she is waiting for the right one. She will make some man very happy—in all ways, Monsieur Henri," and Aunt Maurel poked Heine jestingly. "You would be good to Crescentia. You will save her from the wolves of Paris, *n'est-ce-pas*, Henri? Tell me, what are your intentions? Will you marry her?"

He was taken aback and was silent for a long time before answering slowly, "Marry? Marry? She is in my blood. Marriage? There are problems. I must have time to think. Does she want to marry me?"

"I could talk to her, and she would listen. But I must know that you will not desert my sister's child."

Madame Maurel suddenly became a practical, hard-headed French business woman. Somehow the conversation turned to matters financial, to the problems of a small shop. If a certain number of francs, say three thousand, were put into the shop and used to carry an adequate inventory to supply the customers with the latest styles, why, the shop would prosper. In that event, Henri could rest assured that a generous portion of the profits would go to the benefit of Crescentia. Heine understood. He responded that it would afford him the greatest pleasure to help Madame Maurel with a generous loan, which she need be in no hurry to repay.

The money was forthcoming, and Aunt Maurel began to sing Henri's praises to her niece. But Crescentia shouted, "Yes, he is *très gentil*. But I won't be bought. If I go to him it will be because I love him, because he pleases me more than any other man I know, do you hear?"

"And why shouldn't you love him? You are lucky to be wanted by such a kind and generous man. Where will you find a better one? He will give you what you need. He will be good to you."

"I will not make the mistake my mother made. Before I go to Henri, I want assurances."

"He will marry you."

"He has never asked me to. He only wants me to be his mistress."

"I repeat: he adores you; he will marry you. *Mon Dieu*, if you resist too long, you may lose him altogether.

Perhaps Aunt Maurel's words did their work. Or perhaps it was the duel that finally swayed Crescentia. Late one afternoon, she and Heine had been passing the time at an outdoor café. He was scribbling in his notebook, paying little attention to her endless chatter, or, seemingly, to anyone else. Suddenly he sprang up and strode over to a nearby table where a young man was sitting.

"Sir!" he said, softly but angrily, "you have insulted my companion."

The young man looked at him in astonishment. "How could I have insulted her when I wasn't even speaking to anyone?"

"Do you deny that you stared at the lady sitting at that table in a suggestive way?"

"Is she your companion? I was not aware that I stared at her."

Heine was not at all satisfied with the answer, and he snapped, "You are an impertinent boor." As might be expected, the student, for such he proved to be, rose, saying, "Sir, I consider your remark an insult. I must ask for your card. Here is mine."

The duel was fought with rapiers before a large audience of journalists, students, and ladies. Neither Heine nor his opponent was bloodthirsty. The student had no desire to harm the famous poet, and Heine now felt a little foolish. But he had to go through with it. He was not an accomplished swordsman; nevertheless, his rapier scratched the student's shoulder. The duel was stopped instantly. The surgeon took care of the slight wound, the contestants went through a ritual of reconciliation, the crowd applauded, and the next day a stirring account appeared in the newspapers.

Crescentia was proud of Heine, and she tossed her pretty little head when acquaintances teased the famous inhabitant of their quarter over whom men fought duels. It was a few days later that she moved into Heine's small apartment.

They had a breakfast with a few friends to celebrate the setting up of their ménage. it was a pleasant and merry affair and went off very well. Crescentia was her most charming and natural self, but after the guests left, she suddenly exclaimed, "Listen to me, Henri: you are mine now, mine! I have given you all a woman has to give a man, because I love you. Not because of my aunt or your money. I will never leave you, never, never. Do you think I would have done what I did if I didn't love you? Whether you marry me or not, whether you are good to me or beat me, I shall never leave you. My aunt tells me that you will be good to me, that you will give me fine things, that you are a famous writer. I can't even read. I don't know why you came into my life. Maybe to amuse yourself. But now I am your woman. And if you should try to leave me, I will kill you and then kill myself." Crescentia burst into big sobs, which died down and then broke out afresh as in her imagination she visualized the bodies of two fated lovers.

Heine listened to the outburst, bewildered by its unexpectedness, disconcerted by its threats, and pleased by the revelation that he had won her as a man, and not because of his reputation as a poet. "I am going to give you a new name," he announced, after first repeatedly reassuring her that he would never leave her. "From now on I am calling you Mathilde. Crescentia is an outlandish name that doesn't fit you. Mathilde means mighty in battle. You have overpowered me in the battle of love." She laughed. Thereafter he called her Mathilde, and in time the name Crescentia was forgotten.

It was the most unlikely of relationships. The prince of poets, the wittiest of men, the champion of freedom, bewitched by a woman who had never grown up. They fought and they shouted and they accused each other of unfaithfulness; they threatened to leave each other, and they patched up their quarrels with kisses and tender murmurs. His will, his reason, were helpless before Mathilde, with her laugh, her sensuous mouth, and the seductive way she moved. She was a creature of sensation, emotion, movement. She loved good food and sweet wines. She laughed when men stared at her, and their touch at the dances excited her. She was self-centered as a child and expected her Henri to supply her with all the wonderful things that Paris had to offer: pretty clothes that set off her figure, dinner at fine restaurants, visits to the circus, the vaudeville and the dance hall.

He had always been unusually sensitive to noise; now he lived in a very inferno of sound. He would try to work in his study, but suddenly Mathilde and her parrot would join in a screeching duet. Or Mathilde's friend Pauline, would arrive and a wild pillow fight and screams would ensue. Or she would burst into his room; she wanted to go shopping with Pauline. If he said he did not have money to throw away, she would scream, then scratch at him with her nails or throw herself on the floor, hammering at it with her fists. But he would laugh at her; suddenly she would sit up, dry her tears, throw her arm around him and laugh. Then he would surrender and give her a five or ten franc note, and she would kiss him violently and then run off with Pauline. "We are both happy," he wrote to a friend; "that is, I never have a peaceful moment day or night."

Mathilde had no understanding of Heine's fame. Even after she had been living with him for a number of years, she inquired of a friend whether it was really true that her Henri was a great poet.

He remained terribly in love with her—her primitiveness, her earthiness, her temper, her childishness. The days were filled with clamor, the nights with love. Yet sometimes he wondered how long this kind of life could go on. A feeling of unease, of being trapped in a sensual bog, from time to time gripped him. And then a day came when he tried to escape.

It started with a quarrel. There had been similar ones in the past, and over the same things, but this time they did not become reconciled. She had insisted on going to one of the "disreputable" dance halls. She said she would go, even without him, if he would not take her. She slammed the door as she left. "Don't come back," he shouted after her.

His friends had been right, he told himself. How had he ever permitted himself to be so trapped? Now his eyes were open. Suddenly he saw her through the eyes of his friends, and what he saw was a childish, stupid, slovenly *grisette*, whose chief talent was the way she wiggled her plump behind, who could not read or write, who had not an idea in her head. His friends were too polite to laugh, but they pitied him, a galling thing for a man of spirit. He would leave her.

Heine turned to a woman whom he had once called "the loveliest and most intelligent of women," The beautiful and mysterious Princess Cristina Belgiojoso, who was one of the first friends he had made in Paris. He wrote to her that he had to get away from the bustle and noise of Paris; he yearned to stretch out under the trees at La Jonchère and ease his soul in her company. Would he be welcome?

She answered his letter at once: he would be more than welcome. After telling Mathilde that he did not know when he would be back, Heine left in July 1835 for La Jonchère, the princess's chateau, situated on a spacious estate near St. Germain in the beautiful countryside north of Versailles.

He was greeted with an embrace and a lingering kiss. Her enormous dark eyes shone softly and happily. She held his arm as they walked along shaded paths, and she listened with sympathy to his story, although he did not tell her the full extent of his plight.

He had first met Cristina at one of Lafayette's Tuesday soirees. He had been engaged in animated conversation, but when she entered the room he could not refrain from staring at her. An expression of serene loveliness, warm eyes, a richly molded mouth, coils of lustrous jet-black hair. She wore a long, white satin dress trimmed with lace, and her only jewelry was a brooch of pearls. Heine turned to Gautier, who was sitting next to him, and whispered, "She is like a being from the realm of poetry or of dreams." Gautier replied, "She is a political exile from Italy, and she is as intelligent and noble as she is beautiful. She has written essays and novels; she has studied philosophy and medicine. That tall, gray-haired man who came in with her is Mignet; he is said to be her lover." Heine stared at the famed historian. Mignet's bearing was reserved, and he gave the impression of being a shy person, but when he smiled, his face lit up in a most engaging way. One sensed a fine intelligence. "Introduce me to them," Heine asked Gautier.

Heine had expected to spend no more than a few days at the princess's idyllic retreat, but the days stretched into weeks and the weeks into months. He arrived in the spring, and he was still there in the autumn. He felt healed, and as if he had recovered from a terrible illness. The headaches that had plagued him in Paris disappeared. He felt vigorous and joyous. His appetite was good. He tramped the countryside and reveled in the warmth of the bright sun and the caress of the fitful breeze. With delight he viewed the fields of thick green grass, speckled with yellow dandelions; the white blossoms of apple trees; the dancing flights of white, yellow, and purple butterflies; the somnolent, fat cows. He enjoyed the friendly greetings of farmers to whom he no longer was a stranger from the chateau. With pleasure he listened to the country sounds: the singing of birds, the humming of insects, the occasional rumbling of a passing cart and the greeting of its occupant.

He looked forward to the evenings, when Christina's select circle of friends gathered at the chateau, marvellous people like Chopin, Liszt, Dumas, Gautier, Hugo, and, of course, Mignet. A close relationship sprang up between Heine and François Mignet, and the friendship with the historian, who was the permanent secretary of the French Academy, proved to be of special value to Heine at a later time when he was in serious financial straits.

Autumn arrived. He wondered if people thought that he and the princess had set up a ménage. He did not permit himself to look ahead; while it lasted, he wished to bask in the summer idyll. Cristina brought repose, whereas Mathilde brought turmoil. Cristina recited his poems by heart, while Mathilde wasn't even aware that he was a poet. Cristina, a descendant of one of the oldest and wealthiest of Italy's families, had joined the secret revolutionary *carbonari,* and thereby risked imprisonment and even death, but Mathilde's thoughts did not go beyond the joys of Montmarte.

He knew no woman who combined such beauty and such serenity as did Cristina. They seemed so attuned to each other. Once when he told her, laughing, that he thought of Lord Byron as his English cousin who had given his life for the cause of Greek liberty, she confessed her own passion for the cantos of *Childe Harold.* He asked her what events in her life had influenced her to risk life itself for her cause. She answered that what she had done was not a matter of choice, but that it was as if she had been seized and mastered by an overpowering compulsion. She was the slave of an idea, in the same way that Robespierre was when he said, "I am the slave of freedom."

Her words thrilled him. He said he understood and he agreed. "Yes, we never seize an idea; it is the idea which takes hold of us, enslaves us, lashes us right into the arena, so that we fight for it, gladiators by necessity." "That," she said, "is why you left Germany."

Heine's voice was sad when he answered. "My enemies, even some of my friends, say that I am an enemy of Germany. It is true that I have spoken harshly about my fatherland—but only as one does who loves that which he berates. Because I praise France so highly, I am charged at home with being no patriot. What is love of country? A man can love his country and never know that he loves it, though he lives to be eighty—if he has never left home. You do not realize the meaning of spring until it is winter; and your best songs of May are written behind the stove. The love of freedom is a prison flower, and only in captivity can one feel the worth of liberty. Love of the German Fatherland begins at the frontier, and grows stronger when one looks at German unhappiness from abroad."

"I understand what you say, because I too am an exile"; and a faint sigh escaped Cristina.

They were alone one day, having tea together in the late afternoon. A swirl of feelings crowded in on him. Surely Cristina was the woman for him, Cristina who responded to his every thought, his every mood. She had restored his peace of mind, his calm and dignity. Why did he hesitate? But was she interested in him as a lover, or did she think of him only as a friend? Cristina smiled mysteriously, and she leaned over to pour him some more tea. If he embraced her, he wondered, would she surrender like one of the nymphs of Montmartre, or would she, the gracious princess, reject him? Who would believe it: he the hero of so many romances, afraid of a rebuff?

They had finished their little repast. They sauntered out on the grounds. He placed his arm about her, drew her to him and kissed her—and held the kiss—and felt her return it. She was warm and clinging. But he felt no fire within him, no desire to press further. Cristina was beautiful; she was the ideal woman of poetic invocation; she was his intellectual peer; but, he realized with shock, he could never sensually desire her.

That night his sleep was restless. Toward morning he was awakened by a familiar laugh and a voice that called, "Henri." He jumped up and called out. No one was there. He dressed and quietly left the chateau. He walked along a country road, and the image of Mathilde appeared before him, stayed with him, would not leave him. She was gay, saucy, vibrant. He heard her loud, happy laughter. She refused to depart, this Parisian *grisette* so full of life, and he wanted her, wanted her as she was, with her quick temper, her carelessness, her innocent vanity, her primitiveness. Let his friends smile and his enemies gibe—he was going back to her. He returned to the chateau to say goodby to Cristina.

When he returned to their apartment, Mathilde greeted him with great cries of love. Her Henri had been a bad boy, but she would forgive him. He must promise her that he would never leave her again—and that he would marry her. Heine, who now knew that he was irrevocably tied to Mathilde, agreed. But still he did not hurry, and she did not press him. In fact, the marriage did not take place until 1841, when he married her on the eve of a duel.

That duel was precipitated by remarks he made about a Frau Strauss in his book *Concerning Ludwig Börne*. He had withdrawn the offending statements, but the lady's husband had demanded further satisfaction, and a duel with pistols was arranged. Heine had been in a number of duels, and he faced this one with equanimity, but he was concerned about Mathilde. If he were killed and they were not married, she would have no legal claims upon his estate, and Solomon would certainly not help her. She would be penniless and adrift. The duel was set for September 7, and a week before, on August 31, 1841, he married Mathilde.

When the duel took place, he fired into the air; he explained later, "I was wrong to insult the poor devil's wife, and my anger against him has evaporated." Herr Strauss's bullet grazed his hip but did not strike the bone. He was kept in bed for a few days, and he utilized the rest to send off a few letters announcing the marriage, among them one to Charlotte.

Dear much-loved sister—On the 31st of August I married Mathilde Crescentia Mirat, with whom I have been quarreling daily for more than six years.

She has, however, the noblest and purest heart. She is as good as an angel, and her conduct during the many years of our life together has been so irreproachable that all of our friends and acquaintances praise her as a model of propriety.

In a facetious vein, Heine wrote to August Lewald, "This matrimonial duel, which will not end until one of us is slain, is certainly more dangerous than the short combat with Strauss."

The marriage was solemnized in the Church of Saint Sulpice. Earlier, they had gone through a civil ceremony, but Mathilde said she could not consider herself properly married unless the marriage was performed by a priest. Since Heine professed the Protestant faith, he had to secure a dispensation from the archbishop and give a written pledge that any children of the marriage would be brought up in the mother's faith. "For no consideration," wrote Heine, "would I have shaken this dear being's belief in the religion which she inherited." He always respected her faith; he never permitted a derogatory remark about religion to be made in her presence, and in her room she kept a crucifix and an image of the Christ-child.

Grave and proper people have found it difficult to understand the relationship between the great poet and the simple, uneducated Parisian girl. With horror they have pointed to the fact that Mathilde did not have the faintest notion of Heine's significance as a poet! Once she remarked to Laube: "People say my Henri is a great poet. Isn't it funny I don't understand anything about it?" But when this was reported to Heine, he found it delightful; it showed that she loved him for himself, not for his fame. "You see how my irresistible, highly personal charm triumphs," he laughed.

It was Mathilde's very naturalness and unaffectedness that captivated him. Her unashamed abandonment to passion, her childlike frivolity, her delight in elegant clothes, her unrestrained laughter and chattering were anodynes to his finely honed being. He was the soul and she was the body, and the two are one that cannot be sundered, he wrote.

Her genuineness was a refuge from the hypocrisy and meanness of the world. Laube observed:

Heine always took the greatest delight in Mathilde's happy, unsophisticated nature. It was a joy he never lost. To his last breath he counted himself lucky to have her and he himself had the air of a simple child whenever he spoke of her . . . In no other relationship have I seen him display so many little charms and graces, which in his best poems peep out at us with childlike eyes.

She was true. "Have you ever seen a real Parisian *grisette?*" Heine asked. "Round, buxom, always merry, charming, loyal and honest . . . She is sound through and through; not a mistress in the lyrical sense, but a friend such as only a Frenchwomen can be." (Quoted by Ludwig Marcuse in Heine, *A Life Between Love and Hate*)

When he first met her he wrote to Lewald: "The rosy waves are roaring round me so loudly, my brain is so stupefied by the overpowering scent of flowers, that I am incapable of talking to you rationally. Have you read the *Song of Songs*, which is the *Song of Solomon*?" The waves never subsided, the scent of flowers remained overpowering. "For eight years I have loved her with a tenderness and passion which is almost incredible," he wrote to his brother Max in 1843, and in December 1848 he repeated: "I love her passionately and this emotion is stronger than my sickness."

10
Censorship and Deteriorating Health: *French Affairs*, *Florentine Nights*, *The French Stage*, and *Sundry Women* (1832–38)

Friederich von Gentz, right-hand man to Prince Metternich, called to the coachman to speed up the pace, then sank back into the corner of the cusioned carriage and closed his eyes. He would not be visiting Rahel Varnhagen, his old, cherished friend, after all. An urgent message from Metternich had changed his plans. Perhaps it was just as well. The Prussians didn't like him, and they would have been suspicious of the purpose of his visit; the court would have found it hard to believe that the purpose of his trip was a sentimental one.

He had not seen Rahel since he had fled Berlin many years ago, discredited by his enemies, who charged him with being a man without principles, a debauchee in the pay of a foreign power. But a sudden whim to see her once again had seized him after her last letter. "Dear life-long friend, who once opened my heart to love, how I grieve over our separation. I know you have forgotten me. We still have our circle, but no one holds forth as you once did with the eloquence and discernment that held us spellbound." Ah, she could have had him once, had she set aside her shyness and boldly seduced him.

Those evenings at Rahel's, the high, intoxicating talk! In his youth he had been a disciple of Kant, a favorite pupil of his; he had been thrilled beyond measure when that great philosopher gave him the honor of allowing him to read the proofs of *Critique of Judgment*. In those days he had wept over the sorrows of Werther and had dreamed of renouncing all vain pomp and gold and learning to live simply with four or five friends in a Rousseau-like paradise. He had responded to the French Revolution as rapturously as that fanatical poet, Heine; he had hailed it as "the greatest achievement that History can produce." His enemies still, on occasion, maliciously brought up his early writings. Fools! Should not fallible man be permitted to discard or modify something that he once held to be true but which he now sees differently? Even if our principles remain the same, do not their applications change continually?

He wished he could have seen Rahel. But this was maudlin thinking—the past was past. He put on a pair of big spectacles and turned to the papers that had arrived in the diplomatic pouch. They dealt with the troublemaker Heine and were written with an emotion that was uncharacteristic of Metternich. The time had come, the prince insisted, to put a stop, once and for all, to the incendiary activities of Heine and his cohorts, and particularly to their bold smuggling of revolutionary propaganda across the Franco-Prussian frontier under the guise of literary writings. He wanted Gentz to communicate at once with Baron Cotta, the publisher of the *Augsburg Allgemeine Zeitung*, and express his surprise that such a respected journal would continue to print the poisonous spite of an adventurer like Heine. In addition, commenting that the devil must be fought with fire, Metternich suggested that derogatory remarks about Heine's political and personal conduct be planted in quarters where they would be picked up; he had in mind particularly certain journals that circulated among the German émigré circles in Paris. Included in the pouch was a copy of an intercepted letter that Heine had sent to the Baron Varnhagen von Ense. "I am surrounded by Prussian spies," Heine had written, "They still fear me . . . naturally, since they are making war on me. They know that I shall strike back . . . and with all my might."

Yes, Metternich was right; Heine must be silenced. It should be done in a diplomatic way; by intrigue rather than by the fist, if at all possible. There was always time for action by government edict. One must avoid giving Heine the publicity he wanted. . . .

That letter to Cotta: Gentz formulated it in his mind:

"Baron Cotta, esteemed friend. I fail to understand how you can open your pages to a man like Heine. It is high time that representatives of the middle classes put this monster in his place. True, the nobility and the clergy are no longer popular, and I can accept that. But are the civil servants, the merchants, the landowners, and the bankers to become pariahs too? If so, what dregs will be left to run the country? A party of revolution has been born, that aims at the destruction of all established order, that challenges every traditional form of authority, that poisons the minds of the people, that leads the young astray; and the insolence of this party is abetted by the leniency of the very educated men who should be the first to guard against false doctrines. What can we expect of the uneducated, if respectable journals open their pages to the malicious writings of apostles of revolution, of firebrands like Heine?"

Gentz lay back in the carriage. Well, Cotta would listen to him. He felt sorry in a way for Heine; he undoubtedly would be hurt financially. But did he not realize that these same revolutionaries whom he upheld would cheerfully cut his throat if it suited their purposes? Had not the history of the French Revolution taught him that? What did he think would happen to his *Book of Songs*? He himself bathed his soul for hours in its sad sweet waters. What music Heine spun with the German tongue! And it was not only his poetry. Metternich and he often laughed as they read Heine's witty, barbed sentences in his reports from Paris. That man knew how to hit the mark.

Truth to tell, he felt a secret kinship for Heine. He understood his hatred for the medieval mind, his scorn for stupidity, even his presentiment of a terrible explosion that was gestating in militaristic and mystical Prussia. He wished that he could explain to Heine that he was no enemy of progress, that in fact he joined with him in fearing those barbarian proponents of medieval *Volkstum*, those book-burners who called themselves revolutionists but whose program was based on fanatical nationalism, the extermination of the conquered, and a mad Jacobinism that would climax in the apocalypse of European civilization. Change must come peacefully and must be guided by statesmen.

But did change bring progress? When he looked at the history of mankind, he saw only a cycle of change, but no progress; and when he looked into the future, he saw that the spirit of the age was leading to the destruction of all the traditional and venerable institutions of society and the apocalypse of European civilization. Come what might, he would fulfill the duty that fate had laid on his shoulders: to protect and preserve the religious, moral, and political order against the false doctrines that, under the alluring banner of Liberty, led to unbridled license and anarchy; he would stay at his post to the end.

Half-asleep in the carriage, his red wig askew, Friedrich von Gentz—the man of fame whom kings and queens and bankers sought out, whose smart coach was drawn by two milk-white horses, whose villa was furnished with oriental luxury, who boasted that no one in the world was on such intimate terms with so many important circles and leaders as he was—felt a weariness that was like a poisonous cloud. Yes, he knew them all, and they sickened him, the whole pack of fawners, fanatics, and self-seekers, and (special abomination) the journalists who dogged him. Neither political activity nor poring over Kant or Hegel or Goethe, nor days secluded in the mountains, nor evenings at the gaming tables, nor nights with an actress or a virile young man could ease his soul-sickness.

Baron Cotta heeded Gentz's warning not to publish Heine's reports in the *Augsburg Allgemeine Zeitung;* the last one appeared on June 9, 1832. It was a severe blow to Heine, and not only because he was deprived of a major source of income. No other journal approached the *Allgemeine Zeitung* in prestige and circulation; it had given him a unique forum for interpreting the problems of the times to the people of Germany.

Heine fought back. He selected a number of his articles that had appeared in the paper, edited them to restore to their original form passages that had been mutilated by the censor, and sent the material to Campe to be published under the title *French Affairs.* Before the printer had time to issue the book, which came out later that year, news reached Heine of new repressive actions by the Federal German Diet occasioned by a great demonstration for civil rights in the Palatinate. On May 27, 1832, the anniversary of the winning of the Bavarian constitution, a rally of some twenty-five-thousand men and women had assembled at Hambach and listened to speeches calling for a united free Germany, for an independent Poland, for the emancipation of women, and for other democratic reforms. It was the kind of political event that Metternich and his Prussian henchmen could not tolerate. The following month, on June 28, 1832, the Federal German Diet prohibited popular gatherings, suppressed a number of journals and newspapers, and arrested several of the leading participants in the Hambach festival.

Although Heine thought many of the tactics of the republicans were foolish and unwise, he rallied to their defense. "I took no part in their folly," he declared, "but I shall always share in their misfortunes." He wrote a fiery preface to *French Affairs,* hurling a flaming *"J'accuse"* against the princes of Austria and Prussia: "I accuse them of having abused the majesty of the people. I accuse them of high treason against the German nation. I accuse them."

He directed Campe to publish the preface without any change.

Just because the banner of liberalism is in such a bad way these days everything possible must be done for its sake. I know that I shall never be able to return to Germany if this preface appears, but appear it must, *in its entirety.* I cannot sleep with an easy conscience so long as this preface is not published.

He excoriated the Prussian king and his toadies in words that they and their descendants never forgot and never forgave. He warned against the delusion that a united Germany under the hegemony of Prussia would further the cause of freedom.

I always regarded this Prussian eagle with anxiety. While others boasted that he looked boldly at the sun, I was all the more mindful of his claws. I do not trust this Prussian, this tall, canting, white-gaitered, martinet hero, with his big belly, his big mouth, and the corporal's cane, which he would dip in holy water before applying it. I disliked this philosophical-Christian soldiery, this conglomerate of pale beer, lies and sand. Repugnant, deeply repugnant to me, was this Prussia, this stiff, hypocritical, canting Prussia, this Tartuffe among nations.

He lashed at Prussia for forcing her philosophers and theologians "to betray God and reason, and publicly dishonor themselves."

Hegel was forced to justify servitude and prove it was rational. Schleiermacher had to protest against freedom, and counsel Christian submissiveness to superior authority . . . How great was the name of Arndt before he was commanded to write that shabby little book in which he wags his tail like a dog, and like a Wendish dog, barks at the July sun [the July 1830 Revolution].

And with the most brilliant irony at his command, he exposed the hypocrisy of King Friedrich Wilhelm III, who lied to his subjects who had rescued him from Napoleon.

The King of Prussia is a very devout man; he is a good Christian . . . He has himself written a liturgy, and believes in holy symbols. But, ah, I wish he believed in Jupiter, the father of the gods, who punishes perjury—perhaps then he would give us the promised constitution.

The censors in Germany suspected everyone. A blind hysteria drove them, and it reached a point where the most innocuous and innocent writings of loyal adherents to the crown were labeled subversive of the established order. Heine wrote ironically: "If someone inserts in the *Hamburg Correspondent*, 'My dear wife has given birth to a little daughter as lovely as Freedom,' then the Hamburg censor snatches his red pencil and strikes at the word 'Freedom.'"

It was a climate that bred self-seekers and traitors. Such a one emerged in the person of Wolfgang Menzel, the one-time revolutionary who had won the confidence of the liberals and democrats in Germany and whom Heine had once visited with a letter of friendship from Ludwig Börne.

On September 14, 1835 Menzel betrayed his friends and attacked them in a series of articles in the important *Stuttgart Morgenblatt*. In essence, he charged a number of young German writers, to whom he gave the name Young Germany, with spreading immoral, pro-French, pro-Jewish, and politically subversive doctrines. Hiding his ultimate political objectives under a cloak of moral indignation, he began by directing his fire against *Wally*, a novel by Karl Gutzkow. In issue after issue Menzel hammered away that Gutzkow had written an immoral and wicked book. To prove this, he dwelt on one scene in which the heroine revealed herself naked to the man she really loved, on the eve of her wedding to another. It was the only "sensational" scene in the novel, which on the whole was dull and poorly written. But the book, clearly, was influenced by Saint-Simonism and its doctrine of "rehabilitation of the flesh," and that was enough for the authorities. Gutzkow was arrested, charged with immorality, and sentenced to three months' imprisonment. The way had been prepared for the next step in the campaign to stamp out all liberal ideas that might be considered a threat to the regime.

On November 14, 1835 the Prussian Diet issued a sweeping series of edicts banning all past and *all future* writings of a literary group identified as the "Young Germany" group. When the names of the proscribed writers were published, Metternich was horrified to discover that Heine's name had been omitted from the list, an omission that was all the more regrettable since these writers had acknowledged that they found inspiration in Heine's works. The fact that Metternich dearly loved Heine's poetry did not prevent him from regarding him as a dangerous political foe to be treated accordingly. He therefore made sure that Heine's name was included in the edicts passed by the Federal Diet on December 10, 1835, and on the following day the Prussian Diet hastened to rectify its grievous error of omission and added Heine's name to its list of *verboten* writers. But the Federal Diet went further in its witch-hunt: it sent out directives to the censors in all thirty-nine states under its jurisdiction directing them to eliminate any and all references to Heine in newspapers, pamphlets and books—whether favorable or unfavorable. Heine was to becoem a nonperson in Germany.

The actions of the regime were completely out of proportion to the extent of the danger it faced from Young Germany, a small group of young writers concerned with social and aesthetic questions. They were influenced by the doctrines of Saint-Simonism and the writings of Heine, but actually their works were not widely read. After the full power of the state bore down on them they soon ceased to exist as a movement. A few were arrested, some fled the country, others recanted. Gutzkow, while not going over to the camp of reaction after his release from prison, turned against Heine.

Menzel's infamous articles appeared during the period when Heine, trying to escape from Mathilde, was staying at the chateau of the Princess Belgiojoso. He had not seen a German newspaper for months, and a letter from Laube brought him the first news of Menzel's treachery. This was in November 1835. Heine's reply, as well as a later letter to Campe, indicates that at first he did not realize the full implications of the edicts and of the lengths to which the authorities were ready to go to muzzle opposition. In his letter to Campe dated January 1836, he wrote that there would be such public opposition to the edicts that Prussia would not dare to go so far as to prohibit books not yet written, and that he was of the opinion that Prussia's chief objective was to humble him. However, he declared that he would not be intimidated, but if they did go ahead with the proscription, he believed he was skilfull enough to circumvent the decrees; if need be, he would omit his name from the title pages.

Menzel earned his unmeasured anger and contempt. He wrote to Laube:

> It is disgusting to have to deal with Menzel at this time . . . he is an informer, a shabby scoundrel, an out-and-out hypocritical wretch . . . He is a vulgar, vicious fellow, who should be kicked so that he can never get up again . . . He was never seriously on our side. At the university he bellowed the loudest and got himself elected President of the Student Association. He joined us after the July Revolution when he saw some advantages for himself in the background . . . Take a good, strong cane, and chastise the dirty wretch as he richly deserves, that is, personally . . . The young men of the university will surely give him the physical drubbing.

Later, panic gripped Heine as he realized the full consequences of the edicts of the Diet. Not only did they threaten to cut him off from his German public, but they took away a major source of his income. In his despair he decided to try the tactic of reasonableness and persuasion. He sent the Diet a letter which, he assured Campe, was a sweet and syrupy one that would move the Bundestag so that "six and thirty handkerchiefs will be wet with tears." It is hard to believe that the letter was written in all sincerity. He wrote it on January 28, 1836 in Paris.

You have accused me, tried me, condemned me, without giving me a hearing

. . . The Holy Roman Empire did not act so in similar cases, and the German Diet is its successor. Dr. Martin Luther, of glorious memory, was allowed to appear before the Reichstag provided with a safe conduct and defend himself freely and openly against all charges. Far be it from me to presume to compare myself with that highly esteemed man who won for us freedom of thought in religious matters, but the disciple may well appeal to the example of the master . . . If, gentlemen you will not grant me a safe conduct to defend myself in person before you, at least grant me the right of free speech in the German press, and revoke the ban that you have placed on everything that I may write . . . I hope to show conclusively that my writings are not the fruit of irreligious or immoral caprice, but of a truly religious and moral synthesis . . . But whatever you gentlemen may decide in answer to my petition, you may rest assured that I shall ever obey the laws of my country. The accident of living outside your jurisdiction will never lead me to use the language of strife, for I honor in you the highest authority of a beloved country.

Did Heine really believe that the Prussian government would be moved by his invoking the example of Luther? Or did his sense of humor take a strange turn? He has been criticized for writing a letter that was servile and hypocritical. A letter he sent to Laube in July 1833 may throw light on Heine's tactics, whether or not one approves of them. He warned Laube to

Take care. Even here no one is safe. Last Saturday a number of Germans were arrested. I too am afraid of almost momentary arrest . . . act with caution and moderation . . . Dissimulate. Do not be afraid of being misunderstood. I have never been afraid of that. The publication of my Preface in the midst of the general anxiety will teach my public to trust me in the future, even when I pipe somewhat too softly. In due time I shall sound the great trumpet, and I am now engaged in the composition of a few good trumpet solos.

Whatever the motives behind his letter to the Diet, that body did not answer him, and the Prussian government instructed its envoy in Paris to inform the French newspapers that any journals that printed contributions from Heine would be banned from Prussian territory. This, of course, was treated by the French as an intolerable interference in their affairs, and they paid no attention to the threat.

Campe wrote Heine that in his opinion the Prussian government had gone too far and the ban could not be enforced. He was eager for Heine to send him his latest manuscript, *Florentine Nights*, which he would print and distribute in spite of the edicts. Heine hastened to send it to him, but in his accompanying letter he gave definite instructions that the book must have his name on the title page and "should not be subjected to any censorship . . . This is a point of honor. If you cannot publish the book uncensored, then you must leave it unpublished." But Campe flouted Heine's directives and submitted the manuscript to the Berlin censors. Heine, when he learned of this, was beside himself and wrote Campe:

> Your letter . . . has so shocked me that I cannot collect my thoughts. But one thing remains clear in my mind. I will not betray the German press to Prussia; I will not sell my honor for the price of a book; I will not have the least stain upon my good name . . . If you will not publish the book as it is, then it will not be published at all; and however bitter it may be for me, I shall do without the payment which I had already been counting on . . . Poor wretch that I am. I had so looked forward to another bank draft. I am so pressed for money as you cannot imagine . . . I do not know what I shall do! But first of all, I will save my honor . . . I want my manuscript back.

He saved his honor, but he was in financial distress. His income was cut in half at a time when he had incurred heavy medical bills as the result of a severe attack of jaundice in the fall of 1836. Mathilde had no idea of the value of money, and it pleased him to satisfy her whims. If she wanted to dine out instead of preparing a meal at home, why, life was meant to be enjoyed. And so they drank champagne at Vefour's, and they went to the theater, where they sat in the best seats, and she adorned herself in the height of fashion.

He could not turn to Solomon for help; he was again on bad terms with him. He wrote to Campe:

> [My uncle has] insulted me most shamefully, a thing that one forgives much less easily when one is mature than when one is young. It is bad enough that this man, as I hear, establishes institutions for the rehabilitation of ruined money-lenders, but lets his nephew and his wife-child starve, and for no fault of theirs. I say my *wife*-child; by the first of these words I mean something nobler than a bride procured by money-lenders and priests.

At this time also, foolishness on Heine's part almost cost him the friendship of a generous benefactor, Baron James Rothschild, who might have been of help to him in this difficult period. The baron had from time to time helped him financially. Sometimes he gave him tips on the stock market; on occasion he would hand over to him a sum of money, each time saying that the gift was Heine's share of a business transaction. Yet Heine had let his pen run away with him. He wrote a piece in which he painted a picture of a servant in livery carrying the baron's chamber pot down a corridor while a passing stockbroker respectfully takes off his hat to the awesome vessel. In time Rothschild overcame his anger at Heine and resumed their friendly relationship, but for now Heine was not invited to his dinners.

His situation was desperate. Where to turn?

Heine knew that the French government paid out each year subsidies, or pensions, to a secret list of hundreds of persons, including exiles from every quarter of the globe. As he later wrote, "The high-sounding names of barons, counts, princes, are among them, and of generals, ex-ministers, even priests, forming as it were, an aristocracy of poverty." No conditions of service to the French government were imposed upon the recipients. Reluctantly, he decided to apply for the "alms," as he chose to call the pension. His conscience was clear, yet he had misgivings that some day his action might be used against him.

He needed to find a sponsor to plead his case with the government. He had many friends to whom he might turn. The list included Honoré de Balzac, Alexander Dumas, Victor Hugo, Theophile Gautier, George Sand, Giacomo Meyerbeer, Hector Berlioz, and many others; but it was to the Princess Belgiojoso that he finally went with his problem.

The princess responded without hesitation that she could help him and would be happy to do so; she would speak to François Mignet, who was a close friend of Premier Thiers. Yes, Mignet was the man to speak to. She knew that Mignet admired him. The historian was a defender of the Revolution of 1789, even though he deplored its excesses. She would get him to speak to Thiers, and she herself would second the request. Even though Heine had on occasion criticized Thiers and the government, she was confident that Thiers would be generous.

Cristina held out her arm. "Come, take a turn about the gardens with me," she said. "I want you to be sure to come to the concert I am putting on here in a few weeks for the benefit of the Risorgimento," she went on. "Franz Liszt will play. Do you remember how you described his playing?" Cristina's soft voice lingered over the words. "'When he sits at the piano . . . you can hear the thunder roar across the ivory keys [and smell] the fragrance of the sweetest flowers.'"

Adolphe Thiers, premier of France, and François Mignet, historian and journalist, were life-long friends. They had been the prime figures in the launching of the journal *National,* which had played so important a role in precipitating the July 1830 Revolution. Thiers prized Mignet's opinions, even though they inclined more to the left than his own. When Mignet visited him and over a brandy made the suggestion that Heine's name be placed on the secret rolls of King Louis Philippe's pensioners, he hummed softly. Finally he chuckled.

"He is quite a thorn in the side of the Prussians, François. The Prussian embassy has dropped hints that they would be happy if we deported him as an undesirable alien."

"I should think that an enemy of Prussia is a friend of France."

"That may be. But Heine is also a little too much of a Jacobin."

"He is not a Jacobin. He likes them as little as you do. I have heard him call them riffraff, rogues, liars."

"Yet he chooses to predict the coming triumph of communism."

"He may write so, but he maintains that he prefers a constitutional monarchy. His exact words as I recall them were that a constitutional monarchy is 'the last guarantee of civilization as we know it.' "

"Heine in favor of a constitutional monarchy? I can hardly believe that."

"Perhaps it is his way of saying that he wants stability combined with constitutionalism. He once told me—this was at the Princess Belgiojoso's—that he believed you yourself are in doubt about the royal system as we have it; that you know your French compatriots and the history of the French Revolution too well to believe that the present system is stable. In other words, he is warning that real reforms must come or the Jacobins will triumph."

"So he thinks that about me? Now, about that plea of yours: I wonder what the Prussians would say if they learned that Heine was getting a pension from France? I would like to see their faces."

"Let me warn you, Adolphe; Heine will gladly accept a pension, but he will criticize you whenever your policies displease him."

The Thiers ministry granted Heine an annual pension of 4800 francs, which he received from 1836 to 1848. In 1848 the revolutionary republican government opened the archives of the deposed monarchy and published the names of all the recipients of subsidies from the government of Louis Philippe. When the news reached Germany that Heine's name was on the list, the story quickly spread that he had been bribed and had tailored his articles to suit the French government. One of the first German newspapers to make the charge was the *Augsburg Allgemeine Zeitung*. It had begun printing his contributions again in 1840, for, as Campe had predicted, with the passage of time the Prussians had relaxed their ban on Heine's writings. His sparkling and enlightening articles on the Paris scene had brought added luster to the *Allgemeine Zeitung*, and it was all the more shocking when that paper was one of the first to insinuate that the subsidy had influenced Heine to refrain from writing unfavorably about the government of Louis Philippe. In fact, his stories in the paper had often attacked both Thiers and his successor, Guizot, so sharply that he had laid himself open to the charge that his reports were inimical to the interests of the country that had given him asylum. A notable example was his handling of the frame-up of the Jews of Damascus in 1840. In his report of the debate in the French Chamber of Deputies on the conduct of the French consul in Damascus, Heine had written:

> M. Thiers's reply was a masterpiece of malice and deceit. Through evasion and suppression of the truth, by means of seemingly anxious reservations, he has succeeded in casting suspicion on his adversaries. To hear him speak, one would be led to believe that the flesh of Capuchins was a Jewish national dish.

The charges of wrongdoing against Heine could not hold up. The fact was that he had never allowed concern for his personal welfare to sway him in what he wrote about French politics. But his enemies continued to spread the story that he had been bribed and to impugn his character and his integrity.

And then, just when his financial problems promised to be eased, a new disaster befell him. Early in the year 1837 he was informed that a friend for whom he had acted as surety had defaulted on a loan, leaving him liable for the sum of 20,000 francs. It was an enormous figure for a man of his limited means, and he was in actual danger of being incarcerated in a debtor's prison. Acting on the advice of his friend August Lewald, he turned to Campe for help. He received it, but the publisher drove a hard bargain. In return for 20,000 francs, Heine surrendered all royalties on his collected works for eleven years. But alas, calm and peace were not his destiny. His health now took a sharp turn for the worse.

To the outside world Heine was the picture of physical well-being. Gautier still called him "the German Apollo." Others who met him spoke of his youthful looks, his "muscular figure," his vitality. But as far back as 1832 the first symptoms that all was not well manifested themselves. He made light of them, however, writing to Ferdinand Hiller, "I am swimming up to my neck in the sweetest social life . . . I am now an opera habitue, an adherent of Louis Philippe's, my cheeks are red, two fingers of my left hand are paralyzed." How insouciantly he mentions the paralysis!

It spread slowly, but inexorably. Five years later his letters report an ominous progression. In July 1837 he wrote that his left arm was withered perceptibly up to the elbow. In August he wrote his brother Max that the headaches, which had left him when he first came to Paris, had returned. "They have plagued me for three days and make me unfit for work. And new ills have announced themselves . . . My youth is gone." In September, after returning to Paris from a rest at the seashore, he wrote Campe:

I have been troubled by a soreness of the eyes which grows worse by the hour. When I arrived here I could see nothing with my right eye and very little with my left. The best physician here, Sichel, has so far restored me that I am able to go out today, and even to write. But I am not able to see the letters distinctly. I am weak as a fly. I am bled constantly, and I am able to eat nothing.

Heine was ordered by his physician to refrain from protracted reading or writing; he tried to comply by engaging a secretary, but this was only of partial help because of Heine's habit of ceaselessly correcting his copy.

He had periods of remission, but slowly and relentlessly the symptoms of physical weakening became more pronounced. And from then on the pain was never absent.

Yet, when Laube saw him in 1839 and 1840 during a trip to Paris from Germany, he was hardly aware of Heine's afflictions, so brilliantly did he shine whenever he showed himself.

His spirit was indomitable. Suddenly he undertook to launch a German newspaper in Paris. During 1838 and 1839 he spent many months in an effort to accomplish this. He spent 2,500 francs of his own money and found a financial backer willing to risk 150,000 francs on the scheme. Varnhagen encouraged him, and Heine was led to believe that certain important Prussian officials would not oppose it. But in the end the plan failed; the newspaper could have succeeded only if it had been allowed free entry into Germany, and this the Prussian government would not allow.

His literary output in the face of all his tribulations was astounding. But writing was the very breath of life to him; he could no more cease writing than he could stop breathing. Some of his writings in the two or three years following the enactment of the edicts were potboilers, written because of his desperate need for money, although it must be said that no work of Heine's was ever completely dull or trivial—the spark of his genius flared in even the most uninspired of his writings.

He accepted an offer of 1,000 francs from a publisher in Stuttgart to write an introduction for an illustrated edition of *Don Quixote*. He was half-blind and suffering from an attack of influenza at the time, but, driven by the need to earn money, he labored at it. But he acknowledged to Campe in a letter, "It is the worst I have ever written . . . I did it for money."

The same year of 1838 he was paid 4,000 francs by the French publisher Delloye to write a commentary on a series of engravings that depicted Shakespeare's heroines. This time, too, his eyes were troubling him—in fact, he could hardly see the engravings he was interpreting—and his spirits were at a low ebb. His own comment on his work was, "Between ourselves it is no masterpiece." Yet, whatever may be said of the production as a whole, his essay on *The Merchant of Venice* and Shakespeare is a memorable one.

The great playwright no doubt had intended to write a comedy, Heine suggested, but that was not what he created.

> Perhaps Shakespeare intended to present an unmitigated werewolf, for the amusement of the mob, an abhorrent mythical creature that thirsts for blood, in the end loses his daughter and his ducats, and is made ridiculous into the bargain. But the poet's genius, the universal spirit reigning in him, was always stronger than his own will, and so it happened that despite the exaggerated burlesque, he embodies in Shylock a justification of the hapless sect which for mysterious reasons was burdened by Providence with the hate of the lower and the higher rabble and did not always want to requite this hatred with love. But what am I saying? The genius of Shakespeare rises above the petty quarrels of two religious sects, and his drama in reality shows us neither Jews nor Christians but oppressors and oppressed, and the madly agonized exultation of the latter when they can repay their arrogant tormentors with interest for insults inflicted on them.

With the exception of Portia, the Christian characters are treated with contempt. Antonio is a nerveless creature, Bassanio is a fortune hunter,

Lorenzo under the Prussian Criminal Code would be sentenced to fifteen years at hard labor. These and all the other noble Venetians revile Shylock to their hearts' and tongues' content, which also can be done without danger . . . Except for Portia, Shylock is the most respectable character in the entire play . . .

No, though Shylock loves money, there are things he loves far more— among them his daughter, "Jessica, my child." Though in the great heat of passion, he curses her and would like to see her dead at his feet with the jewels in her ears and with the ducats in her coffin, he still loves her more than all the ducats and jewels. Excluded from public life and Christian society into the narrow confines of domestic happiness, only his family sentiments remained for the unfortunate Jew; and they manifest themselves in him with the most touching tenderness.

The flow of Heine's creative genius was inexhaustible. He once confided to a friend: "So long as my heart is filled with love, and my neighbor's head with folly, I shall never lack material to write about." Another time he remarked that any subject was of interest to him: "It is all God's world and deserving of observation. And what I do not read out of things, I read into them." In the period between 1837 and 1840, amid all his other activities and writings, he published *Florentine Nights, Elemental Spirits*, and *The French Stage*, works that underscored the extraordinary range of his interests and powers.

A highlight of *Florentine Nights* is a description of Paganini playing at a concert in Hamburg. Like a conjurer, Heine takes the reader into the great violinist's mind; the sounds of the violin are transformed into vivid images that come alive like a motion picture in blazing color. The long passage is a master-piece of verbal magic as hypnotic in its effect upon the reader as the sounds of the violin must have been upon the listener.

In *Elemental Spirits,* Heine recounts folk beliefs and superstitions that, he assures the reader, are survivals of the ancient German religion. The pagan German gods were not dead, but survived as goblins, elves, dwarfs, salaman-ders, mermaids and sirens; and the pagan priests became masters of witchcraft. He took the old tale about Tannhäuser and Venus and wrote a new version of the legend. Heine's Tannhäuser has been interpreted by some as a confession of his thralldom to Mathilde, but whether it is indeed so is a matter for the reader to determine. In Heine's poem, Tannhäuser, after seven years in the Venusberg under the spell of Venus, is freed by her to visit the outside world. He makes his way to Rome and there confesses to the Pope that he has escaped from the snares of Venus, but he still dreams of her.

> As the butterfly flutters anigh a flower,
> From its delicate chalice sips,
> In such wise ever fluttered my soul
> Anigh to her rosy lips.

Were all of the boundless heavens mine,
I would give them all to her,
I would give her the sun, I would give her the moon
And each star in its shining sphere.

I love her, I love her with all my might,
With a flame that devoreth me,
Can these be already the fires of hell,
That shall glow eternally?

The Pope raises his hand and answers that for the joys he has loved so well Tännhauser must atone and be condemned into everlasting hell.

But Heine had second thoughts about condemning Tännhauser to eternal servitude. The knight returns to the Venusberg. It is midnight, and his feet are bloody and sore. Frau Venus awakens, clasps him, then goes into the kitchen to prepare bread and a bowl of soup for him. Then she washes his feet and combs his hair, and in a voice that is honey-sweet asks him about his journey. It is a new, confident Tannhäuser who tells her about the outside world; there is a hint that he may wander again.

Lady Venus, my beautiful wife,
I had some business in Rome;
But just as soon as my work was done,
I left and hurried home.

Rome is built on seven hills;
You can see the Tiber flow.
I also saw the Pope in Rome,
He sends you a warm "Hello!"

. . . .

And, standing on St. Gotthard Peak,
I heard old Germany snore;
In the gentle guard of thirty-six kings
It was sleeping just as before.

The *French Stage* was a compilation of thoughtful essays on a variety of topics. In "The Decline of Heroism" he discussed the new aristocracy of wealth, which he categorized as "an aristocracy more repulsive than that older one; an aristocracy which does not even attempt to justify its existence by devotion to an idea, or by an ideal faith in traditional virtues, but whose first and last principles are gain—commonly the fruit of petty possessions, if not of sordid vices—and the possession of money." In "The Empire" he said farewell to his former deification of Napoleon. "Were the days of the Empire in France really as beautiful and blissful as the Bonapartists, great and small, would have us believe? I don't think so. The fields were uncultivated, and men were marched away to the slaughter. Everywhere mothers wept, and homes were desolate."

The *French Stage* also included a number of reviews that Heine had written at different times on the work of such composers as Meyerbeer, Rossini, Liszt, Chopin, and Berlioz. The composer Ferdinand Hiller commented on the essays that, even though he had no technical music training, Heine "because of his imaginative and penetrating mind divined more in music than many so-called musical people."

Heine wrote *The Informer* in 1837 to unmask Menzel. He also hoped thereby to goad him into a duel but was unsuccessful in this aim.

In 1838 Heine became involved in a dispute with Karl Gutzkow, who after his release from prison was engaged as an editor by Campe. The latter showed Gutzkow a sheaf of poems that Heine had sent him, which evidently shocked Gutzkow. He wrote to Heine, claiming to speak in the name of the younger generation of German poets and urging him not to publish them because they would completely ruin his literary reputation. Heine replied on August 23 in a letter that is particularly interesting because of its discussion of the role of art. "You may be right in thinking that certain poems might be used by my adversaries," he wrote, but

> I shall print them with a good conscience, just as I would print the *Satiricon* of Petronius or the *Roman Elegies* of Goethe, had I written those masterpieces. Like the *Elegies*, my poems are not food for the masses. You are on the wrong tack in this connection. Only cultured minds, which can take an intellectual delight in the artistic treatment of a wicked and all-too-natural subject, can find pleasure in these poems. Very few Germans are able to express an individual judgment on these poems since the subject of them, the abnormal amours of a madhouse such as Paris, is unknown to them. The autonomy of art is called in question, not the moral needs of a respectable married citizen of a corner of Germany. My motto is: Art is the purpose of Art, as Love is the purpose of Love, and even as Life itself is the purpose of Life.

Heine had written in a similar vein the year before in *The French Stage*, when he had declared, "I am for the autonomy of art. It is not to be regarded as the handmaiden of religion or politics; it is its own definite justification, just like the world itself."

It would be an error to conclude from these statements that Heine separated art from life. When he wrote that art was the purpose of art, he did not mean by that the sterile aestheticism of "art for art's sake." He considered art that was aloof from life as being just as hostile to art as to life. He insisted that art must not be subordinated to religion or politics or government. Art must be autonomous, but it would retain vitality only if it was connected to life: "Just as the giant Antaeus remained invincible so long as his feet touched the earth, so the poet remains strong and mighty so long as he stands on real ground, but he loses his strength at once when he rises ecstatically into the blue."

11
Emigré Groups: *Ludwig Börne* and *Atta Troll* (1837–41)

There were eighty thousand German emigrants living in Paris in the 1830's, and they belonged to innumerable political groups, factions and associations; they covered the spectrum from Left to Right; they were republicans, monarchists, Saint-Simonists, Proudhonists, Young Germans, Old Germans. A large part of this German colony was composed of journeymen artisans—cabinetmakers, leather workers, and the like—who had come to Paris in the hope of bettering themselves in this center of fashion and the arts and crafts; but they retained the hope of eventually returning to Germany as master craftsmen employing apprentices of their own. They believed that some day soon a democratic revolution would break out in Germany and then they would return to a land rid of its monarchy and outworn feudal institutions.

Among the artisans, a Jacobin movement developed, strongly influenced by competing socialist and communist doctrines. In 1834 a secret organization of German émigrés was organized that soon had a wide membership. It was called The League of the Outlawed, and it adopted a program for the rebirth of Germany upon a basis of social and political equality, civic virtue, and national unity. Within its ranks a bourgeois and a socialist wing competed for dominance.

Since they were fighting a common enemy, Heine tried to remain on friendly terms with the émigré groups, although he soon found many of their tactics unwise. When they pressed him to permit his name to be used by the press union in its struggle for freedom of the press in Germany, he was happy to do so and he even donated money. They were forever coming to him with petitions for him to sign. Finally, when he was asked to protect against the political actions of the Pope in the Romagna, (then part of the Papal States) he declared that he had had enough, that he knew nothing about the Pope's activities.

They insisted that he join their political organization, and when he refused they accused him of cowardice. The Jacobins were determined to force Heine to declare himself openly as either for or against them, and they were ready to resort to any means to achieve their aims. They soon found an opportunity.

When Heine was still Paris correspondent of the *Augsburg Allgemeine Zeitung*, before Gentz's warning to Cotta ended that relationship in June 1832, Heine had written an article (it appeared May 27, 1832) in which he criticized certain actions of King Louis Philippe, the "citizen King" of France. The influential Paris paper *Le Temps* was outraged at the assault on the honor of the royal house, and it criticized the censor for allowing the article to be printed. Replying to *Le Temps*, Heine repeated his charges, but added ironically, "Louis Philippe is honorable as an individual, and he merits esteem as a family man and a worthy husband." The radical newspaper *La Tribune* thereupon reprinted Heine's article in a falsified version, making it seem that he had defended Louis Philippe and adding an accusation that the author was undoubtedly someone in the service of the Austrian government. The allegation spread. An Austrian businessman who had fled Vienna to escape his creditors and who now posed as an exile and fighter for freedom, stopped Heine on the street and asked him whether it was true that he was a paid agent of the Austrians. Heine looked at him contemptuously and said, "I get from the Austrians as much as they are likely to get from you."

Heine accused the Jacobins of acting in collusion with the Right to slander him and declared that he would not submit to blackmail; he would retain his political independence.

He was determined to dissociate himself, once and for all, from the German émigrés. He changed his living quarters, kept his address secret. But they sought him out. The same people who insulted him one day came to him another day and begged him to use his influence in their behalf. If the problem was one such as a threatened expulsion from France, he rarely failed to do what he could for them. Similarly, if the appeal was for money for someone in dire need, he would dig into his pockets. He could not refuse a cry for help; a case of real destitution could reduce him to tears. But his generosity did not put a stop to the calumny and abuse he was subjected to. A serio-comic peak was reached in the relations between him and Ludwig Börne.

The two of them should have been close allies. Both had left Germany as political exiles—actually in the same month, May 1831; both fought for a new social order in which equality and brotherhood and justice would prevail; both were keen observers of the social and political scene; both were Jews from the Rhineland who had turned Protestant and almost immediately regretted the action. But they were incompatible temperamentally, and they soon discovered that they differed fundamentally on the tactics and goals of the revolutionary movement, and on the nature of the good society.

After the July 1830 Revolution in Paris, Börne identified himself with the extreme elements among the German republicans. He often spoke at meetings of the artisans, and his fiery speeches evoked enthusiastic response. His *Letters from Paris* were banned by the Federal Diet, but they were circulated and eagerly read throughout Germany. His writings greatly influenced Friedrich Engels when he became acquainted with them after Börne's death in 1837; he hailed him as a "heroic fighter" for the cause of freedom and justice who had taught him much.

Börne was the political party man; Heine was skeptical of all parties. Börne was committed to a liberal, parliamentary republic for Germany; Heine thought that the best government would be "a republic ruled by monarchists, or a monarchy ruled by republicans." Börne based his program on the principles of the Social Contract and the axioms of the French Revolution; Heine believed that the development of industry and science made it possible and necessary to go beyond the theorems of the French Revolution.

When Ludwig Börne left Germany, he had declared that he expected the revolution to break out any day. "It cannot go on more than four weeks longer; the smoke of indignation will burst into flames behind my coach." Heine was convinced that he would never see a German republic in his lifetime, that the German people were not yet ready for revolution. "In politics, as in life, one should desire only that which is attainable," he observed, and he criticized Börne's penchant for praising any uprising, whether it could have succeeded or not, whether it was a true revolution or the work of demagogy.

Dour, inflexible, and puritan, Börne regarded Heine with growing suspicion and dislike. He charged the poet with being a sybarite; he was willing to grant him talent as a poet but denied him character. When Heine came to write *Atta Troll*, he turned the phrase around and described the hero-bear in that narrative poem as having "no talent, but certainly a character."

In the public mind, Börne's image was that of the noble, dedicated, irreproachable leader, unwavering in his principles; Heine appeared as the cynical, shifting, undependable one. But it was Börne who revealed in his private letters a spiteful, jealous and petty side. Writing to Jeanette Wohl, his platonic friend, he slandered Heine: "I've only just realized, what I hadn't noticed before, that he's handsome and has the sort of face women like. But take my word for it, there's nothing behind the face, nothing. I understand these things."

Börne sneered at Heine for running after women, and for his preoccupation with aesthetic subjects. The poet grew to be an obsession with him. He carried out a veritable spy hunt against him. He wrote to a friend that although he had no proof, he was convinced that Heine received money from tainted sources. He spoke to everyone who would listen about his suspicions. His mania reached a point where he would follow Heine to a café and thrust his company upon him, hoping to trap him into some admission that he could use against him. Heine would try to escape Börne, but, when he saw that he could not, he decided to amuse himself at his expense. He would lean over toward Börne, assume a confidential air, then boast that he was no fool, that he knew how to cash in on his talents. Metternich could buy him any time by giving him all the girls in Paris; how otherwise could he maintain his style of life?—it cost a fortune to support these Parisian dolls (here Heine would leer at his horrified listener). Börne repeated the conversation to his intimates. When they laughed and said it was evident that Heine was making fun of him, that obviously he would keep secret such transactions if they actually took place, Börne muttered: "The fact that he speaks openly, and of his own accord, about his baseness is no proof that these things did not take place. If only half of what he said is true, he deserves five gallows."

Heine continued to exercise self-restraint in the face of Börne's actions. He was both amused and annoyed by his behavior, but he respected the selfless republican, and he did not wish to edify the common enemy by engaging in public controversy.

Ludwig Börne died in 1837 and his influence was greater than ever. His teachings were sacrosanct not only among revolutionaries but also among the widest circles of the democratic-minded population of Germany. But Heine was now convinced that the philosophy of Börne and his close followers had to be debated and refuted; these people would lead the revolution to disaster.

Börne was the incorruptible Robespierre type, who had horrified Heine once when he said: "Marat was quite right; the human race must be bled if necessary. If they had granted Marat the three hundred thousand heads which he demanded, millions of better men would not have perished and the world would have been healed forever of its ancient illness."

Heine realized the enmity he would earn by writing critically about Börne, the revolutionary saint. He would be accused of lèse majesté, of indulging in personal animosity, but he felt that he had to speak out.

Few of Heine's work have been so misunderstood, unjustly treated, and vilified as his *Concerning Ludwig Börne*, which appeared in 1840. His contemporaries greeted it with the most shameless remarks. Gutzkow wrote, "Heine pretends to be a poet, but writes like a vulgar street delinquent." A critic in the *Literaturblatt* revealed his own malice with the comment, "Heine shows here all the ugly qualities of an alien race we shall not mention: deceit, presumption, cowardice, and shamelessness." Ugly envy and hatred prompted the critics: "gilded mud" . . . "betrayed by the kiss of Judas" . . . "insolence" . . . "perfidiousness" . . . "disgusting equivocation" . . . "insane vanity" . . . "stinking wit" . . .

Varnhagen was one of the few who appraised the book at its true worth. He wrote Heine that he had done what he could do to counter the "abominable caricature of the revolutionary party spirit . . . I tried to inject some reason into the mad delusion, but in vain." But he was sure that in time people would see that Heine's book was "a good book and an honest one."

It is sad to realize that even friendly biographers in more distant times have also read the book as a spiteful polemic. Thomas Mann, however, recognized *Ludwig Börne* as being a philosophical examination of opposing world outlooks, a book, written with "deep insight," that anticipated Ibsen and others in the questions it raised about European civilization.

Heine was accused of pillorying a dead man when in fact he was far more generous and open-hearted with Börne than that individual had ever been with him. He began the book with a tribute, sincere and appreciative but without exaggeration.

> We give his statue with his real features without idealizing them; the greater the likeness, the more honor to his memory. For he was neither a genius nor a hero. He was not an Olympian god. He was a man, an inhabitant of this world. He was a good writer and a great patriot . . . perhaps the greatest that ever sucked sweet life and bitter death from the breasts of Germania, his stepmother.

It is true that Heine inserted in the first edition a deplorable insinuation as to the nature of the household shared by Börne with Jeanette Wohl and her second husband, Solomon Strauss, although it should be noted that he regretted the passage and expunged it from later editions of the book. His explanation of how it came to be written certainly makes the offense understandable. The passage had not been in the original manuscript that he had sent to Campe; he added it when he learned that Börne was spreading a story that Mathilde's "thirty charms" could be had by anyone with a few francs. One can easily imagine Heine's fury when he learned of this truly vicious slur. As in the Platen affair, Heine's detractors have been quick to overlook the extent of the provocations he met and have deprecated his readiness to forgive and his action in firing into the air when the duel took place.

In writing *Ludwig Börne,* Heine addressed himself to what he conceived as the fundamental rift of the age: the struggle between the Nazarene and the Hellenic world outlook, between those of an ascetic and abstract type and those who are natural and realisic and rejoice in life. It was from this point of view that he argued against the radicalism of Börne and his followers, who, he declared,

> prescribe a treatment which in the long run works only externally, removing the social scurvy, but not the rottenness inside. Even if they succeeded for a short time in relieving suffering humanity of its most excruciating torments, it could only be at the expense of the last remnants of beauty which the patient still has; he will get up from his sick-bed as an ugly Philistine, and he will drag himself around for the rest of his life in the ugly hospital uniform, in the ash-gray garb of equality . . . For beauty and genius there will be no place in the community of our new Puritans . . . The barren, narrow philosophy of the modern Puritans is already spreading over all of Europe like a gray twilight which precedes a bleak wintertime.

He feared a plebeian society in which utility would be the measure of all things. But he equally rejected the rule of the aristocracy and the plutocracy. Was it possible to achieve a satisfactory mean between the extremes of absolutism on the one hand and collectivism on the other? He was not happy with his own answer that a constitutional monarchy was the best form of government, and he concluded *Ludwig Börne* with the statement, "Alas, it will be many years before we find the great cure." A few years later, under the influence of Marx and Engels, he swung further to the left, but he always remained skeptical of party panaceas. He wanted a world of bread and roses for everyone, and he fought, in the words of Matthew Arnold, as "a brilliant and most effective soldier in the Liberation War of humanity."

In the four years that preceded the publication of *Ludwig Börne* in 1840, Heine wrote little poetry. At times he even questioned the pertinence of poetry in a world of growing materialism, technology, and science. On one occasion he replied to an editor who asked him for some poems, "I haven't much confidence in my poetry any more—perhaps the times we live in are no longer favorable to poetry." In the preface to the third edition of the *Book of Songs*, which came out in February 1839 he lamented:

O Phoebus Apollo! if these verses be bad thou wilt surely forgive me . . . thou knowest well enough why it was that many years have passed since I have busied myself exclusively with the measuring and weighing of words . . . Thou knowest why the flame which once delighted the world with its brilliant display of fireworks was suddenly turned to a more serious blaze . . . Thou knowest why this silently glowing fire is now consuming my heart.

The writing of *Ludwig Börne* served to resolve many of the doubts and questionings that had blocked his creative self. He had tested his ideas and theories of art and society against those of Böne and his school, and after the appearance of the book he was at peace with himself as he had not been for a long time. He felt within the stirring of a new springtime of poetry.

In this pleasant state of mind, he left with Mathilde for a vacation in the French Pyrenees in May 1841. The mountain streams around Cauterets were reputed to have marvellus curative powers, and he hoped that they would benefit him. The wild grandeur of the mountains had something of the same healing effect on his spirit as did the limitless ocean; he felt stirring within him a laughter and a singing, a rebirth of his poetical powers.

One summer afternoon, in the marketplace of the town where he was staying, he saw a performance by a large, brown dancing bear. The animal was a huge fellow. As he danced clumsily to the music, Heine turned to Mathilde and said, "I wonder what he thinks of us?" "What an idea!" she exclaimed, laughing. That day, *Atta Troll*, a mock-heroic poem, was born.

The protagonist of the narrative is Atta Troll, a bear who entertains people by dancing. Suddenly he breaks free and escapes to the mountains, where he rejoins his family. There, in a mountain cave, he dispenses wisdom to his cubs. He discourses in a monotonous growl about liberty, equality, and the great white polar bear who is the ruler of the universe. He exhorts his children not to trust men, not even Germans for they are a miserable lot who have always sacrificed their own offspring to their gods, and now they sacrifice them to their modern god who is a god of gold. They declare that property is sacred, meaning thereby the right to steal, as if, indeed, Nature had brought them into the world with pockets. But we bears, Atta Troll declares, will bring equality into the world for all, except that the bears will forbid the Jews to dance. Eventually Atta Troll is trapped and killed. Mumma, his wife, is dispatched to a Paris Zoo, where a polar bear woos her. His pelt finds its way to the bedroom of Juliette. (Julieete was Mathilde's nickname to her close friends.)

Atta Troll is written in unrhymed trochees. Heine called it "A Midsummer Night's Dream," and it is that. It is wonderfully mischievous and clever, includes many exciting incidents, has enchanting descriptions of marvellous scenery, and tells a tale of fair women. It is a satire aimed both at the superpatriotic *Deutschtumlers* and the narrow-minded followers of Börne who prattled empty slogans and grandiloquent bombast. But even more than satire, the poem is a song of affirmation.

The poet extols his Muse, his Pegasus.

> Pegasus, beloved steed!
> Wingéd horse at his sweet will
> Flies and gallops joyously
> Fabled realm his magic home.
>
> No draft horse of bourgeoisie,
> Nor charger bold of Party strife,
> Stamping and neighing with a blast,
> Furious, rhetorical.
>
> Pegasus disports himself—
> Gold shods the hoofs of my white steed;
> Ropes of pearl the reins I hold,
> Pearled ropes I let hang free.

The poem, declared Heine, was a celebration of life and a championing of the individual against all forms of tyranny. Dedicating *Atta Troll* to his old friend Varnhagen, he wrote: "To my chosen comrade-in-arms who helped me bury the old times, and was midwife to the new."

12

Visits to Hamburg: *Germany: A Winter's Tale, The Silesian Weavers, The Slave Ship, Poems for the Times,* and *New Poems* (1842–47)

On the night of May 5, 1842 a great fire broke out in Hamburg; it raged for four days and destroyed half the town. Heine's mother and sister lived near each other, and when the flames approached the quarter where they lived, Betty fled to her daughter's home. Hardly had she arrived there when she wailed that she had left behind her a bundle of manuscripts that Harry had entrusted to her for safekeeping. Charlotte rushed over to her mother's house, and although flames were already licking at it, she ran inside and rescued her brother's papers; but as she stumbled out to safety a rush of suffocating smoke and ash overcame her, and she fainted. Fortunately, an unknown rescuer carried her to safety; but in the confusion the manuscripts disappeared.

Heine was without news of his family until May 12, when a letter that Charlotte had written on May 7 arrived. The anxiety he suffered in the meantime is reflected in the letter he sent to Hamburg the following day.

> I was beside myself after I learned the alarming news in the papers. I am amazed, dear Lottie, that you could write so calmly and sensibly in view of the terrible fire. I thank you from the bottom of my heart for the reassurance you give me. My wife fell ill with fright after hearing the terrible news. I hope that the terror and agitation will have no harmful effect on any of you. My poor good mother! Do not let yourself be too much upset over the material losses. 'God is a good man.' But this time he placed too much reliance on the Hamburg fire department.

The excitement, the letters, the renewed realization of the depths of his attachment to his dear ones—all intensified Heine's unceasing longing to return to Germany, if only for a short visit. So many years had passed since he had seen his mother, who was now in her seventies, and his sister, who had risked her life trying to save his manuscripts.

He wrote to Hamburg almost weekly: warm, loving, tender letters. "And you, you sweet old puss, how are you?" he began a letter to his mother.

If you die before I see you again, I will shoot myself. Bear that in mind in case the crazy idea should seize you to change your Dammthor dwelling for a worse lodging. Mind that, and you will never commit any such folly . . . Above all things, live as long as possible, and mind what I have told you. Your faithful son.

When Charlotte informed him of the forthcoming marriage of her daughter Marie, he replied:

You will then become a grandmother! And the Old Luck [one of his many terms of affection for his mother] will become one too! Oh, that I had for a moment my old father! How he would have rejoiced . . . oh, that I could pass a few days with you! The hope that Marie will come to Paris delights me to my very soul.

In January 1843, Henry Heine, one of Solomon's five brothers, suffered the loss of a daughter who was only seventeen years old. He and his wife were gentle souls, and their home had been a haven for Heine where he never encountered the affronts he endured from the crowd at Solomon's. Heine was informed of the tragedy by his mother, and he immediately sent a letter of condolence, loving and compassionate. "Heaven sustain and console your kind heart," he wrote his uncle, and asked that Aunt Jette be assured that he, though far away, was sharing her suffering. He wanted to be remembered to Emily and to Hermann, "who was always a fine fellow," and mourned the fact that he could not come to Hamburg. He signed the letter, "I love you very much, Your obedient nephew."

A letter to Charlotte in September is interesting not only because it is one more confirmation of Heine's readiness to respond when called upon for aid, but also because of what it says about Mathilde.

This letter will have been delivered to you by Mdlle. A. de C—, a young person who has as admirable a character as her skin is black. She is of African race, but has been brought up in Paris since her infancy, and in the same boarding school which my wife attended. She is her most intimate friend, and from that you may infer that I know her well, and can commend her with good conscience and cordiality. Her father is a rich merchant from St. Thomas, who recently married a lady of Hamburg, and in order to discuss with him delicate matters Mdlle. de C. is going to Hamburg with her brother. Treat them well from love for us. Your sister-in-law begs the same. You have so good a heart and are so clever that I do not doubt you will be a source of joy and help to our friend.

The sight in his left eye was practically gone, and he felt a leaden pressure above his left eyebrow, a ceaseless pain that had not left him for the past two years. The whole left side of his face was paralyzed. But when he wrote to his mother, he mentioned these things lightly and minimized their seriousness, declaring that the symptoms were temporary and that he was sound of heart and healthier than ever, and that he had a good physical constitution and expected to jump about in this world for a good many years to come.

Suddenly he decided to risk the long-dreamed of visit to Hamburg. Everything was driving him to do so: his longing to see his mother and sister; his concern for Mathilde's future. He had married her on the eve of a duel, to safeguard her welfare if he did not survive it; now he was determined to go to Hamburg and in face-to-face negotiations with Campe and Solomon take care of her beyond his death. That was the duty of a husband. He was haunted by a picture of a lonely and helpless Mathilde in a cold and unfeeling world.

He communicated with Campe about his desire to come to Hamburg and the risks of arrest that that entailed. The publisher investigated and answered that it would be safe for him to come for a short stay, provided the authorities were assured that his visit had no political aims. But the guarantee would apply only in the free city of Hamburg. It would be wise for him to travel by ship, for if he went by land he would have to go through Prussian territory, and all frontier stations had long-standing orders, renewed annually, for Heine's arrest should he have the temerity to cross the Prussian frontier. Nevertheless, in spite of the risks, Heine decided to come by land, for he was doubtful that he could endure the rigors of the rough North Sea at this time of year. He would rely upon Campe's underground apparatus for the distribution of forbidden books to help him evade the Prussian police.

On October 18, 1843, with joyous heart, Heine wrote to his mother that any day she should expect to see him standing before her as large as life. He warned her not to say a word to anyone about his coming, but he reassured her that there was nothing to fear from the government, for he would travel quickly and would say nothing to anyone in Paris about his journey.

As the hour for his departure approached, his impatience to tread German soil reached a fever height. He expressed his feelings in the verses of *Departure from Paris:*

> I'd like to see my mother, too—
> This fact I won't deny;
> Since last I saw her, thirteen years
> Have somehow frittered by.
>
> Farwell, my wife, my beautiful wife!
> You can't know how I grieve.
> I press you so firmly to my heart,
> And yet I've got to leave
>
> How torment drives me from my joys!
> Just once, once more, the breath
> Of German air must fill my lungs,
> Or I will choke to death.

The torment, the pain, the impetuous urge—
How madly they pound and pound!
My feet are shaking—they cannot wait
To stamp on German ground.

Heine left Paris about the twenty-fifth of October, He traveled by fast coach to Brussels, Amsterdam, and Bremen, and arrived in Hamburg the evening of October 29, 1843.

He stood in front of his mother's home. His eyes were misty. He knocked, and she opened the door, and they stood looking at each other for a moment. Then she clapped her hands and cried, "My darling, darling boy!" He had not seen her for thirteen years, and he noticed the wrinkles on her face and hands. He held her frail body in his arms as she repeated, "My darling, darling boy!"; then she wiped her eyes and they entered the house.

She had been waiting for his arrival all day. Her happiness shone in her face, was evident in the tone of her voice, the spring in her walk. She bustled about, setting his favorite dishes before him: fish and goose and kugel and, as a treat, delicious oranges. He ate heartily, praised the food, and gave no indication of the pain that was racking his head. The scene of the poet and his mother is drawn in *Germany: A Winter's Tale*. We see her plying him with food and bombarding him with questions that sometimes he finds embarrassing.

"My poor child! For these thirteen years
In France you've had to live; you
Need a good meal, you must be starved.
Sit down. What can I give you?"

. . . .

"Do you live well in your home abroad?
Are all your troubles ended?
Does your wife know how to run the house?
Are your shirts and socks well mended?"

"The fish is excellent, mother my own,
But the bones are a terrible bother;
I'd hate to have one lodge in my throat,
So let me alone, dear mother."

. . . .

"My child, I'm anxious to hear you name
Your political predilections.
What is your party? What is its aim?
And what are your own convictions?"

"It was most delicious, mother, my own;
The oranges really were fine, dear.
I enjoyed the juice to the last sweet drop
But I'll leave the bitter rind here."

Heine was assured by his mother that she was in excellent health and that she had no money worries. But he wrote Mathilde: "She has shrunk under the weight of her sorrows and old age. Highly nervous, the smallest trifle excites her. Much of her suffering is due to her pride. She does not go out because she has not the means to entertain visitors in her own home."

His visit stretched out for almost six weeks. He was now the famous Heine, and the younger people lionized him. Any number of affairs were held in his honor, and it was a delight to him to meet his many nephews and nieces. Therese's welcome was a very affectionate one. He was pained to observe the poor state of Solomon's health, but the millionnaire embraced him and showed that he recognized that his nephew had made his mark in the world, and he treated Heine as his equal. "I am pampered by everybody," Heine wrote Mathilde. "In return I am ever so amiable. But look out. When I return I shall be ever so unpleasant to make up for the strain of being good-natured."

It was pleasant indeed being so pampered, but then uncontrollable jealous worries about Mathilde plagued him. He watched the dancing at a party, and afterwards he wrote her: "Dear God, how happy it would have made me to see you whirling around there with your fat little behind!" In another letter he pleaded with her. "Stay quietly in your nest, my poor little dove. Don't show yourself in public so that none of my acquaintances may know that you are in Paris without me. For God's sake, do nothing to make me angry when I return. I was crazy not to have brought you with me."

During the entire period of his stay in Hamburg, Mathilde wrote him only rarely. Did the uneducated *grisette* find it too difficult to pen a letter? Was she angry because he had left her behind and stayed on week after week? Was she testing her power over him? Whatever the reason, her failure to write spoiled the pleasure of his visit. On November 25th he wrote her: "Such a long time and still no word from you. My God! Believe me, it is terrible! I shall return straight to Paris, stopping off nowhere."

Still, he could not leave until he had safeguarded the future of that same Mathilde who was presently torturing him with her silence. He already had Solomon's assurance that he would provide Mathilde with a lifelong yearly annuity of 2,400 francs, but the negotiations with Campe were long-drawn-out. Finally, by December he was able to sign a contract with that hard-fisted man. Under the terms of the agreement, he promised to retain Campe as his publisher "for all times," and in return Campe would pay Heine an annuity, beginning in 1848, of 2,400 francs a year until 1853, when it would be increased to 3,000 francs. Upon Heine's death, the annuity would be paid to Mathilde for the rest of her life, but if Heine should die before 1848, Campe would begin payments to his widow at once.

As soon as the contract was signed, Heine wrote to Mathilde, outlining the details and explaining: "It is an undertaking to assure your income after my death—which will not occur so very soon, for I am in excellent health. It is the duty of a husband to provide for his wife in the event of his death . . . This is no merit in a man, but duty."

He packed and said his goodbyes, promising to return the following year with Mathilde. He left for Paris on December 7, journeying by way of Hanover, Bückeburg, Cologne and Brussels, and enjoying the experience of a ride on the pioneer train between the last two cities. At each town he wrote to his mother, telling her that the weather was pleasant and that he felt "happy and cheerful." On December 18 he wrote from Brussels: "I have just arrived here sound and well. I shall continue my journey to Paris, where I shall arrive early in the morning, day after tomorrow, and this letter is my notice to you that I am, as it were, already at home; therefore you can now rest easy."

He was in Paris two days later. Mathilde danced with joy when she saw him; she hugged and kissed and could not have enough of him. She had been a good girl, she assured him, and to celebrate they dined out and drank champagne.

Heine, acute observer of the social scene, was one of the first to draw attention in the press to the fact that a new voice had emerged among the wretched masses of Paris, a far more formidable foe of the existing social order than the Saint-Simonists because it spoke the language of the submerged classes. As early as June 1842, in an article in the *Augsburg Allgemeine Zeitung,* he called attention to this new party.

Communism is the secret name of this dread antagonist setting proletarian rule with all its consequences against the present bourgeois regime. It will be a frightful duel. How will it end? No one knows but the gods and goddesses who see into the future. We only know this much: Communism, though little discussed now, and loitering in hidden garrets on miserable straw pallets, is the dark hero destined for a great, if temporary role in the modern tragedy, only awaiting his cue to make his entrance.

To the extent that the Communists were a threat to the rule of the aristocrats, Heine was sympathetic to them. "Look at their opponents," he wrote.

In the Upper Chamber there sit on the velvet seats guillotined old men with their heads stitched on again, which they nervously feel for when the people raise their voices outside . . . it is dreadful to see these unhappy dead sitting in judgment on the living, on the youngest and most despairing children of the revolution, those neglected and disinherited children whose misery is as great as their madness, the Communists!

But while his sympathy was with them, the romantic poet feared what might follow the triumph of the proletariat.

> Anxiety and terror fill me when I think of the time when these gloomy iconoclasts will come into power. Their heavy hands will ruthlessly shatter the marble statues of beauty which are so dear to my heart. They will destroy all those fantastic and gay arabesques of Art which the poet cherished. They will cut down my groves of laurel, and plant potatoes there. They will root out the lilies that toil not nor spin. A similar fate will overtake the roses, those pampered sweethearts of the nightingales; the nightingales, those unnecessary songsters will be hunted down. (Preface to *Lutetia*)

And then he met the man who was destined to become the most famous of communists. It happened shortly after his return from Hamburg, in the spring of 1844. The visitor introduced himself as the editor of *Vorwärts*, a newspaper devoted to the cause of republicanism. He said that his name was Karl Marx, and that he had admired Heine's writings for many years—in fact, he knew many of his poems by heart. He wished to make his acquaintance and to persuade the most famous of German poets to write for *Vorwärts*.

Marx was twenty-six, but his authoritative manner and his piercing gaze made him seem older. Like Heine, he was an exile from Germany. He had studied law and had earned a degree in philosophy. Two years ago, in 1842, a group of Cologne industrialists had chosen him to be the editor of a liberal magazine, *Die Rheinische Zeitung*, which they envisaged as a voice speaking out against the backward absolutism of the Prussian monarchy. The journal quickly won a wide following, but Marx's outspoken criticism of the regime led to its suppression in the spring of 1843. Marx left Cologne and came to Paris to continue his studies, chiefly in the field of economics. He joined the staff of the *Deutsch-Französische Jahrbücher* and the *Vorwärts*. In articles in the *Jahrbücher*, Marx developed his theories of the class struggle, the limitations of bourgeois democracy, the inevitability of the ascendancy of the proletariat, and the triumph of communism.

In answer to Marx's proposal that he write for *Vorwärts*, Heine replied that his experiences with the German colony in Paris did not predispose him to affiliate with a German political group. As a poet, he could never bind himself to any political party. Marx said he was disappointed but hoped that he could call again, even if only to talk about poetry.

The next time he came, he brought with him his young wife. She was bright, spirited, and charming, and she and Mathilde liked each other at once. Her maiden name was Jenny von Westphalen, and she was the daughter of a high government official. On her mother's side she was a lineal descendant of the earl of Argyll, a member of the Scottish peerage who had been beheaded during the reign of King James II. Jenny was as strong-willed as she was charming, which was evidenced when she took as her husband a young man descended on both sides of his family from a long line of rabbis.

A warm friendship developed between the two families, and during the following year, until Marx was banished from France in 1845, they visited each other quite regularly. One evening when Heine was spending the evening at the Marxs's, the latter's little girl, Jenny, suddenly suffered a convulsion and began to choke. The parents were frantic and helpless, but Heine acted quickly. Drawing a warm bath, he placed the child in it and thereby saved her life.

Marx, who was usually imperious in his personal relationships, chose to overlook Heine's skepticism and doubts. Poets, he said, were unique people who should not be judged by the same standards that applied to ordinary mortals. When he was forced to leave Paris, he told Heine: "I wish I could pack you up and take you with me."

Marx kept urging Heine to write for *Vorwärts*. He held up before the poet his stupendous vision of a complete transformation of society when a new class, the proletariat, would take power, and the ideal of liberty, fraternity, and equality would become a reality.

It was an enchanting picture but. . . . Heine thought of the meetings he had attended, where the thick tobacco fumes choked him, and the long-winded, demagogic speeches stupefied him. He envisioned four hundred thousand hard fists wielded by brawny Parisian workers to bring about an ideal of absolute equality, and he shuddered at the abyss of absolute mediocrity that he saw opening up. Could the revolution keep its promise of a better world or would culture and reason be swept away and be replaced by a new despotism, a new wretchedness, a new oppression?

"I fear your followers," he told Marx. "They distort what I write, they subject me to calumny, they spread rumors that I am in the pay of the Austrian police. You know my poems by heart, but what will happen to them if those Jacobin plotters get control of the engines of power?"

"Every movement has its blockhead fringe. Don't judge us by the blockheads. I must contend with them too."

"Those blockheads by their very numbers will suffocate you. Yesterday one of them wrote, 'A true democrat writes like the people—sincerely and badly.' These ignorant iconoclasts believe that one who loves form for its own self must be an enemy of the people. They despise art, and they will replace all the romance of life with a bleak Puritan night."

Heine's face lit up with amusement, and he went on: "I'm smiling because I've just recalled a conversation I once had with Herr Börne, the king of the German radicals in Paris. What, he asked me, did I do on the first day of my arrival in Paris. Where did I go first? I knew he expected me to name the Pantheon, or the tombs of Rousseau and Voltaire. What a face he made when I confessed that immediately upon my arrival I went to the Royal Library to see with my own eyes the Codex Manesse of the *Minnesinger*, and especially the poems of Walther von der Vogelweide, the great lyric poet. Börne was flabbergasted. What I had done was nothing less than the betrayal of revolutionary principles."

Marx kept bringing him issues of *Vorwärts*, its pages filled with stories of human misery. "Your paper is a master of incitement," Heine declared, but the stories filled him with indignation. Had he not written, "Bread is the divine right of the people?" But if he believed that, then he had to draw the conclusion of the premise.

"The devil is a logician," says Dante. A terrible syllogism holds me in its bonds, and if I am unable to refute the premise that every man has the right to eat, then I am forced to submit to all its consequences. From much thinking about it I am on the verge of losing my reason. I see all the demons of truth dancing triumphantly around me, and at length the generosity of despair takes possession of my heart and I cry "For long this old society has been judged and condemned. Let justice be done! Let this old world be smashed in which innocence is long since dead, where egoism prospers, and man battens on man! Let these whited sepulchers be destroyed from top to bottom, these caverns of falsehood and iniquity. And blessed be the grocer who shall one day use the pages of my poems as paper bags for the coffee and snuff of poor old women who, in this present world of injustice, too often have to go without that solace." (Preface to *Lutetia*)

One day in June 1844, he read in *Vorwärts* a story about the massacre of striking Silesian weavers. It was an impassioned account, and when he laid the paper down he relived the scene: the dark and dusty interior of the factory and the weavers at the looms. He heard the crash and clatter of the machines, and in the background the cries of children and the curses of men and women at the "devils from hell" who drove them. There was a sudden silence followed by the smashing of the machinery—then the crackling of musket fire—and then the screams.

Marx was to have his poem. The words of fury and prophecy wrote themselves, a lamentation of biblical power—*The Silesian Weavers*.

> In gloomy eyes there wells no tear.
> Grinding their teeth, they are sitting here;
> "Germany, your shroud's on our loom;
> And in it we weave the threefold doom.
>   We weave; we weave.
>
> "Doomed be the God who was deaf to our prayer
> In Winter's cold and hunger's despair.
> All in vain we hoped and bided;
> He only mocked us, hoaxed, derided—
>   We weave; we weave.
>
> "Doomed be the king, the rich man's king,
> Who would not be moved by our suffering,

Who tore the last coin out of our hands,
And let us be shot by his blood-thirsty bands—
    We weave; we weave.

"Doomed be the fatherland, false name,
Where nothing thrives but disgrace and shame,
Where flowers are crushed before they unfold,
Where the worm is quickened by rot and mold—
    We weave; we weave.

"The loom is creaking, the shuttle flies;
Nor night nor day do we close our eyes.
Old Germany, your shroud's on our loom,
And in it we weave the threefold doom;
    We weave; we weave!"

His heart beat for all the victims of injustice and tyranny. His vision encompassed the world. If he chanted a dirge for the weavers shot down in Silesia, he also mourned for the blacks sold as slaves. No one but Heine could have written the haunting *Slave Ship* of a decade later; its verses of sorrow and terror and irony are unforgettable.

The poem opens with the captain, Mynheer van Koek, sitting in his cabin, calculating his prospective profits. His cargo consists of rubber, pepper, gold, and ivory, and—best of all—600 blacks he bought on the Senegal in Africa. He purchased them cheaply, with whisky, beads, and trinkets. He figures that even if only 300 of the slaves are alive when he gets to Rio Janeiro, their destination, he will reap a profit of 800 percent, or 300 ducats per piece of merchandise, that is, 90,000 ducats profit on the slaves. These pleasant ruminations are interrupted by the ship's surgeon, van der Smissen, who has returned from a tour of inspection. "Tell me, ship's surgeon, how do you find my dear black merchandise?" the captain asks him. The doctor reports that "tonight the rate of mortality significantly mounts."

"A daily average of two have died,
But seven went today:
Four men, three women—I entered the loss
In the records right away.

I looked the corpses over well.
For many a time these knaves
Pretend to be dead, because they hope
We'll toss them out on the waves.

I took the irons off the dead,
And, as usual, gave an order
Early this morning, that every corpse
Should be cast out into the water.

Sharkfish, whole battalions of them,
Shot swiftly up from the brine;
They love the Negro-meat so well!
They're pensioners of mine."

The captain interrupts to ask what can be done to stop this death rate from getting worse. The doctor answers:

"Through their own fault," the surgeon sneers,
"Many succumb to death;
The air in the hold of the ship is foul
From their offensive breath.

"And many die because they're sad,
For they're kept in a boredom that kills;
A bit of music, dancing, and air,
Will cure them of all their ills."

The captain is enthusiastic about the suggestion and compares van der Smissen to Aristotle. There follows a description of the dance on the slave ship.

Many thousands of stars look out
From the high blue tent of the skies:
Longingly radiant, large and bright,
Like lovely ladies' eyes.

. . . .
There's not a sail on the slave-ship now;
It drifts unrigged and bare;
But lanterns glitter along the deck,
And music's in the air.

The helmsman plays a violin,
The doctor's trumpet sounds,
The cook plays flute, while a cabin-boy
Stands at the drum, and pounds.

A hundred Negroes, women and men,
Are whirling around—insane—
Shouting and hopping; at every leap
A rhythmic clatter of chains.

They stamp the boards with blusterous joy,
And many a naked beau
Embraces his beautiful Negro lass—
Between them a sigh of woe.

The hangman is *maître des plaisirs;*

> And, swinging left and right,
> He's whipped the sluggish dancers on,
> Driven them to delight.

The noise of the music draws the sharks from the deep, and hundreds of them surface.

> They know it's not their breakfast time,
> And open wide their jaws—
> Revealing rows of shiny teeth
> As huge and sharp as saws.

Suddenly, in a lull in the music, the voice of Mynheer van Koek is heard, praying at the bow of the ship.

> "Take pity, O Lord, in the name of Christ,
> And let these sinners live!
> You know they're stupid as cows, o Lord,
> And if they enrage you—forgive!
>
> Spare their lives in the name of Christ
> Who died for us all on the cross!
> For unless three hundred heads remain
> I'll suffer a terrible loss."

The period following his return from Hamburg in December 1843 was noteworthy for Heine's poetic efflorescence. Even an attack of near blindness did not prevent him from starting and finishing the long epic poem *Germany: A Winter's Tale*. He completed it in February 1844 and then wrote a group of boldly satirical poems that were later published under the title *Poems for the Times*. A few of them, as well as parts of *Germany: A Winter's Tale* appeared first in the *Vorwärts*.

The kings and princes declared that the author of these poems was guilty of high treason, but the ordinary folk read them and applauded. They were a new kind of political poetry, polemical and at the same time infused with all the imagery and beauty of true poetry. Heine explained what he sought to do in a letter to Campe.

> It expresses all the ferment in present-day Germany in a most audacious and personal fashion. It is political-romantic, and I hope it will administer a death-blow to the prosaic, bombastic poetry of "tendency." You know that I do not boast, but I am sure that this time I have produced a little work which will create more of a furor than the most popular pamphlets, and yet have the enduring value of a classic.

In April 1844 he sent Campe the manuscripts of *Germany: A Winter's Tale*,

Poems for the Times, and a number of poems that had appeared previously. Campe proposed that he publish all of them in one volume entitled *New Poems,* and also suggested a number of changes in the political poems. This convinced Heine that he could not trust Campe with the editing of the political poems, and that he would have to go to Hamburg to see the book through to publication. Besides, he wanted to see his family again and this time take Mathilde with him. He would have left at once, but the state of his health made it impossible to leave before the middle of July.

They took the steamship from Le Havre and were met at the dock in Hamburg by Charlotte and her husband and their son Ludwig, later the Baron von Embden. The ship was late, but finally it arrived and the famous poet and his Parisian wife disembarked. Mathilde was holding on to Heine's arm. She was tall and full-bodied and moved with voluptuous ease. But above all, the welcomers were dazzled by her "great expressive eyes which flashed fire when excited." Very shortly they saw those beautiful eyes blaze with anger. Moritz, Charlotte's husband, had gallantly led her to a waiting carriage, seated her, and was handing her a box when he let it fall; he had been bitten by Coco, Mathilde's darling parrot, which she had brought with her from Paris. She screamed imprecations upon poor Moritz: "My God, to be so inconsiderate as to frighten poor Coco, and he has been so sick!" Fortunately, the parrot had not been hurt; the beautiful lady was calmed, and soon she returned to her usual bubbly cheerfulness. Heine had been laughing heartily during this episode. Now he turned to Moritz and said, "Dear brother-in-law, you came near being out of Mathilde's good graces forever. I wrote to you that I would come with my wife and Coco, but you took no notice of the parrot until he introduced himself to you by a bite."

The visitors stayed at Charlotte's during the first week, but then they moved into a comfortable, almost luxurious, apartment that Charlotte rented for them in the Esplanade. They had most of their meals with the Embdens. After her initial outburst, Mathilde was on her best behavior, and when she discovered that everyone spoke French, she joked, praised the Hamburg food, and charmed everyone around her.

One Sunday Solomon sent an elegant carriage with a liveried servant to bring them to dinner at his sumptuous home. Heine accepted the invitation with misgivings that proved well-founded. Solomon forbade conversation in a foreign language at his table, and poor Mathilde, knowing no German, was forced to remain silent for two hours. And during the meal she committed a faux pas, although Heine was able by a witticism to turn Solomon's anger into pleased laughter. In his later years Solomon had acquired a hobby: the raising of fruits in his greenhouse. Now, during the dessert, he had a servant bring in a tray and display for the admiration of the guests a cluster of grapes as large as plums from his conservatory. When the tray reached Mathilde, she thought the fruit was being served to her, and she calmly took the grapes and ate them all. Solomon did not notice this, but a little later he asked excitedly where the grapes were. Heine quickly answered, "Dear uncle, the bunch of grapes was a miracle and it caused another miracle, for it has vanished—an angel made away with it!" The old tyrant laughed at his nephew's clever remark, and the bunch of grapes was forgotten.

But Mathilde, as soon as she returned to their apartment, declared that she would never again set foot in that boring place. Heine tried to convince her of the importance of keeping the goodwill of his uncle, but once she had made up her mind nothing could change it. He was forced to concoct the story that Mathilde's mother had suddenly fallen ill and that she had to return to take care of her. Mathilde packed her things and left for home. She said goodby in tears, holding on to Coco, waving at Heine, who stood forlornly on the pier waiting until her boat disappeared.

Because of his practice of ceaselessly revising his work, *New Poems* was not ready for the printer until the fall. He saw his mother every day. A favorite haunt of his was that same pavilion on the Alster Basin where he used to watch the swans when he had come to Hamburg as a youth to make his fortune. Baron von Embden in his recollections describes his uncle whiling away an hour or two of a day with friends at their table there. The young nephew, who obviously idolized his uncle, accompanied him to the pavilion whenever he could. He listened carefully as the poet advised him not to spend too much time reading newspapers, that far more would remain in his memory from the reading of good books. Among the books Heine recommended were the novels of Jean Paul Richter because of their sensitive portrayals of ordinary life, and those of Charles Dickens for their realism and humor.

When *Germany: A Winter's Tale* came out in September 1844, it was an instant success. It was, of course, immediately prohibited in Prussia, which only added to the demand for it. Solomon enjoyed it so much that he again assured his nephew that he could be at ease, that he would provide for Mathilde if she were widowed. And Heine, for the first time in his life, felt financially secure—he now had the pension from the French government, the allowance from his uncle, and a retainer from Campe.

Germany: A Winter's Tale is an epic poem of satire, love, triumph, dreams and prophecies. In a sense it is a sequel to *Atta Troll*. There he had satirized the dull propagandists and party dogmatists, and in turn had been called a turncoat and a false revolutionary; he had even been charged with "ridiculing the holiest concepts of humanity." He retorted in the preface to the French Edition of *Atta Troll,* "But thou liest, Brutus, thou liest, Cassius, and thou liest, Asinius, when you declare that my mockery struck at those ideas which are a precious achievement of mankind, and for which I myself have fought and suffered so much."

In *Germany: A Winter's Tale* the poet is on German soil after an absence of many years, and he compares himself to Antaeus, the fabled giant whose strength was renewed when he touched his Mother Earth:

> Through my veins, since treading on German soil,
> Magical juices flow—

The giant has touched his mother again,
And his power begins to grow.

And he sings a song of promise.

> We mean to be happy here on earth—
> Our days of want are done,
> No more shall lazy belly waste
> What toiling hands have won.

> . . . .

> Wheat enough for all mankind
> Is planted here below;
> Roses and myrtle, beauty and joy,
> And green peas, row upon row.

> . . . .

> Young Europe's betrothed to Liberty,
> That genius of beauty and grace
> They lie in each other's passionate arms,
> They feast on their first embrace.

The customs officer rummages through his bags for contraband. He does not understand that what the poet has hidden is not in his trunk but in his head. In Cologne he dreams of the axe-man who follows him through the streets of the darkened city; he is the poet's alter ego who will carry out the poet's wish to destroy evil:

> He came up close and savagely
> Smashed them, scepter and crown;
> And with one blow those bones of false
> Belief came tumbling down.

The poet continues the journey, and in the forest at night his coach breaks down, and the wolves, howling, gather around:

> Like candles blazing in the dark
> Glimmer their fiery eyes.
> They've heard of my coming, I've no doubt;
> They set the woods afire
> In honor of my visit there—
> And greet me with their choir.

Deeply moved, the poet assumes the proper stance and addresses his fellow wolves:

You never doubted me, fellow wolves,
Never would let them persuade you,
Those villains who called me a renegade,
Who said that I had betrayed you.

. . . .

I am no sheep, no shell-fish, no dog;
I play no Councillor's part;
I've stayed a wolf through all the years,
With wolfish teeth and heart.
I am a wolf, and with the wolves
I'll howl my whole life through.
Yes, count on me and help yourselves;
Then God will help you too.

In Hamburg, the poet delivers many a quip and jest, and gives civic advice as well as dietary suggestions. After the big fire there, 8,000,000 marks had been raised internationally for the victims, food and clothing had been donated, but the people still wailed and wept. He advised them:

Dry your puddles, restore your homes,
And if you're set on vengeance
Let it take the form of better laws
And better fire-engines.

. . . .

Go easy on pepper in mock-turtle soup;
And learn to scale your fish—
Unscaled carp, when it's cooked in grease,
Is not a healthy dish.

He invokes the figure of the red-bearded Barbarossa in a long, satirical passage, calling on him to come and rescue the German people, but at the end he is not so sure that even the best of kings will set them free.

And I don't care much for your flag these days;
No longer am I thrilled
By your black-red-gold—I got sick of it
In the days of the Student Guild.

It would be best if you stayed at home
Here in your mountain-hall—
Considering how matters stand,
We need no king at all.

Clearly Heine's avowal of constitutional monarchy went hand in hand with grave doubts.

The poem culminates in a vision of Germany's future revealed to him by the goddess Hammonia. She tells him to uncover the chamber pot of Charles the Great. The "foul miasmas—monstrous loathsome stenches" cause him to swoon. The horrible scene evokes in a reader the feeling that they are the stench of burning flesh in the ovens of Nazi hell-camps.

Heine concludes the poem:

> There is a new race growing up
> Unrouged, unsinning youth!
> Freedom of thought, and freedom of joy—
> I'll let them know the truth.

He had accomplished his business in Hamburg, and on October 7, 1844 Heine left for Paris and Mathilde. On October 17 he sent an entertaining letter to his mother, telling her he was home and describing the reunion with Mathilde. "We were almost overwhelmed at the joy of meeting. We look eagerly at each other, laugh, embrace, talk about you, laugh again—the parrot screaming meanwhile like mad. How glad I am to have my two birds again. You see, dear mother, that I am as lucky as a man can be."

But before the year's end he received a letter from Charlotte telling him that Solomon had died on December 23. He had been ill for some time and the news was not unexpected, but Heine was overcome with grief. He wrote to his sister:

> Although I expected it to happen, it has shaken me more deeply than anything since father's death . . . My wife is also in tears. Last night she came into my room three times. You are right, only time can comfort us. How poor little Therese must suffer. And Karl too, poor fellow. I won't write to these poor children until I am more composed myself. Dear God, what a sorrow this is.

> Our good Uncle Henry—how upset he must be . . . My pen is shaking as I write. My eyes are in a frightful state . . . Only yesterday I wrote Uncle Solomon, although I had forebodings! Tell me everything about his last moments. He played a great part in the story of my life, and I shall write about him so that none will forget him. What a heart! What a mind! For a long time I have been without anxiety about his final arrangements. He himself spoke to me and referred to them clearly. But I would have given my last penny to have kept him for another five or even three years longer—indeed I would have given half of my remaining years. And how kindly and lovingly he treated my poor mother! He said many harsh things to me; once this summer he even struck me with his cane in a moment of anger. Ah, Lord! how gladly I'd receive such blows again . . . Write to me very soon

how Karl is bearing up, and Therese too, who is still a delicate being and has already suffered so much. Her father was all in all to her.

A short time later, Heine received news—unexpected and unexplainable—that drove him into a frenzy. Solomon's will had been made public. Under its terms Karl had inherited 30,000,000 marks; the sons-in-law and their children had been left several million marks; the gardener, the groom, and the coachman had been remembered; and generous bequests had been provided for a long list of charities. *But there was no mention of a pension for Heine.* Instead, he received a formal letter from his cousin Karl informing him that he and his brothers had each been left a legacy of 8,000 francs; that there was no provision setting aside an allowance for him, but that as the executor he was ready to pay Heine 2,000 francs a year on the condition that in the future Heine submit to him for his approval before publication anything he might write that mentioned Solomon or the family.

Over and over again Heine asked himself what had happened to turn his uncle against him. The will was dated December 4, 1844. Just before he left Hamburg on October 7, his uncle had reassured him that both he and Mathilde would be taken care of in the will. What had occurred between that date and December 4 to make his uncle forget his promise? Solomon had been so pleased with the two stanzas about himself in *Germany: A Winter's Tale.*

> That old noble gentleman
> I also longed to see;
> He never failed to bawl me out,
> Yet always took care of me.
>
> "Stupid fellow!" he used to say.
> Once more I wanted to hear it—
> It always echoed like a song,
> A sweet song, through my spirit.

And there had been tears in Solomon's eyes when he had read *The New Israelite Hospital in Hamburg,* a poem he had written in tribute to his uncle, who had founded a hospital for poor Jews:

> He gave with generous hand—yet richer
> The alms that fell from his eyes: fair and precious,
> Tears he often wept for the vast and hopeless
> Incurable affliction of his brethren.

They must have gathered around his uncle in his last hours; they must have poisoned his mind against the nephew who loved him. "God forgive my family for the sins they have committed against me," Heine wrote to Campe. "Truly it is not the question of money, but the outrage that the intimate friend of my youth and my blood relation did not honor his father's word—that is what has broken my heart." Grief and rage alternated within him whenever he thought of Karl's actions. He had nursed his cousin through the terrible cholera siege in Paris, and Karl had sworn eternal gratitude; yet he had written him this heartless letter.

Heine was frantic with concern for Mathilde, a concern that grew as his health became worse. He wrote to Karl that he would go to court; he had proof in the form of letters from Solomon that he had intended to provide an annuity for his nephew and Mathilde. He intimated to the sons-in-law of Solomon that he was ready to go to court and make a sensational case of the matter—he wasn't afraid of the notoriety, he was used to mudslinging, but could they stand it? But Karl remained obdurate.

Karl had not forgotten how his cousin had risked his life for him in Paris, but what Heine had only a faint suspicion of was that Karl's own family happiness was at stake. His wife, Cécile, came from the Fould and Furtado families, prominent in French public life. Heine had written disparagingly about the banker Fould, Cécile's uncle, and had often sharply attacked two family members for the reactionary policies they espoused in the Chamber of Deputies. Karl's wife and her relatives left him no peace and demanded that he silence this dangerous radical. Cécile was implacable in her vendetta against Heine, to a point where Karl wondered whether she was driven by other motives than family loyalty. He had heard rumors that before he married her, Cécile and Heine had met in Paris and had carried on a relationship that was more than platonic. Was her vindictiveness due to disappointed love? Who knew what Heine might some day reveal in those *Memoirs* he was working on, which were said already to fill four volumes! At all costs he must keep the whip hand over this irresponsible member of the family. He had persuaded his father not to leave a large sum of money to Heine that would free him to write as recklessly and dangerously as he was capable of doing. Karl intended to make sure that Heine would never write anything injurious to the interests of his family or the Foulds and Furtados.

Heine started court action and rallied friends and notables to his support, but Karl remained firm in his course of conduct. When the composer Meyerbeer wrote to Karl that to his personal knowledge, Solomon had declared he was leaving Heine a pension for life, Karl answered that if Heine dared to write a word against his father he would chastise him publicly. He even held back payment of the 8,000 francs that had been bequeathed to Heine in Solomon's will.

Heine's lawyers advised him that his case was weak, and they urged him to settle the matter through compromise, but he said, "I know Karl better. He has only three passions—women, cigars, and tranquil ease. I cannot take the first two from him, but I can disturb his tranquility, and the lawsuit aids me in this."

But it was Heine's own peace of mind that was shattered by the battle to protect Mathilde, and it affected his physical condition. In the summer of 1846 his health took a marked turn for the worse, and on September 1 he wrote to Campe:

> My organs of speech are so paralyzed that I cannot speak, and I have not been able to eat for four months because I find it hard to chew and swallow, and I've completely lost my sense of taste. I am dreadfully thin; my poor paunch has disappeared and I look like a lean, one-eyed Hannibal . . . I am not at all anxious; on the contrary, I am quite composed, and I bear patiently what cannot be altered, and is, after all, man's fate. I believe that I am past saving, and that I can only survive in wretchedness and agony for a short while, one or at most two years. But that does not matter; it is the business of the immortal gods who have nothing to reproach me with, for I have always defended their cause on earth with courage and love. The knowledge that I have lived a good life fills my soul with joy even at this grievous time, and I hope will also accompany me into the white abyss. Between ourselves, this is the least to be feared; dying is a horrible thing, not death—if there is such a thing as death. Perhaps death is our last superstition.

In this condition of extremity, believing that the end was not far off, and concerned above all for Mathilde, Heine set aside all pride and wrote to Karl:

> As regards the pension which my late Uncle Solomon Heine granted me and half of which was to revert to my widow after my death, I beg my cousin Karl Heine to remember the touching and tender regard with which his father always treated my wife. I hope that he will gladly assure her the small sum in a manner which will give rise neither to later humiliation nor to anxiety and care. I do not doubt that your magnanimous heart will remember after I am gone the friendship which so closely united us and the loss of which has caused me such mortal grief.

Whether he was moved by this letter, or whether he feared that, if Heine died before a reconciliation had been arrived at, the *Memoirs* would be published with damaging revelations about the family, Karl acted to heal the quarrel between them. He visited Heine in 1847 and assured him that the full pension of 4,800 francs would henceforth be paid to him, and that if Mathilde survived him she would continue to be paid half that sum. It would have been a generous act on Karl's part if he had stopped at this point. But he added the callous condition that if at any time, even after Heine's death and against his expressed wishes, a writing of his should appear that would reflect against Karl's family or relatives, payments to Mathilde would be cut off at once.

Mathilde's future happiness was at stake, and Heine's relief was so great that he grasped Karl's hand and pressed it to his face in gratitude. After Karl left, he wrote to his mother that he was going through all her letters and Charlotte's and burning any in which there were any references to family matters that could do damage if they got into unfriendly hands. When German newspapers printed stories that the poet was living in great poverty, he issued a public statement on April 15, 1849 denying this and lauding Karl, who, he declared,

since my illness has grown worse, has increased the periodical payments sufficient almost to double the income. The same relative has also rid me of the bitterest worries of my illness by a generous provision for my dear wife, who loses in me her earthly support. The many affectionate inquiries and offers of help which have come to me from Germany are answered in this confession. For the hearts that are bleeding in the Fatherland—greetings and tears!

But these were statements dictated by his fear for Mathilde's future. He did not trust Karl, and when he drew up his will on November 13, 1851, he began it with a long protestation that was like a prayer from the grave. His late uncle, Solomon Heine, he declared, had esteemed Mathilde and has given

many a sign of his affection and regard for her. The fact that in his will he had failed to provide for her could have been due only to an unfortunate accident rather than to the intent of the deceased, for he whose generosity has enriched so many persons who were strangers to his family and to his heart, could not have been guilty of such stinginess when it was a question of the fate of the wife of a nephew who had made his name famous. My cousin, Karl Heine, the worthy son of his father, agreed with me in this sentiment and with noble readiness undertook to pay my wife as a life annuity half the allowance which his late father had provided me.

After this preamble, Heine proceeded with his entreaty.

Unforseen chances and changes, and other weighty reasons compel me to turn once more to the sense of decency and justice of my cousin. I beseech him not to reduce the aforesaid allowance to one half, when he transfers it to my wife after my death, but to pay it to her without curtailment, as I drew it in the lifetime of my uncle . . . It is more than probable that there is no need for this appeal to the generosity of my cousin, for I am convinced that with the first shovelful of earth, which, according to his right as next of kin, he will throw on my grave, if he is in Paris at the time of my demise, he will forget all those painful accusations which I so much regretted and which I have atoned for with my protracted dying; he will then surely remember our former friendship, that relationship and harmony of feelings which united us from our tender youth, and he will accord the widow of his friend truly fatherly protection; for it is well for the peace of the one as of the other, that the living know what the dead demand of them.

Yet Heine never really forgave Karl for the fear and the humiliation he had put him through. One need only read the poem *Spanish Atriden* in the *Romancero* cycle to catch a glimpse of the truth. What adds a special significance to this poem are the two stanzas that were part of the original manuscript but were omitted by Heine from the printed version:

> And he gave me an example
> How Don Pedro mutilated
> Don Gustavus, his own cousin
> And had both his hands chopped off
>
> For the pure and simple reason
> Don Gustavus was a poet,
> And the monarch dreamed his cousin
> Mocked him in his verses.

13
The Mattress Grave:
Romancero and *Memoirs* (1847–54)

Over the years a succession of doctors tried different treatments, but Heine's disease pursued its relentless course. He was the victim of incompetent and primitive medical treatment; some of the methods used seem barbarous indeed to today's practitioners. His back was seared with hot irons; cones of morphine were applied to sores kept open; he was covered with leeches; he was given magic potions; he was promised that cold water baths would cure him. But his sickness was not arrested, and he resigned himself to the inevitable.

The doctors disagreed as to the nature of his illness. Did he suffer from a form of cerebro-spinal syphillis, or was he the victim of a progressive atrophy of the spinal cord, as Dr. Rahmer maintained in his paper on the case? In this connection it is apropos to mention that Heine never exhibited the symptoms of mental deterioration associated with the final stages of syphillis. On the contrary, he was alert and creative to the last and kept abreast of the political, social, and cultural developments of the day. He did not succumb to despair and hopelessness, but faced his plight with a gallantry, a brave humor, and a serenity that have few parallels. He stayed on his feet as long as he could. Above all he worked. "By creating I am able to recover and to become whole," he said in the poem *Songs of Creation.*

He spent the summer of 1847 in the pleasant town of Montmorency situated north of Paris. There Mathilde rented a house; it had a lovely garden where Heine, when he was not writing, liked to recline on cushions piled up on the grass. On Sundays they would be visited by friends. Mathilde was a gracious hostess who greeted each newcomer with an infectious *"bon jour."* Later, she led the guests to their places at the large table decorated with flowers and offering a choice of tempting wines. Heine never failed to inspire laughter and merriment. He was a marvellous story teller. A favorite tale was one about a composer of the day, who he claimed achieved fame by his very dullness. It seemed, he explained, that a group of this composer's enemies planned to create a disturbance by hissing at the end of one of his performances. But they had failed to take into account the maestro's singular genius. The movements were so long and monotonous that one by one the conspirators slunk off until at last only the composer's hired claque was left to cheer the performance. Heine, ill, spread laughter and good feeling about him.

He returned to Paris in the fall of 1847 to his old apartment in the faubourg Poissonière. He was indomitable. He decided to call upon an old friend, the lovely Caroline Jaubert. Unable to mount the stairs unaided, he had a servant half carry him up the stairs to her second story apartment. Once inside, a tearing paroxysm seized him, and he lay doubled up on the sofa. When he recovered, he began joking and threatened that unless she promised to visit him, he would have himself carried in again and she would have a repetition of the distressing scene she had just witnessed. He went on to draw a picture of the embarrasing consequences that would have resulted if he had died on her sofa: "Everyone would have assumed a love affair. What a delightful novel I would have been the hero of." Nor would he leave until she gave him a solemn promise to visit him.

Innumerable stories of this type have come down to us, such as this delightful one by K. M. Kertbeny, a Hungarian poet:

> One day in a fearful snowstorm I was about to take shelter in the reading room of the Palais Royal, when I noticed someone feeling about the glass on the door, trying to take hold of the knob. To my dismay, I recognized Heine. I reproved him for going out in such weather; he excused his act on the ground that he had sat at home all alone for several days, and could not stand the monotony. When he was through reading the German newspapers I went out to get a cab to take him home . . . When I came breathlessly running back, I found him laughing gaily with some grisettes. He was uttering a lot of clever witticisms, and the ladies were all calling him "Monsieur Eine!" (Quoted by Lewis Browne in *That Man Heine*)

Throughout it all, he carefully concealed the real state of his health from his mother. His letters to her were cheerful and sprightly, concerned about her well-being, and expressing interest in all the family doings.

He never failed to include news about Mathilde when he wrote to his mother, and his letters provide a vivid picture of the Heine household. In July 1847 he wrote: "Mathilde sends her love. She loves you and Lottie beyond all telling, and we constantly talk about you. She behaves admirably, except for small whims and great extravagance . . . She and the parrot quarrel all day long, but I cannot do without either of them."

The Heines had moved to their old apartment in the faubourg Poissonière in September, but in the next month there began what must have been a nerve-racking succession of moves from one habitation to another. In October Heine wrote to his mother from 21 rue de la Victoire: "What troubles for my poor wife! In the midst of all this misery I lost my maid, and my wife was for ten days obliged to attend to all her affairs herself. So she is now quite worn out." In November he learned that his mother had been ill, and he wrote to her, "I beg you, dearest mother, write to me at once . . . the real truth how you really are, for I can endure anything except uncertainty." In December he concocted a story for Betty's benefit: "I have not been for two years so fresh and hearty as for the last two weeks, the cause being a certain drink of herbs, which, my physician assures me, will completely cure me, so that I look forward to a happy winter." That same month, he wrote that he would have to move again, "for there is a constant hammering in the house, and it smokes." In January 1848 he informed his mother that although the herbs had not yet cured his eye trouble, they had relieved his stomach complaints and headaches, but that in a few days he would move again. The reason this time was that he was kept awake all night by the stamping and shuffling of the horses that the landlord stabled under Heine's bedroom. Mathilde, too, was not well: "My poor wife was very ill yesterday. She had a nervous attack, and when a tumbler of water was put to her mouth to restore her, she bit it convulsively, and the pieces of glass had to be pulled from her mouth. Think of my terror!" At the end of January, the Heines moved again, this time to 9 rue de Berlin. He wrote to Hamburg: "My dear wife is quite well again, and scolds as of old. We live very harmoniously in general, but she torments me with her love of cleaning and scrubbing. I am now always in good health, but my complete cure has been postponed for the present by the great noise in the house. I love you beyond all words, my dear good mother."

Searching for a suitable place, they moved from one lodging to another. In March 1848, he entered a nursing home owned by a friend. The previous month, Paris had risen in revolt.

Since the enthronement of Louis Philippe in 1830, the upper bourgeoisie had ruled France as an unrestrained plutocracy. They dominated the Chamber of Deputies, and they grew fabulously wealthy reaping the fruits of the growing Industrial Revolution that had come to France. The urban working class grew in numbers, but their standard of living did not improve. In 1846 a severe economic depression was accompanied by a crop failure, and in 1847 two-thirds of the working population of Paris could not find work. Small merchants and artisans went bankrupt. Demonstrations protesting the high prices of food took place in many cities. The government responded by banning meetings and muzzling the press. But it was too late—on February 22, 1848, the people of Paris took to the streets, rose in revolt.

The next day the barricades went up. When the National Guard joined the revolutionaries, Louis Philippe abdicated. A provisional government in which working-class representatives predominated took power; it proclaimed universal suffrage, a ten-hour work day, and other democratic reforms.

From France the revolutionary storm swept over Europe. On May 13, demonstrations in Vienna forced Metternich to flee to London. Uprisings took place in Germany, Hungary, Italy, and Poland. In London the Chartists descended on Parliament with petitions containing six million signatures calling for universal manhood suffrage and other political and economic reforms. The Metternich system of censorship, espionage, and suppression of all liberal and nationalist aspirations was challenged and shaken.

But the revolutions ended in defeat, brought about in some cases by the intervention of foreign armies, in others as the outcome of dissensions and splits among the revolutionary leaders. The Russian army crushed the Poles and Hungarians; the Austrian army ended the revolts in Italy. In Germany and in France, the middle-class representatives allied themselves with the high bourgeoisie and royalty and turned against their working-class allies. In Germany Friedrich Wilhelm IV spurned the crown offered him by the Frankfurt Parliament, the provisional government collapsed, and the old order was restored. In France, the conservative bourgeoisie maneuvered to provoke an uprising by the workers in June 1848, which the army under General Cavaignac crushed in a bloody massacre. Six months later, in December, Louis Napoleon Bonaparte, nephew of Napoleon I, became president of the Second Republic. In 1852, by a coup d'etat, he had himself proclaimed Emperor Napoleon III.

In the first days of the revolution, Heine reacted with his old youthful enthusiasm. He wrote a report for the *Augsburg Allgemeine Zeitung*, beginning:

The three great days of February have left my head in a whirl. There is a constant drumming and shooting going on here, and always the *Marseillaise!* The last—the incessant refrain—almost splits my head, and ah! the treasonable mob of thoughts, which I have kept imprisoned for years, has broken loose again.

But the joyous élan of 1830 was gone. No more would he cry as he had when he heard the news of that revolution: "I am the son of the Revolution . . . give me my lyre that I may sing a battle-hymn . . . I am all joy and song, all sword and flame." He knew the men of the new government, and he was skeptical of them; they were too small, too narrow-minded, too ruled by party dogma. A friend who visited him at this time reported, "All the heroes of liberty, who emerged after February 1848, every single one of them filled him with disgust."

Nevertheless, it would be a great error to think that Heine ever renounced his earlier revolutionary ideals. In his report to the *Allgemeine Zeitung*, he saluted the bravery and selflessness of the "people in blouses and rags" and contrasted their true nobility with the

calculating shopkeeper's spirit, which tells you that you get more customers and greater profits by being honest than by being a thief—for in the end . . . honesty is longer-lived. The wealthy were quite astonished at the fact that the poor starvelings who ruled Paris for three days did not lay hands on other people's property. The rich trembled for their money-chests, and opened their eyes in amazement when they saw that nothing had been stolen

. . . Many objects were demolished by the people in their anger but there was no looting.

But it was clear to Heine that this revolution was doomed to failure. He gave his judgment in a letter to Alfred Meissner in 1849.

> When the Republic was proclaimed a year ago, it seemed to the world as if something which was only a dream, and ever to remain a dream, had become a reality . . . But . . . I am anything but uncertain as to what we have before us. The Republic is simply a change of name, a revolutionary title. How could this corrupt, decadent society change its nature so quickly? To make money, to grab office, to drive with four horses, to have an opera-box and rush from one pleasure to another was till now their ideal. Where did these beings so carefully hide their bourgeois virtues all this time? In Paris, take my word for it, they are good Napoleonists—I mean the napoleon d'or is king here.

In the same letter, he once again proved his keen judgment of men and events, and he foretold the 1852 coup d'etat of Napoleon III three years before it happened.

> A coup d'etat is a public secret. So much is said of it that no one believes in it, but it is being prepared. The President is working after the pattern of his uncle, and will burst out in an Eighteenth of Brumaire [The day on which Napoleon overthrew the Directory and seized power].

Heine was still in the sanitarium when the *Allegemeine Zeitung* in April 1848 had published the false allegation that his pension from the French government was a bribe. He had answered the charges clearly and cogently, but nevertheless the claim was believed in Germany, and it ended his career as a reporter for the *Allgemeine Zeitung* or any other German newspaper.

He had no visitors in the sanitarium, and he felt as if he were in a prison. Outside, the tumult of the revolution had not yet subsided, and occasional street fights still broke out. But he had been confined to the house for weeks, and he felt that he had to venture out, to refresh himself in the balmy spring air, listen to a woman's voice or a child's shout. Nearly blind, using a cane, he made his way along a boulevard. Suddenly he found himself in the midst of a great, wild crowd. Desperately he sought a place of refuge. He looked about and he saw that he was in front of the Louvre. This is what happened next, as described by Heine in the epilogue to *Romancero:*

> It was in May 1848, on the day I went out for the last time, that I said goodby to those lovely idols whom I had worshipped in happier days. It was with difficulty that I dragged myself to the Louvre, and I nearly broke down as I entered the imposing hall where the blessed goddess of beauty, Our dear Lady of Milo, stands on her pedestal. I lay at her feet for a long time, and I

wept so bitterly that it would have melted the heart of a stone. And the goddess looked down at me compassionately, yet so hopelessly, as if she were trying to say, "How can I help you? Don't you see that I have no arms?"

Later in the month Mathilde brought Heine to Passy, a small country town near Paris, in the hope that the clean air and the quiet would benefit him. But Heine was never to walk again.

She insisted that he write to Charlotte and tell her the truth about his condition, and finally he did so. "My wife desires that I should not delude you regarding the true state of my health. For the past two weeks I have been so paralyzed that I have had to be carried about like a child. My legs are like cotton and my eyes are fearfully bad." But even in this letter, Heine went on to reassure his sister. "Heart, head, and stomach are in good condition. I am being well looked after and I have plenty of money to defray all the costs of the illness. Of course I complain a great deal. My wife is behaving admirably, and we are leading a very pleasant life."

In August he wrote to his brother Max: "Even though I may not die immediately, life has ceased to have a meaning. There are no more hill-tops for me to climb, no more women's lips to kiss, not even a good roast beef to eat with light-hearted companions, for my lips are as numb as my feet." But to his mother he wrote, "We have just breakfasted . . . and greatly enjoyed our domestic tranquillity, as well as the fine strawberries and asparagus which we ate . . . the parrot screams and my wife sends greetings." He warned Charlotte, "Let us always keep my illness a secret from mother," and he arranged for Campe to print a special copy of *Romancero* for her without the epilogue that bared the true state of his health, and for the same reason he kept his *Confessions* from her. Responding to a New Year's greeting, he wrote to her in January 1850:

> May the good Lord preserve you, guard you from all sufferings, especially of the eyes; take care of your dear health; and if things do not always go as you would like, console yourself with the thought that few women are so loved and honored by their children as you are, and as you truly deserve to be, my dear, good, upright, and faithful mother. What are others compared to you? We ought to kiss the ground you tread on.

The Heines returned to Paris in September and rented a third floor apartment overlooking a courtyard at 50 rue d'Amsterdam. They chose it because it was in the rear and they thought that the noise of the street would be kept out, but the children shouted and yelled in the courtyard, two amateur pianists somewhere below banged away at their scales, and in the back room the parrot screamed. It was here that, to quote the biographer Brod, "the classic bed of pain was set up . . . the mortally sick man entered a new phase of development, the body wasted away, but new, undreamed-of fields opened out to the hero's spirit and to that of his visitors."

The nights were the worst. Once he awoke from a doze, dreaming that a pack of whirling ghosts was conducting a wild dance in his skull. "A dead poet's skull is just the place they'd choose to have their revels!" he thought. His body contracted with pain, and he groaned. The nurse hurried over. "Morphine!" he gasped. "Pencil. Paper." She applied the morphine to his lacerated back, then helped him sit up. She placed a writing board across his lap and lit the lamp. He held up the lid of his right eye with his left hand, and began to write. He scrawled verses in large letters, to be dictated in the morning to his secretary. In the other room Mathilde slept peacefully. Morphine and poetry—they were the two great healers that enabled him to survive the nights.

His secretary during this period was Karl Hillebrand, a young, devoted acolyte who spent three or four hours daily with the poet and who left this remarkable remembrance of Heine at work:

> His suffering was so intense that in order to get any rest he had to take morphine in three different forms . . . in these sleepless nights he wrote his most wonderful songs . . . He dictated the entire Romancero to me and then he polished it for hours . . . He weighed sound, cadence and clearness; decided with precise care between the present and imperfect tenses; scrutinized each name; cut out every unnecessary adjective; corrected every minute error.

Heine often thought of his father, a being who was plagued by no doubts. When he was five, he had been placed by his father in a cheder. On Saturdays he accompanied his father to the synagogue. At home they celebrated Passover and the other ancestral holidays.

But when he grew up, he had turned to Catholicism, Protestantism, atheism, pantheism. He had come to believe that it was not He who dwelt in Heaven, as his father had supposed, but he himself who dwelt here on earth, who was the Lord God. But now he was laid low.

> When the pain moves agonizingly up and down my spinal cord, I am torn by doubts as to whether man is actually a two-legged god, as the late professor Hegel assured me in Berlin five and twenty years ago . . . I am no longer "the freest German since Goethe" . . . I am no longer the joyous sound Hellene, cheerfully smiling down at the melancholy Nazarene. I am now only a poor Jew, sick unto death, a pallid picture of misery, an unhappy man.

In December 1848 a letter to Max suggested a change in his religious feelings.

> In my sleepless nights of martyrdom I compose many beautiful prayers. All of them are addressed to a very specific God, the God of our Fathers. The old nurse who watches at my bedside said last night that she knew of a very

good prayer against cramps in the knee and I asked her in all seriousness to pray for me, while she was wrapping up my knee in a heated napkin. The prayer was effective, and the cramp vanished. But what will they say in Heaven? Already I can see a number of angels expressing themselves in very scornful terms about me! "There, there, look at that unprincipled fellow! When he is sick, he asks old women to pray for him to the same God whom he scorned bitterly when he was well."

It was not as a penitent sinner that Heine announced with a flourish his return to Jehovah. His laughter and his irony did not abate in the slightest. When he spoke about Jehovah it was in the same intimate terms in which he had formerly conversed with the pagan gods. "Now that I have to think hourly about my death, I often have very earnest discussions with Jehovah at night, and He has told me: 'You may be anything you like, dear doctor, republican or socialist—but please, not an atheist!' " These words to a visitor should not be construed as flippant irreverence. It is a self-mockery that masks a deep emotion. "I have found my way to the good God," he said to Ludwig Kalisch. "He healed my soul; may He be able to heal my body as well. I should be truly grateful for it."

Irony and faith are present in striking juxtaposition in the epilogue to *Romancero* which he wrote in September 1851.

Lying on one's death-bed one become sensitive and sentimental, anxious to be at peace with God and the world. I have not been a lamb; I have scratched some and bitten others. But, believe me, those docile, highly praised lambs would not have acted so meekly if they had been equipped with the claws and teeth of the tiger. I can boast that I have only occasionally employed those weapons with which I was endowed. Since I myself am in need of God's grace, I have granted all my enemies an amnesty . . . I have made my peace with God's creatures and their Creator . . . Yes, I have come home to God, like the prodigal son, after herding the Hegelian swine for so many years . . . I returned to that old superstition, a personal God. I do not want to hush this up, as some of my enlightened and well-meaning friends have tried to do. But I must expressly deny the rumor that my backsliding has brought me to the threshold of any church, let alone into her bosom. No, my religious convictions and views have remained free from any taint of clericalism; no church bells have lured me, no altar candles have dazzled me. I have not toyed with any dogma. I have not altogether renounced my reason. No, I have renounced nothing, not even my old pagan gods, from whom it is true, I have turned away, but have parted in love and friendship.

His God was no milk-and-water God, no pantheistical abstraction, but the God of the Old Testament, the All-Powerful Jehovah. What he needed was a God he could talk to, who was real, he said.

It is a true comfort for me to know that there is someone in Heaven into whose ears I can complain, especially after midnight, when Mathilde has sought the rest she so badly needs. Thank God that I am not alone in such hours, and I can pray and whine without hindrance and shame, and I can pour out my whole heart before the Almighty, and confide to Him some things which one is in the habit of keeping even from one's wife.

He did not tremble before Jehovah. He had never bowed before a king on earth, and he was not afraid to speak openly to the King of Heaven. Oh he had many a complaint to lodge against Him! The heathen gods would never treat a poet the way Jehovah did. Why, He had actually paralyzed his lips so that he could not kiss! Oh, if he were well enough to walk without crutches he would forget all this praying, and saunter along the lovely boulevards and find a lovely girl to laugh with. God would forgive him—that was His business. God would never condemn him for such pleasures. He had placed man and woman on earth to enjoy its fruits and each other. Life itself was holy.

Heine sent a message to Campe that he had a collection of new poems ready for printing. Campe said it was a miracle, rushed off to Paris and offered the poet 6,000 marks, sight unseen, for the complete rights to *Romancero*. He published the book in October 1851; twenty thousand copies were sold in the first two months, and it went through three more editions.

The creation of the poems and their enthusiastic reception did more than his prayers or the doctors to revivify him. "Poetry has remained my best friend," he said. "She has followed me to the edge of the grave, and is fighting for me against death." He wrote his mother that he had stopped taking opiates and seldom saw a doctor.

He bombarded Charlotte with letters requesting her to send him books that were not available to him in Paris. Hillebrand read aloud to him, and Mathilde had improved enough in her learning so that sometimes she read, especially from the novels of Dumas, which were great favorites with Heine. He also enjoyed the novels of Dickens and Thackeray, and the works of Goethe, Schiller, and Schopenhauer. He often had the Old Testament, parts of which he knew word for word, read to him.

He always mentioned Mathilde in his letters to his mother. Sometimes, humorously, he complained of her extravagance. "We live in the greatest harmony, in the most beautiful and expensive peace." Again: "My wife complains that she is no longer so pretty as she was, and that she must therefore dress the more beautifully . . . She has had her portrait taken, but is unhappy with it. In order to have peace I must disapprove of it, but she is really better-looking *en nature* than *en effigie*. Yet I often prefer the picture because it does not complain." But these remarks should be measured against the enduring depths of his love, which he expressed in so many letters as well as in poems and remarks to visitors. Laube quoted Heine as exclaiming, "She's like the angels!" and the poet told Fanny Lewald: "Often in my sleepless nights I am frightened at the idea of such bliss, and I tremble when I think of such overflowing happiness."

The magnificent *Narratives*, the poignant *Lamentations* and *Lazarus*, and the exquisite *Hebrew Melodies*, form Heine's masterpiece, *Romancero*. Gautier read them and wrote: "Like a dead man, the living poet was nailed in his coffin, but when we bent over to listen, we heard poetry ringing from under the pall." It was a new and wonderful poetry that the listeners heard, the vital poetry of a new age. In the words of Kate Freiligrath Kroeker in her *Poems Selected from Heine:*

> Heine may be said to be the last of the celebrated German Romantic School, the funeral pyre of which he himself helped to build up in his youth, only to set it ablaze with the scorching flame of his own remorseless wit. And, behold, from its ashes arose a strange phoenix, the anti-romantic and modern spirit which justly entitles Heine to be called one of the deliverers of thought, the champion of progress, and the sworn foe of all stagnation.

When Meissner read a cycle of the *Lazarus* poems, he was overcome by emotion, and Heine said: "Yes, I know well enough it's beautiful. It's a cry from the grave, a cry in the night from someone buried alive, or even from a corpse, or from the grave itself. Oh, yes, German poetry has never heard these accents, could never have been able to hear them, because no poet has ever found himself in such a condition."

The soul *in extremis* is heard in the *Lazarus* sequence. There are poems of utter weariness and disillusionment with the world, of a suffering beyond all telling.

> The curtain falls upon the play,
> And lords and ladies drive away.
>
> . . . .
>
> . . . now the house has hushed its laughter,
> And all the lights have disappeared.
> But wait! What could that sound have been?
> Close by the empty stage?—perhaps
> It is a feeble string that snaps—
> The string of an old violin.
> Some peevish rats morosely flit
> Backward and forward through the pit.
> The whole place smells of rancid oil.
> The final lamp goes pale, and sighs,
> And hisses bitterly, and dies.
> The wretched fire—it was my soul.

In the *Lazarus* section, too, are the infinitely touching and tender poems in which he broods protectingly over Mathilde, as in To the Angels, wherein he begs them to guard and protect her after his death.

She was both wife and child to me
And when I leave for the realm of shadows,
A widow and an orphan she will be!
I will leave her in this world alone
The wife, the child, who, trusting to my courage,
Carefree and faithful, slumbered by my side.

The powerful dramatic *Narratives* are for the most part based on historic figures. Dramatic genius and psychological mastery combine to create small masterpieces.

In *Charles I*, the fugitive king sits in the charcoal-burner's hut and sings a lullaby as he rocks the cradle of the infant who will become his executioner, and tells of the end of the old faith in God and in the king.

The charcoal-burner's faith is gone;
No more do his children cling—
Lullaby-lulla—to trust in God,
And even less in the king.

. . . .

Lullaby-lulla, what stirs in the straw?
You shall not be denied.
You'll take the empire, and cut off my head—
The pussycat has died.

Lullaby-lulla, what stirs in the straw?
I hear the bleat of the sheep.
The pussycat's dead, the mice rejoice—
Sleep, little slayer, sleep!

In *The Battlefield of Hastings*, Edith Swanthroat searches the bloody battlefield for the corpse of her royal lover. The ground is covered with thousands of mutilated corpses. She has searched the whole day, darkness has fallen. Suddenly there is heard a dreadful scream.

Edith Swanthroat had found the place
Where Harold's body lay.
She did not speak, she did not cry,
She kissed his face so gray.

She kissed his brow, she kissed his mouth,
She clasped the lifeless man;
She kissed the wound upon his breast
From which the blood still ran.

She saw on his shoulder, and covered with
A kiss and another kiss:

Three little scars she'd left there once:
Three monuments to her bliss.

Bitterness is the keynote in *King David.*

Smiling, kings give up their breath;
For they know that with their death
Someone else will shout commands,
And enslavement never ends.

In *The Golden Calf* Heine used an Old Testament story to satirize the worship of gold.

Fiddles, trumpets, and the flute
Make them dance around the brute,
Jacob's daughter as though cursed,
Boom, boom, circle fast and bold.
Calf shaped gold.
Drums are thundering, guffaws bray.

Gowns tucked high up to the loins
Noblest maidens quickly join
Hand in hand the roundelay
And they whirl of madness full
Round the bull.
Drums are thundering, guffaws bray.

Aaron too begins to rave
And the idol dance's wave
Sucks away the holy fellow
Dancing in his high priest coat
Like a goat.
Drums are thundering, guffaws bellow.

The rhythm of this poem brings to mind Vachel Lindsay's *Congo.* If indeed Lindsay was influenced by Heine, he was only one among many twentieth-century poets and writers whose works have been affected by his genius. Among such, the names of A. E. Housman and Bertolt Brecht come to mind.

The poem *Marie Antoinette* led to the immediate banning of *Romancero* in Austria-Hungary. The Hapsburg royalty could not stomach the nightmare of a headless young queen presiding over a headless levee in the Tuileries. In *Miserere,* a procession of dead nuns sing the Miserere as they wend their way through the cloisters of a ruined convent. Countess Jutta, in the poem of the same name, laughs as she sails down the Rhine in the moonlight and the ghosts of the men she has drowned lift their hands in longing. *Vitzliputzli* is an unrelieved account of the horror and savagery of the conquest of Mexico by

Cortez. Sly satire marks *The Knave of Bergen:* The duchess dances wildly with the young unknown "whose eyes flash like dagger blades" behind his mask. He implores her to let him go, but she must see his face before he leaves; she tears off his mask, to reveal the executioner of the town of Bergen! Thereupon the duke, to save his wife from shame, knights the rascal on the spot. Thus the hangman became a noble and the founder of the haughty Von Bergen family.

The God Apollo is a poem of lamentation. Rapture and the yearning for beauty are symbolized in the young nun who has seen Apollo from afar.

> Sweetly, the golden-headed one
> Sings, and plays the lyre;
> And in the heart of the wretched nun
> His ballad burns like fire.
>
> She crosses herself again and again,
> But nothing can suppress
> Her luscious agony of pain,
> Her bitter happiness.

The nun flees the cloister and wanders out into the world to find Apollo. She asks for him everywhere, and everywhere she meets with meanness and vulgarity. The lovely quatrains of the first two sections of the poem change to rough, unrythmical lines; the words are coarse and even revolting. It is a poem of utter sadness. The Apollo whom the nun had seen was a radiant being, a godlike creature. But in the final stanzas of the poem, disillusionment is complete; vulgarity has triumphed. Apollo has been seen, the nun is told.

> Recently he lured some wenches
> From the Amsterdam Casino,
> And he's touring with those "Muses"
> In the role of an Apollo.
>
> There's a fat one, who surpasses
> All the rest in squeaking, grunting;
> For her giant laurel head-dress
> She's been nicknamed the Green Sow.

The most noteworthy of the poems that make up the *Hebrew Melodies* are the *Princess Sabbath* and *Jehuda ben Halevy.* In the first of these, Heine describes lovingly and melodiously the transformation of the humble peddler called Israel when the curse is lifted on the Sabbath and he is changed from an outcast into a prince.

Jehuda ben Halevy, a long, unfinished poem, is in praise of the great Jewish poet of that name who lived in thirteenth-century Spain. The images are striking. The poet mourns for Jerusalem:

> She, the thriving holy city,
> Has become a wilderness,
> Where the satyr, werewolf, jackal
> Carry on their wicked business—
> Snakes and birds of midnight nestle
> In the weatherbeaten walls:
> From the windows' airy arches
> Foxes comfortably gaze.

The tears that Jehuda ben Halevy weeps at the city's destruction are more beautiful than the pearls of the oyster, for they are

> Pearls of tears that, linked together
> On the golden thread of rhyme,
> Came from poetry's gold-smithy
> In the pattern of a song.

The poem tells of his death:

> Calmly flowed the rabbi's blood,
> Calmly he intones his song
> To the last note, and his final
> Death-sigh was Jerusalem!

Choirs of angels greet his arrival in Heaven with songs of his own verses.

He never laid down his pen. *Gods In Exile,* a prose fantasy about the Greek gods, first appeared in a French version in the *Revue des Deux Mondes.* It was well received, and he planned a German edition, but a literary pirate brought out a mangled German translation. Since there were no copyright laws, Heine was unable to obtain redress.

He began work on *Confessions,* a moving account of his exile, his religious searchings, his attitude toward Judaism, and the healing he found in the Bible. He came to see the martyrdom of the Jews in a new light.

> The Jews were always men, mighty, unyielding men, not only in the past, but to this very day, in spite of eighteen centuries of persecution and misery . . . if all pride of ancestry were not a silly paradox in a champion of the Revolution and its democratic principles, the writer of these lines could well be proud that his ancestors belonged to the Noble House of Israel, that he is a descendant of those martyrs who gave the world a God and morality, and who fought and suffered on all the battlefields of thought.

But once a great cry of despair was wrung from him.

What good does it do me that young men and maidens crown my marble bust with laurels, if at the same time the withered hand of an aged nurse rubs my head with cantharides? What good does it do me to know that the roses of Shiraz perfume the air, when Shiraz is two thousand miles from the Rue d'Amsterdam, where I can smell nothing but the perfume of hot compresses. Ah, the mockery of God weighs heavily upon me. The great author of the universe, the Aristophanes of heaven wishes to show me, the little so-called German Aristophanes, that my sharpest sarcasms are feeble little jests compared with His, and how lamentably inferior I am to Him in devising a joke of real dimensions . . . Yes, the derision with which the Master has belittled me . . . is horribly cruel. Humbly do I acknowledge His supremacy and I bow before Him in the dust. But, though I have not His great creative power, yet I have the gift of eternal reason, and I can summon God's jest before that court and subject it to respectful criticism. I dare there to offer the most humble opinion that this cruel game with which the Master is disciplining his wretched pupil is too far long drawn out. It has already lasted over six years, and it is getting to be a little tiresome.

Heine's health took another turn for the worse in the winter of 1853–54. He developed an inflammation of the throat, suffered excruciating chest and bronchial pains, and experienced difficulty in breathing. He had to undergo an operation. He showed a slight improvement but continued writing and revising as assiduously as ever.

In the spring of 1854, he was visited by Charlotte's daughter, Maria, a favorite of his who was now the Princess della Rocca. In her reminiscences we find this graphic account of the last hours she spent with her uncle:

I sat by his bed and his first questions were of the loved ones at home. "Ah, I shall never see my dear mother again. And will my dear Lottie come soon?" he cried. He told me about his youth and his battles with mankind. The sickroom was badly lighted by a lamp and I heard the monotonous ticking of the clock. Suddenly he tried to change his position without the aid of his nurse. He was attacked with agonizing pains, and I was terrified when I saw him struggling for breath. His faithful nurse did what she could to make him comfortable, and assured me that it was only a momentary pain, that she had often seen him in such a state. But I could not stay in the room and I ran out sobbing.

Heine continued to defy death. Hillebrand had left him and he engaged a new secretary, Richard Reinhardt. Heine's courage, serenity, and defiance of fate amazed Reinhardt and inspired in him a feeling that bordered on veneration.

The dread cholera once again visited Paris, and it was particularly virulent in the congested district where the Heines lived. Mathilde wanted to move, particularly in view of her husband's weak condition, and although he dreaded the ordeal of being carried down the narrow stairway and of facing the jolting ride over the rough streets, he told her to find a new apartment for them. He had long yearned to get out of this place he was buried in, where he had never seen the sun or felt the fresh air, and had been forced to endure the infernal piano scales of the amateur musicians who were still practicing somewhere across the courtyard.

Mathilde found a place in one of the suburbs. It had a garden, and at first he was ecstatic. But the autumn brought with it the cold fogs; the dampness penetrated the house, and he contracted another throat infection.

On November 6, 1854, they moved back to Paris, to an apartment on the fourth floor of a building at 3 avenue Matignon, just off the Champs-Elysees. It was spacious, light, airy and quiet, and his face lit up with pleasure when he saw it. It had a balcony and on the first sunny day he was carried out and lay on a chaise longue and enjoyed the outdoors. He held Mathilde's opera glass up to his good eye and gazed at the world before him. He could see the trees and the throngs and the carriages on the boulevard; then he noticed a baker's boy offering his cakes to two ladies in crinoline, and nearby a little dog lifted its leg against a tree. He put down the glass, saying he did not want to see anymore.

14

The Last Years: *Lutetia* and *Memoirs* (1855–56)

Mathilde sat in her room and meditated. When they had brought her Henri home from the Louvre that sad day in 1848, she did not cry out or sob. She knew that her *pauvre garçon* would not want her to weep over him. Without a fuss, she had begun her task of nursing him. Since then Henri had never left his room on his own feet. Many people called her unfeeling. They thought it was disgraceful that of a morning she went strolling with Pauline or some other friend; their idea of the proper thing was for her to be at his bedside night and day. But she knew that Henri wanted no long face to burden him. He wanted her to sing and talk to the parrot, and to tell him all about the silly, delightful things she and Pauline encountered in the outside world. He wanted her to buy pretty frocks and to model them for him. He had insisted that she take the room farthest away from his so that he wouldn't disturb her at night.

The outside world did not understand how deeply she loved him—not with tears, but in her own way, the way he wanted. One night he had had such a terrible attack of pain that she had been frightened. She had sobbed: "No, Henri, no no, you can't do this to me, you can't die! Have pity on me! This morning I lost the kitten, and if you die too, I shall be too unhappy!" Then she had peeked out of the corner of her eye, and had seen Henri smile.

Those stupid doctors. Did all that bleeding help him, she wondered. She had taught one doctor a lesson. When he dared to say that Henri was not properly cared for by her, she gave him a black eye and threw him out.

These fine people did not understand their love. She did not complain. Their marriage had been a wonderful one. He had taken her as she was. He had let her go out with her friends (true, sometimes he was jealous, but that was because he loved her), given her money for clothes and jewels and trifles, taken her to the best restaurants and to other places she liked. He never tried to change her. Yes, in the beginning he had sent her to school, then had given her lessons himself. But when she had tired of learning he dropped the matter. It hadn't all been for nothing, though—she could read Dumas now.

Many fine ladies and gentlemen came to their home. Sometimes they told her how famous Henri was. As if that was why she should take care of him. She didn't care for most of them. Too stuck up and fancy. There were a few, though, that were a lot of fun. Like Alexander Dumas, that big bear, and Hans Christian Andersen from Copenhagen—she really enjoyed their company.

Men still found her attractive—she could tell. But Henri never had any real cause for jealousy, although he was a jealous one. The other day he had complained that she had stayed up all night with the cat, which had hurt itself, but that she never stayed up all night with him. But he probably was teasing.

Really, when she thought about it, she had much more reason to be jealous of him that he of her. Hadn't she caught him with Frisette, her friend the milliner? He had explained that he was so absent-minded that he had mistaken Frisette for her. What kind of explanation was that?

And now Camille Selden, who called every afternoon and sat by his bedside and read to him while they held hands. Henri called her La Mouche. She wondered why. She didn't care for her, but she left them alone. They only loved with words. If that woman eased her Henri's last days, she wouldn't interfere.

Mathilde shook her head and put aside the unaccustomed meditation. Soon a mighty chattering was heard as she and Coco scolded each other, to Henri Heine's delight.

Balzac was dead, and Rahel had died long ago. So many friends had left Paris or forgotten him. But Cristina had not left him. Since her return from Palestine, where she had lived in poverty in a retreat, she visited him regularly. Poor princess, she had lost all her wealth. . . . He thought about his dear friend Gérard de Nerval, gentle de Nerval who had hanged himself. They said he was mad. But was a man mad who shook off his illness when he thought that a friend was calling him for help?

Heine was filled with pity and wonder as he recalled the incident. He and de Nerval had been translating the *Lyrical Intermezzo* into French when suddenly, in the midst of a dispute about the nuance of a phrase, Nerval fell into a stupor. It had happened before, and he had known what to do. He called to Mathilde and they used a gentle hoax to arouse de Nerval. She rang for the concierge, then shook de Nerval, all the time repeating, "Alexander Dumas has been taken ill, he is nearby at the doctor's, and he is asking for you." Her words finally pierced through the mists of de Nerval's mind, and he exclaimed, "Dumas ill? I must go to him." The concierge arrived, took de Nerval by the hand, and gently led him to the office of the doctor who was treating him.

Fewer people were climbing the four flights of stairs to his apartment these days, but those who did were always rewarded with a Heinesque bon mot. When the aged Berlioz suddenly appeared, Heine exclaimed: "What! Someone is actually calling on me! But then, Berlioz always was original." Another caller was greeted with the comment, "Alexander Weill was just here, we had an exchange of ideas, and now I am utterly stupid."

Among the old friends whose company he treasured was Alexander Dumas, whose novels had helped to while away so many a weary hour.

The morning light filtered through the shutters. Heine remembered that Dumas would be calling, and the thought cheered him. He heard Mathilde stirring in the next room. She began scolding Coco and he smiled. He must write a letter to his mother. Her eighty-seventh birthday was at hand; Lottie had written him that her mind was as sharp as ever. He called to his secretary that he had no poems to dictate this morning, but that he wished to send a letter to his mother.

"Dear good mother," he began his usual salutation. The voice coming from the emaciated body was astonishingly rich and warm. Heine did not hear the knock at the door. The maid answered and admitted the visitor. She beckoned the nurse, Catherine, who was reading in a corner of the room. Catherine tiptoed over; her face brightened as she greeted Alexander Dumas.

"Monsieur Dumas, how good of you to come," she whispered.

"Is he well enough to talk to a visitor?"

"He is always happy when you come. He had a good night. He is dictating a letter to his mother. Listen—he is a saint."

Dumas and the nurse stood listening quietly as Heine dictated. Now and then he reached with his hand to lift the right eyelid.

A cough from Dumas, and Heine's face lit up with pleasure when he saw who it was.

"It's you, my dear Dumas! Sit down, my fellow republican, sit down."

Dumas sat down gingerly on the fragile-looking chair the nurse brought him. Heine laughed: "That is one of Mathilde's selections of fine furniture."

"Does your mother have any idea about your condition?" asked Dumas.

"What mother would believe that a son could be so sick?" A pause. "The doctors prescribe morphine to ease my pain, but, Dumas, your novels do more for me than medicine. Mathilde and Reinhardt take turns reading them to me. I devour them all and exclaim to myself, 'What an ingenious poet is this great fellow, the father of Athos, Porthos, Aramis, and D'Artagnan.'"

Dumas's voice boomed. "You are as gallant as all my musketeers rolled into one."

"I was not so gallant the other day. I asked Catherine to carry me to the balcony. From there I looked down and saw a dog running around, and I thought, 'Oh to be able to run around like that dog, to be alive, to fight, to wench,' I thought, 'Let me be scourged, let me be flayed with red-hot tongs, but once more, oh once more let me hold a woman in my arms!'"

A tear formed in the corner of Dumas's eyes. After a moment, Heine resumed, as if he could not stop talking.

"Ah, Alexander, the years come and go. I remember a wonderful summer many years ago in Germany, when I went on a walking tour through the Harz Mountains. I remember leaving Göttingen in the early morning, knapsack on my back, and crossing the stream outside the town, and the fresh morning air, and the singing birds welcoming me on my journey.

"I was a young rascal in those days. I stopped for lunch at an inn and met a gentleman with two ladies. The gentleman asked me to recommend a hotel in Göttingen, and I advised him to ask the first student he met there for the Hotel de Bruhbach. Both ladies then asked me in one breath if the Hotel de Bruhbach was frequented by respectable people. I replied yes, with a clear conscience, and when the trio drove off I waved to them from the window. The innkeeper grinned slyly; no doubt he knew that the students at the university called their jail the Hotel de Bruhbach."

Heine again paused. This time the silence lasted longer. Dumas sat patiently, a gentle, good, loyal giant of a man.

Sitting with his hopelessly sick friend, Dumas thought of all the other friends who had passed away. Balzac was gone, and now de Nerval. Would Heine be next? He felt dispirited. Where had they gone, those magic days that were each a glorious golden glow—those days of love and friendship, good wine and good food, dreams and fame?

His reflections ended as the door to Mathilde's room opened slightly and the sounds of Mathilde and the parrot talking to each other swept in.

"Listen to that delightful chattering," said Heine.

"You love her very much, *mon ami*," Dumas observed.

"Dumas, she is a child who makes me utterly happy. But sometimes she displays a temper, she screams, she throws things about, she even throws herself on the floor. The other day she came home from shopping with a new green frock she had bought. I christened it the Vitzliputzli dress, and told her that it cost exactly what I had been paid for the *Vitzliputzli* poem in *Romancero*. She screamed at me and kicked her heels on the floor."

"Monsieur Heine just laughed at her," the nurse interjected. "Later he wrote a poem about it. He read it to me. It went like this:"

> If your wife a wish expresses
>   for a shawl, why, buy her two;
> Buy her golden brooches, dresses,
>   lace and jewels.

"Oh," the nurse suddenly exclaimed. "I must take him away now and attend to his wants. It is time. I will bring him back soon. You need not leave, Monsieur Dumas." The nurse swooped down, lifted the slight body easily, and bore Heine out of the room, but not before he cried out, "See how the people of Paris carry me on their shoulders!"

Dumas called after him, "Ah, *mon frère*, you have not lost your sense of humor." At that moment, there was a knock on the door, and two little girls entered the room. The secretary placed her arms around the shoulders of the children and told them, "Wait, Monsieur Heine will be back in a minute." She turned to Dumas: "This is Alice and this one is Yvette. They are great playmates of Monsieur Heine. They visit him almost every day." The two little girls stared at Dumas, who winked back at them.

Soon the nurse brought Heine back, Mathilde walking behind her. She was dressed to go out, and gave Dumas an affectionate hug.

"You naughty boy," she scolded him, "not visiting Henri for a long time. I am heartbroken that I cannot stay and talk with you, but Pauline is waiting for me." She bent down and kissed Heine, patted the girls, and left.

Alice leaned up against Heine and Yvette stood at the foot of the bed.

"Alice, I promised you a story, didn't I?" Heine asked.

She nodded.

"And I will keep my promise, *ma petite*. Alice, I know of a place that is so glorious and lovely, with the most beautiful flowers that have the most wonderful colors, and there is a house there that belongs to God. His house is called Heaven. And the kitchen maids are angels. And they like to eat chocolate cake from morning to night, and they wipe their mouths on their white wings. Now what do you think of that?"

Alice gazed at Heine wide-eyed, but Yvette declared emphatically, "Dirty little things!" and was surprised at the laughter her remark prompted. Dumas's infectious merriment filled the room. After a while, the children left, but they promised Heine to return the next day.

"They bring you great joy, don't they, Henri?" Dumas observed.

"They are two faithful friends," said Heine softly. "They are two flowers that blossom in my sickroom."

"Tell me, *mon ami*," said Dumas, "What is happening about your religion? All kinds of rumors are floating about. They say that you have repented all your sins, although I suspect that would be a rather long list. The Protestants, the Catholics, the Jews—each group claims you."

"How the devout souls yearn for me to reveal some miracle, that like Paul I have seen a light on the road to Damascus, or that like Balaam I rode a stubborn ass who suddenly began speaking like a man. I have never seen an ass—at least not a four-legged one—who spoke like a man; although I have met plenty of men who, whenever they opened their mouths, spoke like asses."

Chuckling, Dumas said, "So there is no truth in the report of your salvation?"

"If by salvation is meant a vision or a voice from Heaven or an extraordinary dream—no. But illumination, transformation brought about by the reading of a book, yes."

"A book?"

"Yes, an old and simple book. I have been reading it a lot these days. It is a simple book, as unpretentious a book as the sun that warms us, as the bread that nourishes us, a book that looks at us with as much blessed kindliness as an old grandmother, who has herself read it every day, with her dear, trembling lips, and spectacles on her nose. This book is the Bible. It holds sunrise and sunset, promise and fulfillment, birth and death—the whole dream of mankind."

Heine closed his eyes and Dumas waited. Finally Heine stirred.

"Dumas, you divine heathen, are you still there?" he whispered.

"Yes, my dear friend, right here."

"A thought just came to me. What is the most beautiful word in the human language?"

"An interesting question."

"There are many beautiful words. 'Friendship' is beautiful. So is 'love.' Is it not true that 'joy' is beautiful? But the most beautiful word, Dumas, is 'freedom.' Freedom of mind and spirit. And how is this freedom manifested?"

Again a pause, and again Dumas waited. After a while, Heine continued:

"Let me tell you a story. Many centuries ago my great ancestor—I am speaking of Moses—took a poor shepherd tribe and from it he created a nation that was to defy the centuries—a great, immortal, holy people, the people of God. He created Israel."

"You were speaking of freedom."

"I was speaking of freedom and Moses. Freedom was always the great emancipator's leading thought. His love of freedom glows in his statutes on pauperism. He would have wiped out slavery, if he could, but it was too deeply rooted in the customs of that primitive age. He had to confine his efforts to ameliorating by law the conditions of the slaves, rendering self-purchase by a bondsman less difficult, and limiting the period of bondage. But listen well, Dumas. If a slave was freed by law, but refused to depart from his master's house, then Moses commanded that the incorrigibly servile villain be nailed by his ear to the doorpost of his master's house and, after being publicly exposed in this shameful manner, be condemned to lifelong servitude. Would that I could nail to the Brandenburg gate by their long ears our complacent German slaves in their liveries of black, red, and gold!"

Heine closed his eyes and whispered, "I am tired." After a while, Dumas rose and murmured, "Goodby, old friend."

Suddenly once again the carriages were crowding each other in front of his dwelling.

It started when the Exposition of 1855 opened in Paris. Tourists from across the Rhine came in large numbers, and among them were many old friends from Germany whom he hadn't seen in years. To 3 avenue Matignon came Leopold Zunz, with whom he had worked in the Society for Jewish Culture and Science and who had encouraged and helped him in the writing of the *Rabbi of Bacherach;* and Elise von Hohenhausen, who had dubbed him "the German Byron," after he read his poems aloud in her literary salon in Berlin. So many visitors came that he quipped that he had at last become a holy saint, for the callers would enter his living tomb as reverently as if they were approaching a sacred shrine.

Paris too was acclaiming him. In April a French version of *Lutetia* appeared. He had taken the articles he had written for the *Augsburg Allgemeine Zeitung* in the period from 1840 to 1844 and revised them. Freed from the German censorship, they constituted a fascinating history of contemporary France—

brilliant and perceptive of leaders and institutions. Discussing censorship, he wrote with a truly Gallic touch about the *cancan*.

The *cancan* is a dance never seen in respectable society but only in common dance halls, in which whoever is dancing it is promptly seized by the police and thrown out . . . But Parisian light-heartedness capers most joyfully when in a strait-jacket; even though the stern eye of the law prevents them from dancing the *cancan* with all the cynical precision demanded, the dancers know how to express their forbidden thoughts in all sorts of capers and exaggerated propriety . . . I do not think that morality profits from this governmental interference and its show of arms at these dances. Forbidden fruit is sweetest and most tempting; and the subtle, often quite witty circumvention of the censorship frequently has a more harmful effect than openly sanctioned licentiousness.

In July 1855, the publication in French of *Poems and Legends* brought him new fame. The collection included *Lyrical Intermezzo, North Sea, Atta Troll, Germany: A Winter's Tale, Lazarus, Ballads,* and a number of other poems from *Romancero.* Among the French poets who had collaborated with him in the translations were Gérard de Nerval, Saint-René Taillandier and Edouard Grenier.

Heine was now known in distant lands and across the ocean. In the United States, twelve editions of *Germany, A Winter's Tale* had been published, and lectures about his work were being given in New York. In 1855 a Philadelphia publisher brought out a translation of *Travel Pictures,* which met with a warm reception. Polish, Hungarian, and Czech fighters for liberty recited his stirring songs of freedom—the Czech poet, Bozena Nemcová called him "our brilliant Heine." In Germany, the Teutomanians and the aristocrats still hated him, but burghers and peasants sang his poems as folksongs. In 1850 a visitor brought Heine musical arrangements of his poems by Mendelssohn, Loewe, and Schubert. In 1855, members of the Cologne Male Choir, which was in Paris for the Exposition, visited him and sang a number of musical versions of his poems. He was particularly delighted with Klein's arrangement of *The Two Grandiers.* Yet it is sad to think that Heine never received a word of appreciation from the composers, let alone money, for all the hundreds of songs his poems inspired. According to the biographer Max Brod, a letter in Heine's posthumous papers indicates that Schumann in 1840 sent the poet the *Heine Lieder Cycle, Op. 24,* but it is doubtful that the package reached Heine, for no acknowledgment from him was received by Schumann, although Heine was very conscientious about such matters.

In August 1855, a letter from Heine to his mother was filled with happy anticipation.

I have thought of nothing since your last letter but the joyful meeting with my darling sister. Everything is ready for Lottie's arrival. She will have a comfortable room. It would be an infinite delight to see if she will bring one of my nieces, no matter which, Anna or Lena, since both are equally dear to me . . . We have plenty of room, and all visitors here admire the fine view and the excellent air which we enjoy, so that while in the most brilliant central point of Paris, we still seem to be in the country . . . My wife is well and very cheerful . . . She sends greetings and kisses from the heart . . . I embrace you tenderly, my good, most admirable mother, and remain ever, with deep love, your faithful son.

Charlotte actually did not come until November, when she arrived accompanied by Gustav, the reactionary brother whom Heine loved to twit and whom Mathilde disliked. One wonders why Charlotte had not visited him in all the years of his grave illness—it would have brought him so much happiness. Still, now that she was here, not a word of reproach escaped him; he was beside himself with delight. Here is her description of their meeting:

When I approached his bed, he cried, "My dear Lottie," and embraced me and held me long in his arms without saying a word for a long time. After what I had previously learned about the illness of my brother, I feared the first sight of his suffering would shock me terribly, but as I saw only his head, which smiled at me with a wondrous glorious beauty, I could abandon myself utterly to the first delight of seeing him again. But when later on, his nurse carried him in her arms to a chaise-lounge in order to make the bed, and I saw his shrunken body from which the limbs hung down as if lifeless, I was compelled to summon up all my strength to endure the terrible sight. During the night it was agonizing to hear how he suffered from terrible pains in the chest.

But there were moments when he was free from pain. Then they talked of memories of bygone years. Sometimes they would laugh, and if Mathilde was present she would join in the laughter, and then ask, because she did not understand German, what it was they were laughing at.

Charlotte stayed for about a month, when she received word of the illness of one of her children. She was assured by her brother's doctor that, unless something unexpected occurred, he would live another two or three years, and when she told Heine that she would be back in the spring, she fully expected to see him again. He was downcast but realized it could not be helped. He obtained her promise that she would bring her son Ludwig with her when she returned, for he had appointed him in his will as his literary executor and there were matters he wished to discuss with him. Heine then handed his sister a poem. He told her that it was a humorous piece about the reception she would receive when she arrived home. She left it on the desk, intending to pick it up when she departed the following day. But when she looked for it in the morning she discovered that the maid had used it to light a fire. Charlotte was inconsolable, but Heine comforted her: "Console yourself, dear sister, when you return I will write you a poem which shall be even far more full of fire."

But Charlotte never saw her brother again, for before the spring he was dead.

She has come down to us by the name Heine gave her: La Mouche, because she flitted about like the fly that was engraved on her signet ring.

He was on the verge of the grave, but she resurrected him. She appeared at his bedside one June day in 1855. Eight months later he was dead; but in those last few months of his life he experienced the saddest, the sweetest, the tenderest love he had ever known.

Her background was rather obscure. Born in Prague of German ancestry, she had been adopted by a well-to-do couple, who provided her with a large dowry when she married. Her husband was a Frenchman who turned out to be a scoundrel. After running through her fortune, he managed through trickery to commit her to a mental institution in London, but she escaped to Paris and secured a divorce. Her past included a love affair with Alfred Meissner. When Heine met her, she was earning a living by tutoring.

She had loved Heine's poems since her youth. While visiting in Vienna, she was asked by a Viennese composer to deliver some sheets of music to Heine, whose poems he too loved. When she presented herself at the apartment at 3 avenue Matignon, the nurse took the manuscripts and was about to turn the visitor away when a deep voice called to Catherine to let her in.

La Mouche carefully made her way through the darkened room to Heine's bedside. Recalling the moment twenty years later in her book, *Last Days of Heinrich Heine,* she wrote that he looked much younger than he really was, that his features were fascinating—"the head of Christ with the smile of Mephistopheles." (Gautier, who saw Heine for the last time in January 1856, wrote: "Illness from the statue of a Greek god shaped a Christ . . . Thus ravaged he was still beautiful. When he raised his heavy eyelid a flash shot from his half-blinded pupil. Genius resuscitated this dead face. Lazarus came forth from his grave for a few minutes.")

When La Mouche got ready to go after a short conversation, Heine asked her to leave her address. She did not expect to hear from him again, but something about her had attracted him. It might have been her roguish eyes, her graceful, youthful figure, her sweet voice with its German accent. She was about twenty-five.

He did write to her, a day or two later.

My very gracious and charming young woman: I am deeply sorry that I could see you only for a few moments recently. You left an extremely favorable impression, and I am looking forward to the pleasure of seeing you again soon. If you can, come tomorrow; in any case, come as soon as your time allows . . . I don't know why your kindly sympathy does me so much good, but superstitious man that I am, I believe that a good fairy has visited me in my hour of sorrow. It was the right hour. Or are you a wicked fairy? I must know that soon.

The good fairy answered his call, and thereafter she visited him almost daily. Mathilde quietly walked out of the room whenever La Mouche came.

When Charlotte arrived in November the two became close friends. She found La Mouche to be

"a singularly gifted, pleasant creature . . . who combined French vivacity with German earnestness . . . a charming, youthful being . .– of medium height, more pleasing than pretty . . . her mischievous eyes looked out at you over a retroussé nose, and she had a little mouth, which, in speaking or laughing, revealed her pearly teeth. Her hands and feet were small and dainty, and there was something unusually graceful about all her movements." (Ludwig von Embden, *The Family Life of Heinrich Heine*)

La Mouche was skilled in both German and French, and, when Reinhardt had to leave the poet's services, she took over much of the work of the former secretary, refusing to accept any pay for her labor. When Heine finished dictating or going over proofs, he enjoyed having her read to him on the balcony. Sometimes he clasped her fingers in his and nothing was said for long minutes at a time. He called her "the last flower of my mournful autumn," and he sent her absurd, gallant little notes; she should not come on Wednesday because a bad headache was already dawning, but she should come on Friday—and thereafter more often. Meanwhile he dreams of her: "Flutter around my nose a bit with your little wings, my good, delightful, lovely Mouche. I know a song by Mendelssohn with the refrain: 'Come soon, you!' The tune is forever running in my head: 'Come soon, you!' And another note: "It makes me happy that I shall soon put a chaste kiss on your sweet face. The words would suggest something less platonic were I a man. Alas! I am only a spirit. This may please you, but it does not please me at all. I am a dead man who longs for the most ardent pleasures that life can afford. It is horrible." He calls her his lotus flower, then in his wretchedness he ridicules both of them.

> Truly the two of us offer
> The oddest sight you can see:
> One, I'm afraid, has lumbago
> And one sighs rheumatically.
>
> The lotus flower uncovers
> Her sweetness at evening time;
> But all that's born of this loving
> Is a bitter and frustrated rhyme.

He drops his mockery. He is overcome with tenderness. She is not taking care of herself, and therefore he must protect her. "Imagine! going out in this bad weather—getting your feet cold, even wet, and being stubborn as a mule and not listening to reason! And surely running a fever by now. Oh, you naughty lotus flower! She is not to come unless the weather is fine."

It is New Year's Day, 1856. He sends her chocolates and a note. "I feel my pains lessen when I think of your loveliness, of the charm of your mind. Unfortunately, I can do nothing for you but send you words like these—I can only coin words." Again and again the thought tortures him: "*Je pose une empreinte vivante* upon all your glories—but only in my thoughts; they are all that you can have of me, poor girl!"

By the beginning of February it was evident that he did not have much longer to live. He himself was aware of this. The nurse was in constant attendance. On February 3, he worked on his *Memoirs* for six hours. When the nurses begged him to rest, he said: "I have just four more days to work—then I am finished."

La Mouche came the next day. She had been sick but had not wanted to tell him of her illness. He received her irritably: "So at last you've come!" She could not tell him that she had dragged herself from her bed to see him; she sobbed silently. "Take your hat off so that I might see you better," he whispered. He placed his hand on her hair; they gazed at each other in silence.

When she left, he called after her, "Till tomorrow, then, and don't be late." But the next day she was ill and could not get out of bed. She did not see him again.

The man on the mattress stirred. A groan. "Mouche!" Mathilde!" The nurse, nodding in her chair, awoke.

"Yes, Monsieur Heine?"

"Catherine."

"Yes, what is it?"

"I do not have much more time. I want to see the dawn before I go."

Catherine started to weep softly.

"Do not cry. I have lived a full and rich life."

"Shall I call Mathilde?"

"No. Poor child, let her sleep. Later, tell her that I will be looking down from Heaven to watch my plump and breathless pigeon strolling upon Montmartre with Pauline. Now, come Catherine, take me out to the balcony."

The nurse wrapped him in a blanket and carried him to the balcony, where she carefully set him down in the chaise longue. The day was mild. He lifted the eyelid of his good eye and hungrily stared at the sky, then murmured:

"Catherine, see how the sun awakens the earth with jubilant beams and palpitating glow. It will be a beautiful day. The sun of freedom will warm the earth. A new race will rise, engendered in free embrace, and not in forced nuptials. Ah! they will not understand how horrible was the night in whose darkness we were compelled to live, how bitterly we had to fight with frightful ghosts, stupid owls, and sanctimonious sinners."

Suddenly he half lifted himself and placed one hand on the railing. Catherine hastened to support him. In a trancelike state, he chanted the words of his *Hymn.*

I am the Sword, I am the Flame.

I've lighted your way in the darkness, and when the fight began, battled ahead in the front lines.

Here round about me lie the bodies of my friends, but the victory was ours. The victory was ours, but here round about lie the bodies of my friends. Amid the wild paeans of triumph sound the chants of the funeral rites. But we have time neither for grief nor for rejoicing. The trumpets sound anew, fresh battles must be fought—
I am the Sword, I am the Flame.

(Hymn)

The nurse carried him back into the room, then sent for the doctor. Heine kept repeating, "I shall never be able to write to my mother again." A little later he said, "I am so happy that I saw my dear sister once more—for I am a dead man." The doctor came, but there was little he could do beyond easing the pain of the sufferer with sedatives.

The end came early on the morning of February 17. The nurse, Catherine Bourlois, saw that the end was near, but she did not call Mathilde, for, as she explained later, she felt that that was Heine's wish, and she was afraid that Mathilde would lose control, which would only add to the dying man's agony. Shortly before dawn, he woke and tried to tell her something. It seemed to her that he was saying, "Write, write," but she did not understand what he meant. Then he strained with all his might and gasped, "Paper! Pencil!" With tears in her eyes, she hurriedly placed a pencil in his hand, but the next moment he dropped it. His struggle was over.

About two hundred people joined the procession to the Montmartre cemetery where Heine had expressed his desire to be buried. Mathilde was missing. She had left the house a half hour before the funeral and was not seen again for the rest of that month. Her whereabouts during that period remain a mystery.

Dumas, Gautier, and Mignet were among the mourners, but there were no ceremonies, for that was Heine's stated wish in his will.

I expressly forbid any speeches whether in German or French. I have never cared to devote my person to political mummery. It has been the greatest task of my life to work for a cordial understanding between Germany and France, and to frustrate the plots of the enemies of democracy, who exploit national prejudices and animosities for their own use. I believe that I have deserved well of my fellow countrymen and of the French people, and the claim which I have on their gratitude is no doubt the most valuable legacy which I can bequeath to my universal heirs.

As they left the cemetery, Gautier said to Dumas, "A king of the mind has been buried."

After Heine's death, Mathilde loved no other man. Her beloved Henri had fought fiercely to the end to provide for her after he was gone, and she was able to live comfortably—with her friend Pauline, her parrot Coco, three lap dogs, and a flock of fifty canaries.

She enjoyed having company. One of her favorite visitors was Heine's nephew, Ludwig von Embden, the son of Heine's beloved sister. Embden never failed to call on Mathilde when he came to Paris, and he grew very fond of her. In his *Family Life of Heinrich Heine*, Mathilde comes to life, the *grisette* who had won the poet's heart.

> Her amusements consisted in visiting the circus, or a small theater of the Boulevard where a comedy was showing, or taking a walk with Pauline on the Champs Elysees . . . When I was a guest she always prepared some dish which had been a favorite one with her pauvre Henri, and believed in her childlike manner that she had thus honored his memory. It was touching to hear with what devoted love she spoke of him and confided to me that many men had sought to marry her, but that she would never forget her Henri and give up his celebrated name. When her pauvre Henri was very angry with her because she had spent too much money, or he thought sadly of his mother and sister in Germany, a single caress of love was always enough to awake in him joy and merriment.

Mathilde died on February 17, 1883, on the anniversary of Henri's death. Embden wrote in loving tribute, "After twenty-seven years she was reunited with the loved husband whose life she had made beautiful by her amiability and gaiety, and whom she had helped to forget so many hours of great suffering."

In the century that followed Heine's death, thousands of pilgrims who had fallen under the spell of his poetry and prose made their way each year to his grave in Montmartre. They came from every country, and they blanketed the grave with flowers.

Then, in the third decade of the twentieth century, evil men took power in Germany. They banned Heine's books and tried to root out from the hearts of the people his poems and songs. In the school books, *The Loreley* was described as "a popular folk song, author unknown."

Later the book burnings came, and Heine's books were thrown on the bonfires. When he was still a young man, Heine had written the drama *Almansor*, in which a Moorish warrior reports in horror that the Koran was burned by the Christians in the marketplace, and the Moor Hassan observes somberly. "The burning is but a prologue: where books are burned, people in the end are burned too." How well Heine prophesied!

In March 1941 a German army entered Paris. Acting under the directives of Adolf Hitler, the German High Command ordered the obliteration of Heine's grave. No trace of it exists today.

Selected Bibliography

Translations from Heine

Heinrich Heine. *The Complete Poems of Heinrich Heine. A Modern English Version.* Translated by Hal Draper. Boston. Suhrkamp/Insel. 1982.

————. *Doctor Faust,* A Dance Poem. Translated and edited by Basil Ashmore. London and New York: Peter Nevill, 1952

————. *Heinrich Heine, Works of Prose.* Edited by Hermann Kesten. Translated by E. B. Ashton. New York: L. B. Fischer, 1943.

————. *Poems of Heinrich Heine.* Translated by Louis Untermeyer. New York: Henry Holt, 1917; New York: Harcourt, Brace, 1937 and 1945.

————. *Poetry and Prose of Heinrich Heine.* Selected and edited by Frederic Ewen. Poetry translated by Louis Untermeyer, Humbert Wolfe, Emma Lazarus, Margaret Armour, and Aaron Kramer. Prose translated by Frederic Ewen. New York: The Citadel Press, 1948.

————. *Religion and Philosophy in Germany.* Translated by John Snodgrass. Boston: Houghton Mifflin, 1882; Beacon, 1959.

————. *The Sword and the Flame, Selections from Heinrich Heine's prose.* Based on a translation by Charles Godfrey Leland. Edited with an introduction by Alfred Werner, New York: Thomas Yoseloff, 1960.

————. *Travel Pictures,* including *Tour In the Harz, Norderney, Book of Ideas,* together with *The Romantic School.* London: George Bell & Sons, 1901.

Biographies

Bieber, Hugo. *Heinrich Heine, A Biographical Anthology.* Philadelphia: Jewish Publication Society of America, 1956.

Brod, Max. *Heinrich Heine, The Artist in Revolt.* New York: University Press, 1957.

Browne, Lewis. *That Man Heine.* New York: Macmillan, 1927.

Butler, Elizabeth M. *Heinrich Heine.* New York: Philosophical Library, 1957.

Embden, Baron Ludwig von. *The Family Life of Heinrich Heine.* Consisting of commentary and conversations, and including 122 letters addressed by Heine to different members of his family. Translated by Charles Godfrey Leland. London: William Heinemann, 1893.

Fejto. Francois. *Heine, A Biography.* London: Allen Wingate, 1946.

Marcuse, Ludwig. *Heine, A Life between Love and Hate.* New York: Farrar and Rinehart, 1933.

Untermeyer, Louis. *Heinrich Heine, Paradox and Poet.* New York: Harcourt, Brace, 1937.

Vallentin, Antonia. *Poet in Exile, The Life of Heinrich Heine.* London: Victor Gollancz, 1934.

Index